NAMING THE ROSE

NAMING THE ROSE
Essays on Eco's
The Name of the Rose

EDITED BY

M. Thomas Inge

UNIVERSITY PRESS OF MISSISSIPPI

JACKSON & LONDON

Library of Congress Cataloging-in-Publication Data

Naming the rose : essays on Eco's The name of the rose / edited by M.
  Thomas Inge.
      p.   cm.
    Includes index.
    ISBN 0-87805-345-X
    1. Eco, Umberto.   Nome della rosa.   I. Inge, M. Thomas.
  PQ4865.C6N636 1988
  853'.914—dc19   87-27681
                                                                          CIP

Excerpts from *The Name of the Rose* by Umberto Eco, copyright ° 1980 by Gruppo Editoriale Fabbri-Bompiani, Sonzogno, Etas S. p. A.; English translation copyright ° 1983 by Harcourt Brace Jovanovich, Inc. and Martin Secker & Warburg Limited. Reprinted by permission of Harcourt Brace Jovanovich, Inc.

iv

Contents

Introduction

Umberto Eco's *The Name of the Rose* is a major and most unusual literary phenomenon of the 1980s. Written by a professor of semiotics from the University of Bologna who had already attracted international attention for his scholarship and critical commentaries, the novel was an immediate bestseller when published in Italian in 1980 and was subsequently translated into twenty languages. When the English translation appeared in the United States in 1983, *The Name of the Rose* remained on the hardcover best-seller list for forty weeks, with half a million copies sold. Paperback publication rights brought $550,000, reportedly the highest price ever paid for a translation in paperback; and the initial print run was over 1.2 million copies. The book stayed at the top of the paperback bestseller list for weeks, was widely read on college campuses, and in 1986 became a motion picture.

What is to account for such success for a detective novel set in a medieval monastery, a work which not only has a compelling narrative but in the process of working out the intricacies of its plot deals with such unlikely topics as early church history, theology, philosophy, language, humanism, art, the Enlightenment, literary criticism, theories of comedy, and the structure of libraries? How did Eco succeed in producing that rarity to highbrow critics—a widely popular work of fiction that addresses themes of considerable intellectual consequence? Answering these questions will require a good deal of thought and time, if indeed they *are* answerable.

In the meantime, we can at least begin to explore the complexity and cultural significance of Eco's remarkable novel in terms of its background and literary context. Focusing less upon the public response (although one essay surveys a selected group of readers), the essays gathered in this book examine the novel in light of some of the various traditions from which it draws, theories of detective fiction, comedy, postmodernism, the Apocalypse, semiotics, and literary criticism, all areas of inquiry in which Eco is something of an authority himself.

The essays in the first section place Eco's novel in the broader traditions of Western thought and literature. Hans Kellner notes the various works and writers that have influenced Eco—Lewis Carroll, Jorge Luis Borges, and Sir Arthur Conan Doyle among them—and identifies some of the medieval sources of names and ideas. He examines political and theological influences but focuses finally on the function of laughter in the novel. After surveying the sources of thought on the subject among medieval thinkers and modern critics, Kellner decides that the readers are, finally, the butts of the humor for their willingness to participate in the games and misleading trails of the playful narrative.

Lois Parkinson Zamora addresses the extent to which Eco uses the themes and ideas of the apocalypse as reflected in the Book of Revelation and other texts and suggests that it is the shared sense of dangerous times and threatening transition that joins our world with Eco's fictional one. Images of chaos preceding the end of the present world have a continuing strong appeal for readers, as demonstrated not only by the success of Eco's novel but the popularity of such writers as Walker Percy, Gabriel García Márquez, Carlos Fuentes, and Mario Vargas Llosa. Mark Parker takes another tack in examining *The Name of the Rose* as a conscious example of postmodern fiction, that is, an ironic retort to the tradition of modernism, which itself had been an effort to achieve an abrupt break with all previous tradition. This means that postmodern writers lack a strong system of values or standards against which to rebel. Postmodern critics, however, have looked to mass culture as a gesture of affirmation. Parker analyzes Eco's critical statements on these matters as a way of coming to terms with *The Name of the Rose*, a fulfillment of Eco's stated belief that it is possible to write a novel that is both aesthetically valid and popular entertainment.

The most obvious genre of popular literature to which *The Name of the Rose* belongs is, of course, the detective novel, and the second group of essays examine the several ways Eco has used and played with the venerable form. Michael Cohen believes that Eco not only borrows creatively from and pays homage to the great practitioners—from Voltaire and Doyle to Borges and the hard-boiled school of writers—but that he uses the failure of his detective, William of Baskerville, as a way of questioning the rationalistic premises on which the form depends. Joan DelFattore, however, notes that Eco has conflated classic detective methodology with the theological methodologies of Roger Bacon and William of Ockham, supporters of experience and logic and the two theologic masters of William of Baskerville. She concludes that it is not the method of detection that fails William but, rather, he who fails the method.

Pierre L. Horn finds that, whereas Eco has drawn on all the theories of classic detection, he has carried them into the realm of humanism through the difficult moral choices and rationalistic dilemmas posed by the plot and circumstances. The reasons for the deaths and disasters in the novel ultimately are related to William and Adso's humanistic pursuit of knowledge. H. Aram Veeser argues that Eco refuses to accept the rigid, rational conventions of detective fiction and its movement from chaos and obscurity to order and clarity, offering instead the open, medieval countertradition of carnival and laughing satire derived from Lucian, Rebalais, and others.

It is only natural that most of the essays in this book contain references to semiotics (the study of language as a system of signs), since Eco is one of the contemporary masters of the field. Although he declaims any intention to produce a novel consistent with his semiotic theories, Eco acknowledges that there are bound to be relationships. The essays in the third section consider some of these connections. Helen T. Bennett goes back to the fourteenth-century work of William of Ockham to discover parallels between his medieval nominalism and the twentieth-century semiotic theories of Charles Sanders Peirce. These parallels make the medieval setting a suitable one for the actions of William of Baskerville, a reader of signs caught in what is actually a modern semiotic dilemma rather than a simple murder mystery.

True to the semiotic ideas that inform the novel's structure, Jocelyn Mann, in her essay, suggests that Eco displays in *The Name of the Rose* the theory that signs can both mislead and inform. "Although the signs themselves can be useful and valid," she notes, "the idea that it is possible to create an *enduring* thread of meaning by linking them together and following them to a permanent truth is an illusion." Deborah Parker, responding to some of Eco's statements in his semiotic studies, challenges his refusal to designate the novel as closed or open (that is, as a work that allows little freedom of interpretation or one that has many possible meanings or inexhaustible interpretations). She locates the tension between the open content and the closed form as central to the novel's meaning, the one serving to complement rather than cancel the other.

In a postscript, Roger Rollin discusses the status of *The Name of the Rose* in the context of popular culture and fiction and reports on the results of his survey of selected readers in a limited area. His findings suggest that the popularity of the novel may be attributable in part to its unique combination of elements drawn from historical fiction, the detective novel, the philosophical tale, and the novel of initiation. Thus it has something for nearly everyone, but especially for those who can fantasize and identify with the innocence or experience of Adso of Melk or William of Baskerville.

The variety of approaches represented here demonstrate the extent to which Eco has constructed a successful work of fiction which stimulates and intrigues readers and critics alike. These writers are among many at work on analyses of the novel, which is already the subject of several book-length studies underway, numerous essays in the critical quarterlies, and at least one special issue of a scholarly journal. The annotated checklist presented in the Appendix by Jackson R. Bryer and Ruth M. Alvarez is an indication of what has already been written in English about Eco and his work. *The Name of the Rose* appears to hold great riches, which will provide Eco's fellow critics with a good deal to speculate on for years to come.

Most of the essays in this volume resulted from a general call for papers to be read at a meeting of the Modern Language Association for a special session arranged by the editor. Only five papers could be accepted for the session, but the quantity and quality of the proposals were so high that many were invited to submit essays for this book. Eco himself was invited to appear as a respondent at the MLA program, but he was unable to attend. He did agree, however, to write a response to the essays which follows the introduction to this book. Critics seldom have the benefit of an immediate response to their commentaries on the part of the author about whom they are writing. We are grateful for Eco's courtesy in performing this task.

The editor is also grateful to Hunter Cole and Seetha Srinivasan for their faith in this project, and to John Baldwin for his usual helping hand. The contributors have not only made my job a pleasure but an unusually stimulating one.

M. Thomas Inge
RANDOLPH-MACON COLLEGE

Prelude to a Palimpsest

Umberto Eco

Over the past six years, I have repeatedly tried to avoid any statement about the possible interpretations of my novel. My opinion is that a narrator should never provide interpretations for his own text. I do not say this as a radical deconstructionist. On the contrary, I believe that a text—as an object (a textual linear manifestation), insofar as it is referred to in an encyclopedic background, comprehending in some way both the encyclopedia of the time in which it was written and the encyclopedias of its readers—can work as the public parameter of its interpretations.

When one has the text to question, one need not question the author. In my *Postscript to "The Name of the Rose"* I show how and to what extent an author can be unaware of the effects his text has.

In several of the essays in this book I found brilliant, possible readings of my novel, readings I cannot absolutely challenge because they are rooted in the text and of which I became aware only by reading the readings of my readers.

Sometimes I recognized something I wanted to put in the book and was proud to see that it had been noted. At other times, I was sure that what others saw was far from my intentions. I would be the first to stress that the author's intentions *(intentio auctoris)* have nothing to do with the intention of the text *(intentio operis)*. For instance, I was delighted by the allegorical meanings that one of the contributors to this volume[1] found in such names as Umberto da Romans, Milo Temesvar, and Nicholas of Morimondo. Milo Temesvar I shall discuss later. As for Umberto da Romans, he was a historical figure who actually wrote sermons for women. (But why did I choose this author among so many others?) And Nicholas of Morimondo; it is astonishing that a character bearing this name (which undoubtedly suggests "death of the world") is the one who utters "The library is on fire!", thus acknowledging the fall of the abbey as a microcosm. As a matter of fact, I christened Nicholas from the name of the well-known abbey of Morimondo, in Italy, founded in 1136 by Cistercians coming from Morimond (Haute Marne). When I christened Nicholas, I did not as yet know that he had to pronounce his fatal statement. Furthermore, I am not sure that the etymology of

Morimond comes from the verb *mori* and the noun *mundus* (I ask the experts for alternative explanations). In any case, when I invented Nicholas I was concerned neither with the world nor with death. I realize, however, that a reader with a certain knowledge of Latin or Italian cannot escape such a semantic association. The text says that there is something in the name of Nicholas that recalls the death of a world. I was not responsible for this allusion. But what does "I" mean? My conscious personality? My id? The play of language (of *la langue*) that was taking place in my mind when I was writing? The text is there; the rest (at least on my part) is silence.

In the same vein, I would not like to speculate about the other essays, especially those in the semiotics section, which reveal to me many things that I was not thinking of when writing. I never suspected that my novel was so consistent with my research in semiotics, because I told my story by accepting a split personality, and I did not (consciously) try to put in my novel the theories I had developed in my scholarly writings. I will admit, though, that even the most schizophrenic personality cannot be as split as that. A good reader can understand the relationships between my various books better than I can.

When one writes fiction, one constructs a world, one that readers are persuaded to take seriously. And to take something seriously is to take it as a situation from which to infer everything that can reasonably be inferred.

Let me tell you about Milo Temesvar. In the early sixties, at the Frankfurt Book Fair, four distinguished publishers met for lunch. I remember only that one of them was my publisher, Valentino Bompiani (at that time I was working as the nonfiction editor for his publishing house); the others were perhaps Gallimard, Fischer, Weidenfeld, and/or Rohwolt). It was a moment in publishing history when people were paying enormous sums of money to buy the rights to any book, and these publishers were preoccupied with that irresponsible trend. Thus one of them said, "I bet that if we invent an author—let us say, Milo Temesvar—who has written a new novel, let's say 'Let Me Say It Now,' and that the New American Library has just paid a $50,000 advance for an option on the manuscript, before this night is over, everybody will rush to obtain the foreign rights." Valentino Bompiani went back to our booth and told me the story. I started circulating through the fair, asking people about that mysterious Temesvar and dropping vague bits of information. The rumor did indeed spread; by 6:00 P.M. practically everyone was ready to sell his own soul in order to have Temesvar, and at 8:00 P.M. a well-known Italian publisher boasted at dinner: "Stop. I have just bought the foreign rights for the whole world."

I began to like Milo. Two years later I wrote for a magazine a fake review about the new book of Milo Temesvar, *The Patmos Sellers*. My review was a piece of academic chicanery intended to mock the positions of Adorno and Marcuse. I inserted in my review numerous signals of forgery. I said, for instance, that Milo Temesvar was an Albanian who had been charged with "leftist deviationism" and expelled from his country, that the book was published by Snoopy & Snoopy Inc. All in vain. A prominent publisher took my review seriously and sent his editors a memo instructing them to buy the book at any cost.

Milo Temesvar did not exist, at least in the sense in which common people understand the verb *to exist*; but in some way I set up around this *flatus vocis* a believable world. I could no longer control the movement of people in *that* world.

Since I want to keep playing the role of storyteller and not semiotician, let me continue my game.

Few if any critics have questioned the figure of the Abbé Vallet who appears at the beginning of my story as the author of the French translation of a Latin manuscript. By quoting Abbé Vallet, I paid an old debt.

The following story concerns a book written in 1976, in which I quoted the story of a book written in 1954. Please follow me.

In 1976, I published *Come si fa una tesi di laurea* (How to Make a Doctoral Dissertation),[2] a small book written to provide students not only with a "manual of style" but also with a sort of philosophy of doctoral dissertations, that is, a series of reflections about what it means to do scientific research.

In this book there is a chapter on "scientific humility." I explained that one should never despise any source, because even the least important and least original authors can sometimes suggest an interesting idea. In order to explain what I meant, I told the story of the Abbé Vallet and of my own doctoral dissertation, written in 1954.[3]

It was December of 1953. I was in Paris, trying to finish my dissertation. Aquinas never wrote *ex professo* about aesthetics, so my job consisted of putting together scattered remarks that appeared here and there in his immense opus, when he was dealing with other subject matter. I wanted to show that all these pieces could be organized into a coherent theory and that all the previous efforts to do so were inconsistent.

During two years of hard work, I had encountered many difficulties. I had all the elements for solving my puzzle but one. It was like having a chemical formula but with an empty space in the middle. If I did not fill this gap, the formula was devoid of any sense.

To put it in technical terms, all the previous scholars who studied the aesthetic thought of Aquinas explained his notion of beauty in terms of the first operation of the mind, known in the scholastic tradition as *simplex apprehensio*. For reasons difficult to explain (or difficult to tell in a few lines), this solution was unsatisfactory.

Walking along the banks of the Seine one day, browsing in the boxes of the *bouquinistes*, I came across a nineteenth-century book, finely bound. The author was P. Vallet, "pretre de Saint Sulpice, Professeur de Philosophie au Seminaire d'Issy," and the title was *L'idee du beau dans Saint Thomas d'Aquin*. It was rather expensive, and I was a penniless student. Before buying it, I cursorily read enough pages to understand that it was one among many neo-scholastic, secondhand compilations produced in nineteenth-century seminars, which repeated old ideas without providing any new ones. But I believed in scientific humility, and I felt it a duty to read everything that was written on my subject. Thus, that evening, I went without dinner and bought the book.

I read it. As expected, it was boring; but I kept going through it. Then, on page 49, I found the seminal, decisive idea I was desperately looking for: the experience of beauty does not take place during the first operation but rather in the second operation of the mind, that is, the *compositio et divisio*, or judgment. Vallet did not prove that idea; but as soon as I returned to the Thomistic texts, I found persuasive evidence of it. I had my thesis finished, and I still think that this idea is my most original contribution to Thomistic scholarship.

Thus, in 1976, I told my readers the story of the Abbé Vallet, who had told me that we can and must learn from everybody, provided we read everybody's texts with patience and humility.

When my book was published that same year, Beniamino Placido, a dear friend of mine, reviewed it in *La repubblica*. Though positive, the review suggested, tongue-in-cheek, that I presented the activity of research as a fairy tale. Placido said that my book was based on the narrative functions of Propp, that I presented the student as a hero fighting for the beloved one. As happens in every fairy tale, my hero at a certain point meets a Magic Donor, in my case the Abbé Vallet, who gives him the Magic Ring. Obviously the Abbé Vallet was an astute invention, a magnificent piece of fiction.

Some months later, Beniamino Placido came to my place. Pouring him a double scotch, I told him that he was wrong. Not only did the Abbé Vallet exist, but I had his old book, which I was prepared to show him. I added that I had not opened the book for twenty years, but I had a good visual memory, and I remembered vividly the crucial page, with the double underscoring in pencil I scribbled in 1953.

I rummaged in my shelves, and read to Placido the passage. There was no trace of the splendid idea that had seduced me twenty years earlier! The Abbé Vallet had never said what I was convinced he had said.

On this page (and in the rest of the book, of course), Vallet was saying something else, something absolutely irrelevant. It was only then that I understood I had extrapolated *my* idea while reading him, probably because some of his words had triggered in my mind a sudden association, had provided the starting point for an inference, obliging me to move my thoughts in a given direction. Who holds the rights for that idea? P. Vallet? Myself? Vallet's book?

I think the third answer is the most likely. The book served as a machine for producing interpretations. I insist that Vallet's book *contained* that idea because (and I checked afterward) nothing in the preceding or following pages disproves it. The book did not spell out that idea but strategically provided the possibility of extrapolating it. Naturally, the poor, forgotten, irrelevant Abbé Vallet had no responsibility whatsoever for what I made out of his book. He did not know what his book could do. But it did it.

That is why I put the Abbé Vallet at the gate of my narrative abbey, and this is why I still thank him for having told me what he did not mean to tell but should have told.

My dream is to play the role of the Abbé Vallet for many of my readers.

Umberto Eco
Milano
October 1986

Notes

1. I would like to name each of them, but if I quote somebody I cannot do it without expressing or suggesting agreement or disagreement, and if I do so I shall indirectly or directly support one or another interpretation, thus contradicting my theoretical assumptions.

2. Milano: Bompiani, 1976.

3. *Il problema estetico in San Tommaso* (Turin: Filosofia, 1956); revised edition, *Il problema estetico in Tommaso d'Aquino* (Milano: Bompiani, 1970); English trans., Harvard University Press, forthcoming.

TRADITIONS

1 "To Make Truth Laugh": Eco's *The Name of the Rose*

Hans Kellner

The ruses of the narrator of *The Name of the Rose* reach an exquisite level of absurdity in his preface.

> If something new had not occurred, I would still be wondering where the story of Adso of Melk originated; but then, in 1970, in Buenos Aires, as I was browsing among the shelves of a little antiquarian bookseller on Corrientes, not far from the more illustrious Patio del Tango of that great street, I came upon the Castilian version of a little work by Milo Temesvar, *On the Use of Mirrors in the Game of Chess*. It was an Italian translation of the original, which, now impossible to find, was in Georgian (Tbilisi, 1934); and here, to my great surprise, I read copious quotations from Adso's manuscript, though the source was neither Vallet nor Mabillon; it was Father Athanasius Kircher (but which work?). A scholar—whom I prefer not to name—later assured me that (and he quoted indexes from memory) the great Jesuit never mentioned Adso of Melk. But Temesvar's pages were before my eyes, and the episodes he cited were the same as those of the Vallet manuscript (the description of the labyrinth in particular left no room for doubt). [1]

This paragraph, a labyrinth in itself with many passages I cannot venture into here, leaves us with one lingering question: What, besides pure contiguity, has Adso's manuscript to do with mirrors and chess? This readerly conundrum leads us to the major work in the Western literary tradition dealing with a mirror-image chess game, namely *Through the Looking-Glass* by Lewis Carroll, particularly the version edited by Martin Gardner and called *The Annotated Alice*. In this volume, Alice's adventures, which take the form of a mirrored chess game played on a giant chess labyrinth of brooks and hedges, are presented with annotations that comment extensively on the philosophical problems that dominate *The Name of the Rose*. Obviously, Alice passes through the looking glass as William and Adso must do to enter the end of their labyrinthine library. When Alice enters the wood in which things have no names, she muses on the absence of names, the need to rename things, and her attachment to her own name.

"This must be the wood," she said thoughtfully to herself, "where things have no names. I wonder what will become of *my* name when I go in? I shouldn't like to lose it at all—because they would have to give me another, and it would be almost certain to be an ugly one. But then the fun would be trying to find the creature that got my old name! That's just like advertisements, you know, when people lose dogs—'*answers to the name of "Dash": had on a brass collar*'—just fancy calling everything you met 'Alice,' till one of them answered! Only they wouldn't answer at all, if they were wise."[2]

Aside from describing the situation in which William of Baskerville first impressed the monks of the abbey by identifying a lost horse, Alice's plight is put in a philosophical perspective by Gardner's note:

> The wood in which things have no names is in fact the universe itself, as it is apart from symbol-manipulating creatures who label portions of it because—as Alice earlier remarked with pragmatic wisdom—"it's useful to the people that name them." The realization that the world by itself contains no signs—that there is no connection whatever between things and their names except by way of a mind that finds the tags useful—is by no means a trivial philosophic insight. The fawn's delight in recalling its name reminds one of the old joke about Adam naming the tiger the tiger because it *looked* like a tiger.[3]

Adso, the naive realist, sounds a similar Adamistic note when he notes that the lamb, *agnus*, got its name from its character because it recognizes, "agnoscit," its mother in the flock; he infers from his meditation on naming the goodness of the Creator and "the greatness and stability of Creation" (280–282). William, on the other hand, demonstrates in his fancifully learned speech on politics and representation, that God's decision to give Adam the responsibility for naming things was his sign that men should rule themselves: "So that surely the word 'nomen' comes from 'nomos,' that is to say 'law,' since nomina are given by men ad placitum, in other words by free and collective accord" (351).

The philosophical world of *The Name of the Rose* frequently mirrors Alice's encounter with Humpty-Dumpty. Humpty's views on language dismay Alice, reversed as they are in the mirror world, but they are much the same as those of William of Baskerville. As Gardner puts it: "Humpty takes the point of view known in the Middle Ages as nominalism; the view that universal terms do not refer to objective existences but are nothing more than *flatus vocis*, verbal utterances. The view was skillfully defended by William of Occam and is now held by almost all contemporary logical empiricists."[4] Yet Alice is still befuddled by the White Knight and his song.

"The name of the song is called '*Haddocks' Eyes.*' "

"Oh, that's the name of the song, is it?" Alice said, trying to feel interested.

"No, you don't understand," the Knight said, looking a little vexed. "That's what the name is *called*. The name really is '*The Aged Aged Man.*' "

"Then I ought to have said 'That's what the *song* is called'?" Alice corrected herself.

"No, you oughtn't: that's quite another thing! The *song* is called, '*Ways and Means*': but that's only what it's *called*, you know!"

"Well, what *is* the song, then?" said Alice, who was by this time completely bewildered.

"I was coming to that," the Knight said. "The song really is '*A-Sitting On a Gate*': and the tune's my own invention."[5]

Finding the basis of nomination here is as frustrating as finding the source of the narrator's text (found in Argentina, the Castilian version, in an Italian translation of the Georgian "original," which cites an unknown reference to a missing text), yet, according to Gardner, Alice's conversation is perfectly sensible to a student of logic and semantics. Mirrors, labyrinths, and nominalism link *Through the Looking-Glass* with *The Name of the Rose*.

Nomination is itself a labyrinth; *The Name of the Rose* makes naming most important and the lack of a name a deep tragedy:

"You bear a great and very beautiful name," he said. "Do you know who Adso of Montier-en-Der was?" he asked.

I did not know, I confess. (83)

Adso's ignorance of his own namesake when queried by Jorge (who was himself, no doubt, ignorant of Dr. Watson) is one of his few modern traits. Etymology and onomastics, the study of the origins of words and names, were fundamental categories of thought in the Middle Ages, in which the ancient question whether the names of things originated in "nature" or in "convention" was a living debate, usually decided in favor of nature. Dante's formula—"*Nomina sunt consequentia rerum*"—could hardly differ more from the modern Saussurian notion of the arbitrariness of *both* parts of the sign; but it was an inescapable part of reading the medieval world, even practiced by the arch-nominalist William of Baskerville, albeit in jest.

William of Baskerville is not *named* by chance or nature but, rather, by referential conventions. His relationship to Sherlock Holmes, the hero of *The Hound of the Baskervilles*, is clear and the references to Conan Doyle numerous in *The Name of the Rose*. Not only does the description of William match Holmes (thin, beaky nose, penetrating eyes, long face covered with freckles—a true Basil Rathbone type), but his habits are Holmesian. William at

times indulges in certain herbs, which, he remarks, are good for an old
Franciscan but not for a young Benedictine (16). Sherlock Holmes, however,
is but a part of William's identity. His own master is William of Occam, the
great Franciscan philosopher. Occam (and sometimes the Franciscan empiricist Roger Bacon and Jean Buridan) are the intellectual guides for
William of Baskerville, whose methods, statements, theology, and metaphysics are faithfully Occamite. Occam maintained that "no universal is
existent in any way whatsoever outside the mind of the knower."[6] This
philosophy maintains that universals (of which *names* are the most striking
example) are created by people.[7] Thus "dog" or "rose"—Occam's usual
examples—do not exist except as a convenience in ordering the similarities of
individual beasts and flowers. The *dog* is in William of Baskerville's name, the
rose in the "name" of Eco's book. It is this philosophy of "nominalism"—as
opposed to the "realism" which maintains some eternal reality for the
concepts "dog" and "rose"—that makes possible modern semiotics as the
study of human systems of meaning. Occam's theology held that neither the
existence of God nor the immortality of the soul could be demonstrated by
reason, and that the great logical structures of scholasticism were quite
without foundation. Thus, God is not bound by any strictures, is unknowable and absolutely free.[8] William of Baskerville repeatedly suggests the
unknowability of great truths, the lack of perceivable order in the world. His
nominalism is absolute; in this regard, he, like his scholastic namesake, is
almost a modern man.

Adso of Melk, on the other hand, remains a man of his time. His faith in
the rational demonstrations of the Thomistic tradition has been shaken by his
brief time with William, but he is no empiricist, and, despite his uncertainties, no skeptic. He grasps William's ideas but is trained to want more, to
seek ultimate truths, which William refuses him. Adso asks, "Then I can
always and only speak of something that speaks to me of something else, and
so on. But the final something, the true one—does that never exist?"
William replies, "Perhaps it does: it is the individual unicorn" (317).
Nevertheless, Adso remains of the old ways; after recounting his great sin, a
brief moment of love with a young woman whose name he never learns, he
gives a lengthy disquisition on naming which is scholastic and Thomistic
throughout and concludes with praise for "the greatness and the stability of
creation" (184). This divine, natural (and not human, conventional) theory of
names is revealing:

> I saw the lamb, to which this name was given as if in recognition of its
> purity and goodness. In fact the noun "agnus" derives from the fact that this
> animal "agnoscit"; it recognizes its mother, and recognizes her voice in the

midst of the flock while the mother, among many lambs of the same form, with the same bleating, recognizes always and only her offspring, and nourishes him. (282)

Adso's faith and innocence are the basis of his charm, and most of the humor in the book comes from the indirection of Adso's narration. When William learns the identity of the inquisitor sent by the pope, his displeasure is marked by an Anglo-Saxon expletive, which we learn of in the following terms: "William made an ejaculation in his own language that I didn't understand, nor did the abbot understand it, and perhaps it was best for us both, because the word William uttered had an obscene hissing sound" (210).

Eco presents several scenes in which etymological discussions take place. He also asks his readers for a bit of etymological and onomastic inquiry. The dozens of references may be as clear as Jorge of Burgos or William of Baskerville or as whimsical as the name of Humbert of Romans (Umberto da Romans), but they are ubiquitous. The names are often obscure references to medieval arcana, which usually offer clues or develop semiotic, theological, or political themes in the novel. For example, the names of Adelmo and Berengar, whose illicit love caused so much trouble, come from prominent eleventh-century clerics. Berengarius of Tours (d. 1088), Archdeacon of Angers, held ideas about transubstantiation that were seen as heretical by some; the name *Berengarians* was given to all in the Middle Ages who denied the substantial presence of the body and the blood of Christ in the Eucharist. His "early friend and school companion," the Archdeacon of Liège who tried in vain to change Berengar's views, was *Adelmann*. Adelmo of *Otranto*, whose death sets *The Name of the Rose* in motion, also alludes to the first Gothic mystery, Walpole's *The Castle of Otranto*, while Berengar of *Arundel* comes from the mythic kingdom where another illicit lover, Tristram, performed great feats recorded in Mallory's *Morte d'Arthur*.

The major characters of *The Name of the Rose* often bear the names of earlier churchmen who played important roles in the conflict between the sacred and secular powers, which is a thematic center of *The Name of the Rose*. Benno of Uppsala bears the name of the Bishop of Meissen (1010–1106) who took the papal side against the emperor in the struggles of the eleventh century, for which he was later sainted (to Luther's disgust). Severinus of Sankt Wendel, the herbalist of the abbey, has the name of a seventh-century pope whose consecration was delayed a year and a half by the emperor; as Pope Severinus, he served only three months. Abo, the abbot (Benedict's *Rule* gives a full etymology of the word *abbot*, beginning with the Hebrew), suggests the tenth-century abbot of Fleury, Abbo, who was twice sent to Rome by the French king to ward off a papal interdict and was twice successful. The cellarer Remigius bears the name of the famous French saint Rémi (437–533), the friend of Clovis, founder of the French monarchy; it was Rémi who converted Clovis to orthodox Christianity.

Medieval humorists are covertly represented throughout the somber abbey. Venantius, whose corpse is found in the barrel of pig's blood, bears the name of Fortunatus Venantius (530–609), the Bishop of Poitiers and the friend of kings who celebrated the marriage of his friend King Sigbert and Brunhild and who wrote a mock epic on kitchen humor and other ridiculous subjects. Also, the abbot mentioned above bears the name of Abbo of St. Germain, whose historical epic of 897 also contains kitchen humor.

The web of reference may be more hidden and theological. The librarian Malachai of Hildesheim bears the name of the last book of the Old Testament; thus it seems theologically fitting that he should be the pawn of Jorge of Burgos, identified so completely with the last book of the New Testament, which completes and in every way provides "meaning" for the Old Testament in the Christian figural tradition. Further, the "book" mentioned prominently in Revelation is "figured" in Malachai 3:16. "Then they that feared the Lord spake often one to another: and the Lord hearkened and heard it, and a book of remembrance was written before him for them that feared the Lord, and that thought upon his name."

Milo Temesvar's text—found in Buenos Aires in the Castilian version, which is an Italian translation of the impossible-to-find Georgian original—is another clue of the sort that writers of mysteries love. The name *Milo* itself is a topos of medieval misattribution. Milo was a Frankish bishop whose exploits have been confused with and attributed to the famous Turpin of the *Song of Roland* and is thus linked with the inauthentic *Historia caroli magni*. And Buenos Aires is the city of Jorge Luis Borges, whose Castilian "version" is Jorge da Borgos, and the Italian translation, perhaps, is *Il nome della rosa* (The Name of the Rose). The Georgian original, as noted, is indeed "impossible to find."

If we can readily understand the propriety of using the Gospel and Apocalypse of John as a focus for this medieval mystery, the importance given to Jorge Luis Borges needs some elucidation. Borges was a unique and irreplaceable voice in modern literature. He was a writer of fragments, brief pieces, odd, tiny tales that must be called Borgesian in the same sense that Kafka's work is Kafkaesque; like Kafka, Borges created a world that was unique to his work and that corresponded to nothing outside the imagination and desire of its maker. These works were gathered and published under the titles *Labyrinths* and *Other Inquisitions*. It would thus seem that the very actions and location of Eco's novel are taken from Borges' titles. The Borgesian references are many. The structure of Eco's book, however, is built on a central opposition of ideas. Borges is the reverse of St. John, who wrote of the Word made Flesh, for the Argentine wrote of the transfiguration of all things, including Flesh, into the Word. Borges was a man of the library—in fact, like Jorge of Burgos, a librarian for much of his life. This world of books was for him the real world, or at least *a* real world. His theology followed Mallarmé's notion that the world existed to be put into a book, the flesh become word.[9] Thus, just as the Apocalypse of John guides the detectives through the library-labyrinth and seems to structure the nature of the murders, and just as the Gospel attributed to John provides Adso his narrative opening, so the work of Borges may be taken as the absent guide for readers of *The Name of the Rose.*

Borges said of himself, "First and foremost, I think of myself as a reader. . . . I am not a thinker. I am merely a man who has tried to explore the literary possibilities of metaphysics and religion."[10] Any reader of Borges will be struck at every turn with moments that reappear in some form or other in *The Name of the Rose.* However, a central core of themes appears throughout Borges' work: his philosophical realism, his repeated discussion of roses, and his illusionism, which weaves the symbols of words, labyrinths, libraries, and mirrors.

In his "Poema de los dones" (Poem of the Gifts), Borges points to the irony of his status as blind librarian:

> No one should read self-pity or reproach
> Into this statement of the majesty
> Of God; who with such irony
> Granted me books and blindness at one touch.
>
> Care of this city of books he handed over
> To sightless eyes, which now can do no more
> Than read in libraries of dream the poor
> And senseless paragraphs that dawns deliver
>
> To wishful scrutiny.[11]

God is the author of the catechresis of a blind librarian. Another poem by Borges seems a gloss on the line of Bernardo Morliacense (*"stat rosa pristina nomine, nomina nuda tenemus"*) that ends *The Name of the Rose.* In this poem we see an opponent of William of Baskerville's (and of Occam's) nominalism.

> Rose,
> the unfading rose beyond my verse—

rose that's full and fragrant,
rose of the black garden in the deep of night,
rose of any garden and any night,
rose that's born again by the art of alchemy
out of tenuous ash,
rose of the Persians and Ariosto,
rose that's always by itself,
rose that's always the rose of roses,
the young Platonic flower,
the blind and burning rose beyond my verse,
unattainable rose. [12]

Here, it is the *name* of the rose that Borges rejects; *his* rose is precisely what is beyond the name—the reality, unattainable. Borgesian metaphysics are clearly antagonistic to the Baskervillian metaphysics of empiricism. Borges wrote elsewhere, almost sadly, of the defeat of realism.

> A thesis that is inconceivable now seemed obvious in the ninth century, and it somehow endured until the fourteenth century. Nominalism, which was formerly the novelty of a few, encompasses everyone today; its victory is so vast and fundamental that its name is unnecessary. No one says that he is a nominalist because nobody is anything else. [13]

The mark of this transformation, Borges notes, is the "passage from the allegory to the novel."

Not surprisingly, Borges the allegorist wrote no novels; but Eco has, and when we come across the tiny reference to a scholastic "Humbert of Romans" in his text, we see the trace of Umberto the novelist-etymologist. The end of the world perhaps *is* to become a book; the destruction of a book is a figure for the end of the world. I mention here the fine scene in Victor Hugo's novel *Ninety-Three*, in which two children, locked in the library of an ancient castle, destroy a magnificent old book, the prize of the collection, out of joy and innocence. This symbol of the end of a world of feudal privilege and beauty, and the subsequent burning of the castle, are as clear ancestors of *The Name of the Rose* as the legendary destruction of the library of Alexandria and others. (The *Stift* at Melk, Adso's abbey, burned at the end of the thirteenth century, a few decades before the action of *The Name of the Rose*.) The *end* of the world is to create a book; the destruction of a book is the end of a world.

We are left with a choice. William, the former inquisitor, remains an inquisitor, both of nature and of books. He tells Adso that a book is not to be believed but questioned (316). In this, he is like Bernard of Gui, whose thirst for truth rivals William's. Is the passion for truth which they share in different ways wrong? Is there a case for Jorge's position? Is Adso wrong to insist on the cheapening of learning passed from hand to hand for anyone's use?

> There, I said to myself, are the reasons for the silence and the darkness that surround the library: it is the preserve of learning but can maintain this learning unsullied only if it prevents its reaching anyone at all, even the monks themselves. Learning is not like a coin, which remains physically whole even through the most infamous transactions; it is, rather, like a very handsome dress, which is worn out through use and ostentation. Is not a book like that, in fact? (185)

By leaving the question open, Adso questions the role of the reader in good realist form: "*videmus nunc per speculum et in aeniqmate . . .*" But he has lost Paul's optimism about ultimately seeing "*facie ad faciem.*"

William's spectacles seem a banal symbol of his insight against the blindness of Jorge. His choosing among the lenses ground for him at the abbey after his own pair has been lost figures both his empiricism and his abductive method. The lenses, however, are philosophically relevant both to the medieval discussions in the novel and to the looking glasses in the book. Roger Bacon believed that to choose optics meant choosing experience over traditional authorities. For him, only *visible* things existed:

> This science is indispensable to the study of theology and the world . . . and because it is in itself almost infinitely delightful and immensely useful, therefore do I enjoy explaining it to the full and with particular care, because without it one cannot learn anything marvelous. This is, in fact the science of vision, and a blind man cannot know anything of this world. Sight shows us the variety of all things, and opens the way to a knowledge of everything, as experience teaches. [14]

Fascination with lenses and fascination with mirrors went together in the Middle Ages, explained by the treatise of Alzaher. Jean de Meun's *Roman de la Rose* has a canto in praise of mirrors. [15] Consequently, when William cites the great contributions of the infidels to optics and the science of vision (87), and repeats Roger Bacon's notion that a value of glasses is that they prolong human life (74), he has focused on the physical emblem of empiricism and of the conflict between Jorge's blindness and his own search for insight.

What precisely is the nature of this search for insight symbolized by the lost and then replaced spectacles? William of Baskerville and Adso, nominally identified with Sherlock Holmes and Dr. Watson, use a method of reasoning described and demonstrated by Charles Sanders Peirce, who, with Ferdinand de Saussure, stands as the founder of modern semiotics. [16] This form of reasoning Peirce calls abduction or retroduction. In brief, it differs little from what is commonly called the educated guess but differs a great deal from either deduction (as Adso, to his dismay, clearly realizes) and from induction in the proper sense.

According to Peirce, "Abduction seeks a theory. Induction seeks for facts."[17] It is a preparatory sort of reasoning, or an "Originary Argument," which sets the stage for induction as a process of elimination. As Sherlock Holmes put it: "Eliminate all other factors, and the one which remains must be the truth." Yet Holmes only tacitly recognized the necessity of abduction, the "chief elements" of which, in Peirce's words, are "its groundlessness, its ubiquity, and its trustworthiness."[18] Holmes explains his reasoning to Watson thus: "Ah, . . . that is good luck. I can only say what was the balance of probability. I did not expect to be so accurate.[19] He denied, however, that he had guessed: "No, no: I never guess. It is a shocking habit—destructive to the logical faculty." William of Baskerville explains himself to Adso in a more clearly Peircean way, but he is no less Holmesian for that:

> "Perhaps this is the right track. But it could also be just a series of coincidences. A rule of correspondences has to be found. . . ."
> "Found where?"
> "In our heads. Invent it. And then see whether it is the right one." (166)

Like Holmes, William notes the element of luck in formulating abductive hunches: "I won, but I might also have lost. The others believed me wise because I won, but they didn't know the many instances in which I have been foolish because I lost, and they didn't know that a few seconds before winning I wasn't sure I wouldn't lose" (305). Holmes formulated his abductions during the "extreme languors," often drug-induced, that made him formidable. Peirce names this process Pure Play, or Musement.[20] Adso describes William's state after chewing on certain herbs:

> In fact, he seemed absent, but every now and then his eyes brightened as if in the vacuum of his mind a new idea had kindled; then he would plunge once more into that singular and active hebetude of his. (213)

Like Holmes the chemist, William is an amateur herbalist and forms a close relationship with the abbey's herbalist, Severinus. Peirce noted that the roots of semiotics are to be found in ancient medical treatises, which display a logic of their own and lead toward the modern sciences. "Speaking in a broad, rough way, it may be said that the sciences have grown out of the useful arts, or out of arts supposed to be useful."[21]

The nominalism of Occam and the empiricism of Roger Bacon, the two Franciscan giants of the late Middle Ages, lead directly to William's Holmesianism. "And I, on the contrary, find the most joyful delight in unraveling a nice, complicated knot. And it must also be because, at a time when as philosopher I doubt the world has an order, I am consoled to discover, if not an order, at least a series of connections in small areas of the world's affairs" (394). These consolations of philosophy are semiotics.

The secret cipher that is the key to the mystery of the library is a set of anagrams drawn from quotations from the book of Revelation. The code is found by using the first letters of the citation, associating these letters with the room in which they are found, and deriving full names from the relation of the rooms (now alphabetic signs) to each other.

"The system of words was eccentric," Adso says.

> At times it proceeded in a single direction, at other times it went backward, at still others in a circle; often, as I said before, the same letter served to compose two different words (and in these instances the room had one case devoted to one subject and one to another). But obviously there was no point looking for a golden rule in this arrangement. It was purely a mnemonic device to allow the librarian to find a given work. (320)

In this code Eco does homage to the other "founder" of modern semiotics, the Swiss linguist Ferdinand de Saussure, whose obsession it was to discover anagrams, hypograms, and anaphonies (as he called them) of names in the verses of Greek and Latin poets. Saussure believed that the ancients wrote in secret anagrams even in their most casual writing—"second nature" it was to them, he believed. The many dozens of unpublished notebooks Saussure devoted to his studies of anagrams seem an odd aberration to some; as Saussure himself pointed out, critics find it either too hard to locate such anagrams, suggesting that his contention that they were universal is wrong, or too easy to find them, suggesting that they are, rather, a product of language itself, not a special device. The study of Saussure's anagrams by Jean Starobinski, however, underlines one lesson his work has to teach us:

> Decipherers, whether they be cabalists or phoneticists, have a free range: a reading which is symbolic or numeric or systematically attentive to a partial aspect can always bring to light a latent depth, a hidden secret, a language within the language. And if there is no cipher? The constant attraction of the secret, of anticipated discovery, of steps astray in the labyrinth of exegesis—all these would remain.[22]

Here, the image of the labyrinth, so central to *The Name of the Rose*, reappears. It is the sort of repetitive clue any detective finds helpful—when it is not a false scent.

The words beneath words that William of Baskerville finds are both revelatory and derived from the great Revelation, the end of the sacred book. The labyrinth of language stands for the labyrinth of the library, which is itself a figure of the labyrinth confronting a life seeking salvation, or a text its ending, or a mystery its solution. At each step, and at many more I have not suggested, the imagery points two ways: on the one hand, toward the *end*, the solution, meaning, closure which readers have sought in books for millennia as seriously and cleverly as William seeks the murderer or as Adso seeks salvation; and on the other, away from the end, toward the beginning, closer to the primal stuff from which the whole is made, the chaos from which God made order in the book at the opposite end—that is, the beginning—of the Christian Bible. This latter path, which notes "that behind each phrase lies hidden the multiple clamor from which it has attached itself to appear before us as an isolated individuality,"[23] leads to riddles, not solutions, and finds that every text is to some extent "open." A sign that points two ways is, in fact, no way out of a labyrinth. Adso's poor harvest of fragments at the end of the book—the library, the abbey, the age of realism, and so forth—merely repeats the coded mystery of the library labyrinth, but it has been thematized into a generalized search for meaning, sealing, as it were, the decodable solutions of the limited fourteenth-century allegories of Dante, the soluble crimes of Sherlock Holmes (as approached through Peirce's "abductive" reasoning), and the describable structures of Saussure. Semiotics, like Jorge of Burgos, is a "sort of ghostly presence" behind all human endeavor, because it is nothing less than the "historical and social result of the segmentation of the world" which makes any human consciousness possible.[24] Adso's dilemma is truly one of dissemination in the sense of Sollers and Derrida.

Umberto Eco's participation in politics—which, like semiotics, is the result of the "historical and social segmentation of the world"—has led to speculation on the "leftist" aspects of *The Name of the Rose*, with its references to Italian politics, to the confrontation of "open" systems with the great institutions (American and Soviet), the weight of which would prevent change and in effect close the text of history. These allegorical readings (the stuff of book jackets) can, like most interpretations, lead almost anywhere. Both a liberal and a communist can identify with the good guys and can describe his opponent in such a way as to conjure up the forces of repression.

Eco himself has written, in articles published in the mid-1970s in the

Italian magazine *Espresso*, of matters treated in *The Name of the Rose*. In an "Elogio di San Tommaso," Eco reflects on Thomas's great accomplishment and its unfortunate effects on Catholicism; the energy and inquiry of Thomas becomes in Thomism a system that paralyzes the future of Catholic thought. "That is, Thomas furnishes to Catholic thought a grid so complete, in which everything finds a place and an explanation, that from then on Catholic thought cannot displace anything." To symbolize for the readers of *Espresso* the immobilism of creative thought after the death of Thomas Aquinas, Eco cited the great problem faced by the monks of Fossanova in moving the fat man's corpse down the narrow stairs. In *The Name of the Rose*, the abbot, who wants to forbid inquiry and hush up any scandal in his abbey, has acquired his fame precisely by carrying Thomas's body down those stairs. The closure of Catholic thought after Aquinas leads to a displacement of the "tension and anxiety for learning" into the heretical movements and the Protestant Reformation. The Thomistic "grid" remained but not the energy that had been expended to make it. Henceforth, when it was a question of choosing between "yes" and "no," the latter always prevailed. Yet, in Thomas's time, according to Eco, to say "no" was a dialectical act, one that "did not mean to stop, but rather to take a step forward and to turn over the cards on the table." A modern Thomas Aquinas, Eco maintains, would be more combative and less conciliatory. "He would come to grips with Marxism, with relative physics, formal logic, existentialism, and phenomenology. He would not write on Aristotle, but rather on Marx and Freud." And any *summa* he might write would be looseleaf, with pages that could be substituted.[25]

In "I fratelli del libero festival," which appeared in *Expresso* in 1976, a meditation on the apocalyptic movements of the Middle Ages leads Eco to contemporary Italian terrorism and to some specific political advice for the Left. He leaves no doubt where he stands on the status of history: "without fear of seeming ridiculous," he writes, "history is the teacher of life." He quickly contradicts Marx on the nature of historical lessons. "And it is not at all true that events repeat themselves twice, once as tragedy and again as farce. Sometimes certain events repeat themselves cyclically, and always as tragedy." Eco's analysis of the apocalyptic movements of the Middle Ages, drawn mainly from Norman Cohn's *The Pursuit of the Millennium*, suggests that revolutionary eschatology in general is based on a misreading (we would say, an allegorical reading) of John's text, which refers specifically to events of his own time, to, for instance, the Roman emperors. Neither John nor, later, Augustine necessarily meant that temporal powers should always be associated with Satan. Nevertheless, groups of the elect, believing themselves "pure," prepared for sacrifices and, ready for martyrdom, set themselves against the powers, including the Church. "They are Christians, but against the Christian party."

Beside these groups, other, marginal ones arise, "in which hope and practical action prevail over doctrine." Composed of the bottom of society, these autonomous groups have little interest in doctrine. They identify the Antichrist with the clergy, cities, merchants, Jews. Bit by bit, they admit all sorts to their bands of the "pure." Sexual anarchists or sodomites, they will dress against the norm, either poorly or richly, and live apart. These groups have no real doctrinal discipline and may be given to such scapegoating as anti-Semitism. They have little to do with the revolutionary groups that were their inspiration. To public opinion, however, they are indistinguishable from them, and this perception can be used by those in power to bring about the extermination of *all* apocalyptic revolutionary groups. Eco's lesson, which addresses the problem of the Red Brigades for the Italian left, is precise:

> And if past events have any usefulness, they should show that the first duty of a revolutionary group is to define itself publicly with extreme exactness and rigor, in respect to spontaneous groups that objectively expose it to unconditional repression and isolate it in respect to observers foreign to the situation.

A sense of brotherhood should give way to one of doctrinal rigor. "Not all the poor help the poor, not all the desperate are brothers of the desperate."

Eco's critical politics, particularly his experience as a member of the leftist avantgarde Gruppo 63, seem to have left their mark in *The Name of the Rose* as well. Eco describes his former comrades in terms of medieval heresy:

> With Sanguineti, dialectic leads to a taste for compromise which is followed through to the ultimate acceptance of the historical impossibility of rebellion; it gives him a tinge of the gnostic and at one stage I insinuate this without ever getting a clear refutation of my suspicion. In fact, he gave me a shifty smile when he heard me suggesting it aloud.
>
> For the gnostic Carpocrates, the only way to deliver himself from the tyranny of the angels, lords of the cosmos, was to give in to the worst ignominies they could force on him in order to release himself from the debts contracted with each individual one of them. It's only by committing all possible actions that the soul can gain release from action and recover its original purity. By this interpretation, Jesus became the man who came to know all possible forms of evil but was able to triumph over it.
>
> Now Sanguineti's poetic theory, deriving as it does from a Marxist type of historical judgment, recognises the existence of a state of alienation which it

is the main undertaking of poetry to represent objectively. But poetry can only record the historical alienation by way of its reflection on language, language as a historical depository. The historic exhaustion of language, its ability to play out every variation, though in a deceptive style, its potential evocation of myths which no longer offer us any release—these are Sanguineti's themes, and he brings a prodigious verbal *virtuosité* to play on the double keyboard of an individual nervous breakdown and the collective nervous breakdown of Western history. One must cross the whole rotten swamp of language to reach a subsequent release: *Palus putredinis, Laborinthus* these are the recurring formulae in Sanguineti's work. Quotations from such medieval poets as Benvenuto da Imola and Evrard the German. In this swamp of culture a whole range of alchemical and Jungian symbols seethe like larvae made up of quotations from Pound, Eliot, and Marx. Sanguineti's language has all the feature of high middle-age *pastiche*; it achieves a grotesque, tragic-comic levelling of any myth that has ever nourished our hope for redemption. The historical avant-garde, with its taste for contamination, multilinguism, scissors-and-paste work, clever collage and all the rest, in fact attempts to reach its point of no return here.[26]

The description of Sanguineti's politics foreshadows Fra Dolcino's call to antinomian indulgence, while the poetics resemble the language of the onetime follower of Dolcino, Salvatore (whose speech has been described as Joycean). It is the language of the Apocalypse.

The vision of the end of the world has long been on people's minds. Each age seems to attribute the destruction of things to that power deemed strong enough and uncontrollable enough at any moment, whether it be nature or God or time or technology. Each age seems to believe that the danger it confronts is the most horrifying, the ultimate danger. The end of the world is always at hand; it is always taking place. "The end of the ancient world," "the world of yesterday" (ended by definition), "O brave new world" (replacing an old one), "the world we have lost"—all these expressions suggest that the image of the end of the world is indispensable to our historical notions of time and culture. At least in the West, the end of individual human life prompts an awareness of cultural change cast in its likeness: I die, and my world will also pass.

People, however, usually do not at the time notice the passage of historical "worlds." No news headline would have read "Roman Empire Falls," or "Age of Reason Over," because both the concept of the empire and the age are historical constructs, and so is the notion of beginnings and endings. Representation and its modes here define the past they create.

The end of the medieval world was unusual in that it came at a time when people were peculiarly attuned to the notion of ends. First, of course, there is the notion of Apocalypse, the physical ending of creation, an event that is metahistorical because it encompasses the idea of the closure of history. Second, there is the notion of the end of an age, a world in the sense of a culture; this is the end of the world as historians speak of it. Finally, there is the sense pointed out by Otto Friedrich in his recent history of thought on the end of the world. "The end of the world is, in a way, a pun. The end can mean not only the conclusion but also the purpose of the world."[27] *The Name of the Rose* weaves these three "ends" closely into its text.

The reality of the Apocalypse is taken for granted in the monastery of *The Name of the Rose*; its millenarian character is not deterred by the failure of the world to end after the thousandth year since the birth or crucifixion of Christ, since the date of the Donation of Constantine had been substituted as a point of origin. Clearly the end of the world is always at hand, as the parents and grandparents of the odd Salvatore concluded from the many doomsayers of their experience (187). The Apocalypse of St. John was the apparent directive force behind the murders in the abbey and a clear sign that the end of the world was closer and closer at hand, as each new corpse experienced the catastrophe of another day of the last moments of earth. The terrible sermon of Jorge of Burgos near the end of the book says: "And the times of the end will have come, and the end of time . . ." (404). All in divine retribution for the sin of pride precisely spelled out in the book of Revelation.

The end of time, however, is not the same as the end of *a* time, the sense that a form of life with focus, meaning, and accomplishment was dying. This is a sentiment very much based on the experience of human life; surely the young are less likely to believe that their age is an old one than are the elderly. The sense of an impending Apocalypse, however, led the aged Adso to write: "Because of mankind's sins the world is teetering on the brink of the abyss, permeated by the very abyss that the abyss invokes. And tomorrow, as Honorius would have it, men's bodies will be smaller than ours, just as ours are smaller than those of the ancients. *Mundus senescit*" (36). Discussions of the aging of the world are found throughout Eco's novel. Even William of Baskerville, who keenly sees through this metaphoric vision of the world which gives it the form of a human life, will admit that some forms of devotion are dead in his day and that the talk of penitence is mere nostalgia (118). However, William also notes—in a phrase as anachronistic as the notion of nostalgia—that even the dwarfs of his own age may see further than the giants of the past because the lesser men stand on the shoulders of the greater (85–86). Adso never accepts this idea of progressive knowledge. It remains for him intellectual pride. "Quite different was the scribe-monk imagined by our sainted founder, capable of copying without understanding, surrendered to the will of God, writing as if praying, and praying inasmuch as he was writing. Why was it no longer so? Oh, this was surely not the only degeneration of our order!" (184)

The debate in the fourteenth century about the status of learning, a particular historical issue, leads to the metahistorical debate about the third sense of the "end," the purpose of the world. About this there are several opinions. Jorge, of course, believes that the world is a closed form, God's perfect creation, to be known by revealed truth. William doubts that the world has a form at all. As a good Occamite, he feels that any notion of an "end" is contrary to the notion of God, who "is something absolutely free, so that if He wanted, with a single act of His will He could make the world different" (207). Between these positions we find Adso, trying to make sense of the scattered bits of experience he has and—like the initial narrator, who has found the remains of Adso's tale—ultimately resigned to simple narrative. Seeking the sense of these endings, so clearly tied together in the holocaust of the library—it is Nicholas of Morimondo, of the "dead world," who utters the words, "The library is on fire!" (486)—leads Adso to despair, or at least resignation. Another sort of reader, a postmodern one perhaps, is led instead to laughter.

What is the "sheer narrative pleasure" (5) described by the narrator? Is it more than the sensual delight of writing in "those large notebooks from the Papeterie Joseph Gibert in which it so pleasant to write if you use a felt-tip pen" (1)? This witty example of what Roland Barthes called the "reality effect" clearly foreshadows the thematic importance of the physical objects pertaining to writing, with a nod to Barthes, who best describes the sensual nature of writing and reading; but there seems to be more at work here than a tribute to the philosopher of the book and the body, the text of pleasure and the text of bliss. There is a darker side to this book as a human product, suggested in a trivial way by the old Adso at the end of the book when he complains, "It is cold in the scriptorium, my thumb aches" (502). The book serves as a substitute for a loss, in fact a double loss, in fact a doubled double loss. For the narrator, the book coincides with the loss of love.

> Before we reached Salzburg, one tragic night in a little hotel on the shores of the Mondsee, my travelling-companionship was abruptly interrupted, and the person with whom I was traveling disappeared—taking Abbé Vallet's book, not out of spite, but because of the abrupt and untidy way in which our relationship ended. And so I was left with a number of manuscript notebooks in my hand, and a great emptiness in my heart. (2)

It also coincided with the Soviet occupation of Prague, a major political loss for the left in Western Europe. This book, then, is as much pain as pleasure, meant to fill the personal and political gaps left in the course of personal and political history.

If history and life are the realm of the individual, the unique, what are we to make of the fact that the story which the narrator brings to us as a response to his loss is itself a response to another personal and historical loss, the experience of Adso of Melk? The battle Adso and William fought against the papal inquisitors was clearly lost, and their hopes for compromise and toleration of a different idea of the religious life were crushed just as surely as the "socialism with a human face" of the Prague spring in '68. History becomes repetition, and so does individuality, because Adso is also writing to fill a personal loss, the tragic loss of the young woman, his only carnal experience, who will be burned as a witch for her poverty and weakness. Her memory is immediately turned into a book by Adso, long before his labor of old age. As part of the universe, "a book written by the finger of God," she has her place "(sinner though she may have been) . . . nevertheless a chapter in the great book of creation, a verse of the great psalm chanted by the cosmos " (279). Here, I am not far from suggesting that Adso created his text simply to place his beloved, whose *name* he would never know, in it. History as repetition, individual life as repetition—even the book is repetition, if we are to believe Borges, who has written precisely that "Dante, when Beatrice was dead, when Beatrice was lost forever, played with the idea of finding her, to mitigate his sorrow. I believe that he erected the triple architecture of his poem simply to insert that encounter."[28] Adso, too?

The language of Adso's passion is couched in terms that seem, and are, mystical in a conventional religious sense; but there are also clear traces of Derrida. It is Derrida who has questioned the privilege given to "presence," which, he claims, is the effect of innumerable traces of absence, and to identity, which he views as always undermined by the repetition that constitutes identity, even in denying it. Adso, in his romantic rapture, asks himself whether divine and sinful delight differ. "At that moment the watchful sense of difference was annihilated in me. And this, it seems to me, is precisely the sign of rapture in the abysses of identity" (245). At another point, Adso seems to make sport with Derrida's play of presence and absence when he writes, ". . . I suffered from an absence, though I was happy with the many ghosts [*fantasmi*] of a presence" (279).[29]

The *fantasmi* of presence-as-absence returns at the end of *The Name of the Rose*, when Adso returns to the site of the events and begins to gather scraps.

Some fragments of parchment had faded, others permitted the glimpse of an image's shadow, or the ghost [*fantasma*] of one or more words. At times I found pages where whole sentences were legible; more often, intact bindings, protected by what had once been metal studs. . . . Ghosts [*Larve*] of books, apparently intact on the outside but consumed within; yet sometimes a half page had been saved, an incipit was discernible, a title. (500).

When Adso runs about after the great conflagration, gathering up any bit of charred parchment or paper that may have survived in the hope that some final meaning may be drawn from these remains, he is unknowingly reenacting the story of St. Francis of Assisi, who picked up every piece of written matter from the ground, pagan works included. When asked why, he replied: "Fili mi, litterae sunt ex quibus componitur gloriosissimum Dei nomen."[30] Adso, of course, comes to quite a different conclusion about the "kind of lesser library, a symbol of the greater, vanished one: a library made up of fragments, quotations, unfinished sentences, amputated stumps of books" (500). These scraps also allude to Dante's vision at the end of *Paradiso* of a volume in which Love has bound together in one volume what is scattered in leaves throughout the universe.

> Nel suo profondo vidi che s'interna,
> > legato con amore in un volume,
> > ciò che per l'universo si squaderna:
> sustanze e accidenti e lor costume,
> > quasi conflati insieme, per tal modo
> > che ciò ch'i'dico è un semplice lume.
> > > [XXXIII, 85–90]

In its depth I saw that it contained, bound by love in one volume, that which is scattered in leaves through the universe, substances and relations as it were fused together in such a way that what I tell of is a simple light.

Adso has no such vision; he finds no message in his collection of scraps, nor in the tale he has told. He confronts, with discomfort, the situation that is the discomfort of modern criticism. "And it is a hard thing for this old monk, on the threshold of death, not to know whether the letter he has written contains some hidden meaning, or more than one, or many, or none at all" (501). Yet his book exists, bound (like the narrator's) by (lost) love— like Dante's, too, if Borges' suggestion is to be believed. And, like *Through the Looking-Glass*, of which Hélène Cixous has written:

Thus it is that the reader-pursuer almost lays hands on the escaped text, but never completely. In the same way it will never be exactly time for Alice to

eat the jam if she enters the service of the White Queen; symbolic of the
interdiction which weighs on all food, and on consumption in general or on
reward, is the offer of employment which the queen makes to the little girl
("twopence a week, and jam every other day, — jam yesterday and jam
tomorrow, but never jam today?"). This stresses allegorically the nongratifying
relationship which this book establishes with the reader: no day will be the
day of meaning, but there is meaning on the one side and on the other of the
time of reading, meaning both promised and inaccessible.[31]

Adso's book, born of both a holocaust and the traces of other books, brings
us back to the problem of postmodernist and poststructuralist literature. It is
an allegory of the deconstruction of the book undertaken by Derrida but even
more specifically undertaken by Edmond Jabès, the Egyptian-born fran-
cophone poet whose influence on Derrida is clear. Jabès writes of the book as
shattered and dispersed, eternally recomposed from the scraps of earlier
books. The model for this is the destruction of the first tables of Mosaic law.[32]

> One passage of particular importance to me, as you know, is where I say
> that the Hebrew people gave Moses a crucial lesson in reading when they
> forced him to break the tablets of the law. Because they were not able to
> accept a word without origins, the word of God. It was necessary for Moses to
> break the book in order for the book to become human. . . . This gesture on
> the part of the Hebrew people was necessary before they could accept the
> book. This is exactly what we do as well. We destroy the book when we read
> it in order to make it into another book. The book is always born from a
> broken book. And the word, too, is born from a broken word. . . .[33]

The ironies of attributing the French translation of Adso's manuscript to the
presses of *l'Abbaye de la Source* have been noted in Walter E. Stephens' excellent
essay, "Ec[h]o in Fabula."[34] The many feints of the narrator's introduction to
The Name of the Rose obscure its origins; it has no beginning. It is always born
from a broken book.

We are back to a teleological discussion: what is the relation between the
end of the book, the end of this book, and the end of the world, in all the
senses of that expression? The political end of human power and dignity was
asserted by William because God gave Adam the right to name his world, an
incomparable freedom to create. Yet, as Aristotle must have said in his
forbidden book, the poor and lowly will have a different truth, and different
names for their world; surely part of this response will be found in the playful
misnaming and renaming that comes from metaphor and in the radical,
cathartic power of comedy. As Jorge knew, laughter is always an attack on
power. Poverty is also an attack on power, insofar as it is a principled refusal of

corruption. Still, as Remigio the heretic said, "As you grow old, you grow not wise but greedy" (273). Perfection is not for humans. And this is why the open world, the open library, the open debate, and the "open work" are so important. Our nominalism is a nominalism of readers of the world, of semioticians who will always want to know the names of things, and know as well that these names are *our* names, ready to be changed for human needs. As the legendary fourteenth-century girl from Verona said (in a later, and surely corrupt translation of her words): "What's in a name? A rose by any other name would smell as sweet."

At the conclusion of *The Name of the Rose*—that is, after the holocaust—Adso thematizes the reader's plight as he puzzles over the remaining scraps of the library and the culture destroyed by Jorge's laughing hatred of laughter. Like Adso, we are reminded here that the role of the reader is to find senses, the role of the critic to undo them, and that all of this is actually rather funny, or, at least, laughable. A droll battle of books within *The Name of the Rose*, a *bibliomachia*, lends a precarious structure to the ostensible theme of popular culture and its tragic links with laughter.

The intrusion of laughter into the somber abbey of *The Name of the Rose* is an odd note. How does this lost part of Aristotle's *Poetics*, sought by so many and by one with a consuming passion, lead Eco's book toward its end? Laughter is forbidden by the Rule of St. Benedict, and the outbursts among the monks always prompt censure and explanation. The first appearance of Jorge of Burgos finds him not only scorning laughter but associating it with the "modern," fanciful art of the abbey's manuscripts and sculptures, and with figural language in general. He sees all anti-mimetic representation as dangerous in the same way that laughter is dangerous. Here, Jorge is the spokesman for "realism" in both its philosophical and aesthetic form:

> "And as there is bad speech there are also bad images. And they are those that lie about the form of creation and show the world as the opposite of what it should be, has always been, and always will be throughout the centuries until the end of time." (79)

When William and Adso find the notes taken by the murdered Venantius from the mysterious book, the fragments, though meaningless, contain "references to the simple folk and to peasants as bearers of a truth different from that of the wise" (285). Laughter is thus related to heresy and to inquiry; it is the preface to doubt and to the open world of discovery. Those who would add to the world read it as an "open work"; they must laugh at it. In doing so, they inevitably undermine whatever structures of authority exist.[35]

The discussion of laughter proceeds at the level of ancient authorities among the monks in *The Name of the Rose*. Their most Christian concerns, such as whether Christ or the saints ever laughed, are direct descendants of Plato's worry about the moral effects of representing the gods or persons of worth overcome with laughter. What is implicit in these discussions (and in the ancient authorities) is political power, a different sort of authority. The practice of power in the Middle Ages existed in intimate dialogue with laughter, which was its "other."

In thematizing the subversive role of laughter as a metaverbal commentary, as opposed to a verbal metacommentary (which always proves authoritarian), Eco introduces into his text the problematics of the Russian critic Mikhail Bakhtin. In *Rabelais and His World*, Bakhtin sketches a history of laughter and a theory of laughter and the carnivalesque. According to Bakhtin, the Middle Ages was the high point in the history of laughter, which served a role at once universal, philosophic, and essential. To a large extent, subsequent history has been the story of the limiting, interpreting, marginalizing, and degrading of the grotesque, comic, and carnivalesque, leading to a modern world which, by implication, has no general response to the totalitarian demands of authority. Bakhtin's emphasis on laughter as a political act, which some have seen as a response to the Stalinist regime which for so long delayed the publication of *Rabelais and His World*, provides the view from below of the classical (and modern) restrictions on laughter in the interest of class and *dignitas*.[36]

Medieval laughter had three basic aspects, which it bequeathed to the Renaissance but which would later be lost. First, it was universal; it was never aimed at merely a part of society by another. "One might say that it builds its own world versus the official world, its own church versus the official church, its own state versus the official state." Second, medieval laughter retained an "indissoluble and essential relation to freedom." Finally, and most important, laughter was the form of the unofficial truth of the people as William and Adso learned from Venantius' notes.

> The serious aspects of class culture are official and authoritarian; they are always combined with violence, prohibitions, limitations, and always contain an element of fear and intimidation. These elements prevailed in the Middle Ages. Laughter, on the contrary overcomes fear, for it knows no inhibitions, no limitations. Its idiom is never used by violence and authority.
>
> It was the victory of laughter over fear that most impressed medieval man.[37]

In other words, Bakhtin sees the universal counterworld of laughter as fundamentally dialectical, creating the "other" voice confronting authority, a second voice which history must unfold. Hence, the emphasis on time, change, death, and rebirth. Bakhtin wrote of the "dialogization" that takes place when a word or a discourse enters the world of other words and discourses, with which it must interact in an open-ended way that brings language into the marketplace, carnivalizes it, and removes its static sacredness by submitting it to laughter, which is the emblem of change in the world.[38]

Within *The Name of the Rose,* such a carnivalized, learned dialogue proceeds between the *theory* of laughter, drawn from the ancients and represented by the allusion to E. R. Curtius' magisterial *European Literature and the Latin Middle Ages,* from which the debate between William of Baskerville and Jorge of Burgos and a great deal of other information are drawn,[39] and the *practice* of medieval laughter stressed by Bakhtin. It is the nature of this folk laughter that provides the subtext for the entire discussion of learned theory and citation of ancient authority.

Yet the final terror of Jorge's laughter as he begins the conflagration that will destroy the world of the library seems inadequately accounted for by Curtius or Bakhtin. It is Baudelaire who points out the satanic quality of laughter, who links it with the contradictory essence of humanity; it is a sign "at once the sign of an infinite grandeur and of an infinite wretchedness, a wretchedness relative to the absolute Being, which conception it possesses, a grandeur relative to the animals."[40] For Baudelaire, laughter is a sign, a semiotic index of both the greatness and the wretchedness of the human condition, of both mind and death.

The semiotic function of laughter is described by Georges Bataille in an essay "The Labyrinth." Following Baudelaire, Bataille places laughter at the demonic pole of life:

> But laughter is not only the composition of those it assembles into a unique
> convulsion; it most often decomposes without consequence, and sometimes
> with a virulence that is so pernicious that it even puts in question
> composition itself, and the wholes across which it functions. Laughter attains
> not only the peripheral regions of existence, and its object is not only the
> existence of fools and children (of those who remain vacant); through a
> necessary reversal, it sent back from the child to its father and from the
> periphery to the center, each time the father or the center in turn reveals an
> insufficiency comparable to that of the particles that orbit around it. Such a
> central insufficiency can be ritually revealed (in saturnalia or on a festival of
> the ass as well as in the puerile grimaces of the father amusing his child). It
> can be revealed by the very action of children or the "poor" each time
> exhaustion withers and weakens authority, allowing its precarious character to
> be seen. In both cases, a dominant necessity manifests itself, and the

profound nature of being is disclosed. Being can complete itself and attain the menacing grandeur of imperative totality; this accomplishment only serves to project it with a greater violence into the vacant night.

THE UNIVERSAL resembles a bull, sometimes absorbed into the nonchalance of animality and abandoned to the secret paleness of death, and sometimes hurled by the rage of ruin into the void ceaselessly opened before it by a skeletal torero. But the void it meets is also the nudity it esposes TO THE EXTENT THAT IT IS A MONSTER lightly assuming many crimes, and it is no longer, like the bull, the plaything of nothingness, because nothingness itself is its plaything; it only throws itself into nothingness in order to tear it apart and to illuminate the night for an instant, with an immense laugh—a laugh it would never have attained if this nothingness had not totally opened beneath its feet.[41]

Jorge saw himself as a narrative victor, ending the story with the last laugh ("You did not expect this conclusion, did you . . ."). But no story can end while there is still laughter, the deconstructive power of which, according to Bataille, never quite permits the *universalizing* closure that offers meaning. Adso tries and gives up—the story is all there is, and it will not stop; the writer simply gets tired (and a sore thumb).

Jacques Derrida also focuses on laughter in his discussion of Bataille and Hegel, pointing out that Hegel failed to admit laughter into his system because the system knows only knowledge, it does not recognize the sacred laughing nature of the *Aufhebung*, which also, we might say, refuses to let the story end.[42]

Eco has distinguished between three varieties of labyrinth. First is the Greek labyrinth (Theseus and Ariadne), a canny sort of maze, with one way in and one way out. The terror comes from knowing that there is a minotaur at the center. Second is what Eco calls a "mannerist labyrinth," a root structure with many dead ends. Finally, he mentions what Deleuze and Guattari call the rhizome, which has no center, no periphery, no exit and is potentially infinite. Eco comments: "The labyrinth of my library is a manneristic labyrinth, but the world in which Guglielmo realizes he is living is already structured like a rhizome: that is, it is structurable but never definitely structured."[43] Considering what Bataille wrote about the monster in the laybrinth, I would add that the library is all three forms at once.

And to say this, to chase down the references and games and trails of *The Name of the Rose*—should not this readerly activity provoke its own sort of laughter? *The Name of the Rose* casts each reader as Adso, as Dr. Watson, as the butt of many jokes, the biggest of which is the process of reading the novel at all. To cite Eco on Derrida on Bataille on Hegel on laughter is rather droll; at best, it is Adso-izing, at worst a sort of Hegelian Jorge-ism, a search for the authority that will end the story by giving it meaning (and us knowledge), the universalizing monster of narrative closure. Like Adso, the wiser we become, the more foolish we feel.

Notes

1. Umberto Eco, *The Name of the Rose*, trans. William Weaver (San Diego: Harcourt Brace Jovanovich, 1983), 3. Subsequent citations appear in the text.

2. Lewis Carroll, *The Annotated Alice*, ed. Martin Gardner (New York: C. N. Potter, 1960), 225.

3. Carroll, 227n7.

4. Carroll, 268n6.

5. Carroll, 306.

6. Cited in David Knowles, *The Evolution of Medieval Thought* (Baltimore: Helicon, 1962), 322.

7. "A given thing, a dog or rose, evokes in the human mind a mental 'sign' (*signum naturale*) which is the same in all men, as is a laugh or a cry; each race of men then gives to this sign a verbal sign or term or name in its own language, which we attach to our mental image and which recalls that image to our mind. . . . In other words, the universal only exists because it is framed by the mind, and the term or word (dog, rose, &c.) is a sign which we attach to our mental intuition, and which recalls it to us." Knowles, *Evolution of Medieval Thought*, 322.

8. Knowles, *Evolution of Medieval Thought*, 329.

9. Umberto Eco, *The Role of the Reader: Explorations in the Semiotics of Texts* (Bloomington: Indiana University Press, 1979), 56.

10. Borges, *Selected Poems: 1923–1967* (New York: Delacorte, 1972), xv.

11.

> Nadie rebaje a lágrima o reproche
> Esta declaración de la maestría
> De Dios, que con magnífica ironía
> Me dió a la vez los libros y la noche.
>
> De esta ciudad de libros hizo dueños
> A unos ojos sin luz, que solo pueden
> Leer en las bibliotecas de los sueños
> Los insensatos, párrafos que ceden
>
> Las albas a su afán. . . .

Translated by Alastair Reid.

12.

> La rosa,
> la inmarcesibile rosa que no canto,
> la que es peso y fragancia,
> la del negro jardín en la alta noche,
> la de cualquier jardín y cualquier tarde,

> la rosa que resurge de la tenue
> ceniza por el arte de la alquimia,
> la rosa de los persas y de Ariosto,
> la que siempre está sola,
> la que siempre es la rosa de las rosas,
> la joven flor platónica,
> la ardiente y ciega rosa que no canto,
> la rosa inalcanzable.

Translated by N. Thomas di Giovanni.

13. Borges, "From Allegories to Novels," in *Other Inquisitions: 1937–1952*, trans. R. C. Simms (Austin: University of Texas Press, 1964), 157.

14. Umberto Eco and G. B. Zorzoli, *A Pictorial History of Inventions from Plow to Polaris*, trans. A. Lawrence (New York: Macmillan, 1963), 106.

15. Eco and Zorzoli, 105.

16. The debt of modern semiotics to Peirce and Saussure, "predecessors to be honored," is described in Jonathan Culler, *The Pursuit of Signs* (Ithaca: Cornell University Press, 1981), chap. 2

17. Thomas A. Sebeok, "You Know My Method: A Juxtaposition of Charles S. Peirce and Sherlock Holmes," in *The Play of Musement* (Bloomington: Indiana University Press, 1981), 34.

18. Sebeok, 24.

19. Cited in Sebeok, 19.

20. Sebeok, 35.

21. Cited in Sebeok, 36.

22. Starobinski, *Words Upon Words: The Anagrams of Ferdinand de Saussure*, trans. O. Emmet (New Haven: Yale University Press, 1979), 129.

23. Starobinski, 122.

24. Umberto Eco, *A Theory of Semiotics* (Bloomington: Indiana University Press, 1976), 315.

25. Umberto Eco, *Dalla perifero dell'impero* (Milano: Bompiani, 1977), 132–133. I thank Professor Mary P. Aversano for her translations.

26. Eco, "The Death of the *Gruppo 63*," in *20th Century Studies* (Sept. 1971): 65.

27. Friedrich, *The End of the World: A History* (New York: Coward, McCann, and Geoghegan, 1982), 12.

28. Borges, "The Meeting in a Dream," in *Other Inquisitions: 1937-1952*, 100.

29. In Derrida, writing finds a champion who privileges it over speech, which he considers to be but a special form of writing. If bibliolatry seems scarcely too strong a term for this attitude, it is clearly part of Eco's world. The epigraph to *The Name of the Rose* reads, "Naturally, a manuscript," suggesting that writing is a part of *nature*, not a mere human supplement. To be sure, nature herself is in question in the book; to the mystic Ubertino's comment that Nature is good because she is the daughter of God, William pointedly responds, "And God must be good, since He generated Nature" (61).

30. E. R. Curtius, *European Literature and the Latin Middle Ages*, trans. W. R. Trask (Princeton: Princeton University Press, 1953), 319.

31. Cixous, "Introduction to Lewis Carroll's *Through the Looking-Glass* and *The Hunting of the Snark*," *New Literary History* 13 (1982): 237 (French original, 1971).

32. The vital importance of the destruction of the tables in Derridean thought derives from its representation of his view of all human writing:

> Poetic autonomy, similar to no other, presupposes the broken Tables.
>
> *"And Reb Lima: 'Liberty was originally engraved ten times on the Tables of the Law, but we deserved it so little that the Prophet broke them in his anger.' "*
>
> Between the pieces of the broken Tables the poem sprouts and the right to the word takes root.

Jacques Derrida, "Edmond Jabès et le question du livre," in *L'Ecriture et la différence* (Paris: Seuil, 1967), 102.

33. From Paul Auster, "Book of the Dead: An Interview with Edmond Jabès," in *The Sin of the Book: Edmond Jabès*, ed. E. Gould (Lincoln: University of Nebraska Press, 1985), 23.

34. *Diacritics* (Summer 1983): 51–64.

35. The debate over laughter is a forgotten but vital element in Christian tradition. From the early church fathers to the Puritans, the ban on outward displays of frivolity has been an essential part of piety because it points to the tragic aspects of earthly life, the fallen nature of man, and the concentration of the believer on higher matters. According to Ernst Robert Curtius, early Christian monasticism took over the ancient (Roman) ideal of *dignitas*, so that Benedict's momentous stricture follows the model of Athanasius, Sulpicius Severus, Ephraim, Basil, and Cassianus. As late as the seventeenth century, Jansenist writers could warn "Malheur à vous qui riez." E. R. Curtius, *European Literature and the Latin Middle Ages*, trans. W. Trask (Princeton: Princeton University Press, 1953), 420–422.

Plato's view of laughter was generally negative, though he granted that serious things cannot be known without their opposites. Nevertheless, in the *Laws* [V, 732C] he would ban laughter on serious occasions and would require slaves and foreigners to play comic roles, since virtuous men cannot take an interest in the subjects of comedy [VII, 816–817]. In the *Republic* this socio-moral division demands that the guardians not laugh, nor may persons of worth or the gods be shown overcome with laughter [II, 388E]. Clearly, this disqualifies much of Greek literature as we know it.

Aristotle's discussion is more varied and psychological. The origin of genres is found in the distinction of the less worthy comic from the higher seriousness [*Rhetoric*], yet there is pleasure in imitating even the ugly and grotesque matters which comedy concerns, the pleasure in learning [*Poetics*]. In the *Ethics*, Aristotle follows Plato in noting that amusement is valuable as relaxation because it better enables one to be serious; he carefully distinguishes the buffoon and boor from the truly witty person, who is a law unto himself. The danger implicit in this last point also surfaces in the *Rhetoric*, where it is noted that the young love laughter while the old are not witty. See the discussion in M. A. Grant, *The Ancient Rhetorical Theories of the Laughable*, (Madison: University of Wisconsin Press, 1924), 17–32.

36. Hayden White, "The Authoritative Lie," *Partisan Review* #2 (1983): 307–12.

37. Mikhail Bakhtin, *Rabelais and His World* (Cambridge, Mass.: M.I.T. Press, 1968), 88–90.

38. On Bakhtin, see Dominick LaCapra's essay, "Bakhtin, Marxism, and the Carnivalesque," in *Rethinking Intellectual History: Texts, Contexts, Language* (Ithaca: Cornell University Press, 1983).

39. For example, the exchange on pages 130–32 in *The Name of the Rose* comes directly from Curtius, 417-22.

40. Charles Baudelaire, "De l'Essence de rire," in *Curiosités esthetiques, Oeuvres complètes*, ed. J. Crépot (Paris, 1923), 379.

41. Bataille, *Visions of Excess: Selected Writings, 1927–1939*, ed. A Stoekl (Minneapolis: University of Minnesota Press, 1985), 176, 177.

42. Derrida, *L'Ecriture et la différence*, 378.

43. Stefano Rosso, "A Correspondence with Umberto Eco," trans. C. Springer, *Boundary 2* 12 (Fall 1983), 7.

2 Apocalyptic Visions and Visionaries in *The Name of the Rose*

Lois Parkinson Zamora

Readers of Umberto Eco's novel know that the seven trumpet woes listed by John of Patmos in the Book of Revelation provide what William of Baskerville mistakenly believes to be an explanatory pattern behind the series of murders taking place in a great abbey in northern Italy in 1327. It is after two monks have been murdered and a third is missing that an emerging pattern, based on apocalyptic symbols, is suggested to William by the old monk, Alinardo of Grottaferrata.

> "Too many dead," he said, "too many dead . . . But it was written in the book of the apostle. With the first trumpet came the hail, with the second a third part of the sea became blood; and you found one body in the hail, the other in blood. . . . The third trumpet warns that a burning star will fall in the third part of rivers and fountains of waters. So I tell you, our third brother has disappeared. And fear for the fourth, because the third part of the sun will be smitten, and of the moon and stars, so there will be almost complete darkness. . . ."[1]

Alinardo's intuition of an apocalyptic progression appears to be confirmed by subsequent events—the third victim, Berengar, is indeed found drowned in the balneary, the fourth, Severinus, is murdered by a blow to the head with an armillary sphere representing the vault of heaven, and the expiring Malachi refers enigmatically to the scorpions described by the fifth trumpet. Thus William (and the reader) accept the hypothesis that John's enumeration of the plagues preceding the end of the world describes not only God's plot but the murderer's as well. Along with William, we begin to interpret, and even anticipate, clues according to the seried apocalyptic prophecies of disaster.

It is when one of the murderers hears that William is pursuing this apocalyptic pattern that cause and effect, crimes and clues begin to blur. Jorge of Burgos finds that it serves his purposes to conform to William's hypothesis, and he obligingly leaves apocalyptic symbols along his way. Thus, what is posited as a means of detecting the murderer becomes in part his motivation, because the spurious link to Revelation gives Jorge's actions the seeming stamp of divine direction, and allows him to justify himself in these terms. He consciously elaborates and extends the apocalyptic pattern William seeks in his symbolic warning to Malachi that the book in his possession has the lethal power of a thousand scorpions; and he seems to respond unconsciously to that pattern in his final, desperate eating of the text which he himself has poisoned. Just as the murders have been linked to John's apocalyptic vision, so this final image of the murderer links him ironically to John himself, who, in Revelation 10:10, obeys the divine command to eat the book he has written. As if to confirm the apparent pun on the consuming quality of the apocalyptic text (as well as to explain his mistaken imposition of the apocalyptic pattern on events), William observes, "Everyone nowadays is obsessed with the book of John" (470).

The apocalyptic vision of *The Name of the Rose*—the fiery end of the abbey and the novel is no less apocalyptic for William's deductive error—makes the character's word "nowadays" almost amusingly self-conscious. Umberto Eco has often observed that what joins the world depicted in the novel to our own is precisely our shared sense of impending apocalypse, our common perception of living in a dangerous time of transition. Surely the immense popular success of this difficult novel must be attributed at least partially to this similarity.[2] Eco's writings on medieval philosophy and cultural semiotics attest to the fact that he himself has long been fascinated by apocalyptic texts. In this essay I will refer to his book-length study of the tenth-century Mozarabic San Isidoro illuminations of the eighth-century commentary on Revelation by the Asturian abbot, Beatus of Liébana; and to his very different use of apocalyptic archetypes in discussing the cultural implications of Superman and other such contemporary mythic heroes.[3] Eco's familiarity with apocalyptic texts explains far more than just the iconography of disaster that so richly furnishes his novel. More important, *The Name of the Rose* is also informed by the narrative assumptions and historical consequences of Judeo-Christian apocalyptic tradition. But before illustrating this assertion, a working definition of *apocalypse* may be useful.

The word itself comes from the Greek word meaning "discovery," "disclosure," "revelation," and refers to texts that share certain recognizable narrative subjects and conventions. In the canonic Hebrew apocalyptic texts—Ezekiel, Zachariah, Daniel—and in the Christian canon—the thirteenth chapter of Mark, the twenty-fourth chapter of Matthew, the Second Epistle of Peter, the Revelation of John (perhaps the finest and most complete example of the genre)—the apocalyptic narrator describes God's revelation of the turbulent events leading up to the end of the present world, the subsequent millennium—a thousand-year period ruled by Christ—a last loosing of Satan, then the New Jerusalem, the timeless paradise promised to God's elect. Apocalypse is eschatological (here the root is *eschatos*, "furthest," "uttermost"); it is concerned with the end of the present age, the Last Judgment, and the age to follow.

Biblical apocalyptic visions are binocular in nature, simultaneously entertaining images of cataclysm and millennium. While the apocalyptist describes in lurid images the upheavals by which he believes God signals the end of human history, he also foresees a realm of timeless perfection beyond the end of his own troubled times. In the Revelation of John, this duality of moral forces and temporal orders is embodied in the metaphoric contraries of Christ and Antichrist, bride and whore, the New Jerusalem and Babylon. Of course, the biblical apocalyptist and his audience believed they would be included among those to inhabit "the new heaven and new earth": the plagues and wars and upheavals were reserved for their enemies and for those who faltered in their faith. Thus, disaster becomes the visible sign of God's imminent justice and of his promise to his followers of a transcendent future.

Herein lies a central irony of apocalyptic texts: images of chaos—war and pestilence, earthquakes and floods, beasts, dragons, swarms of insects— served to reassure the believer of God's divine order and to reinforce his faith in God's ultimate triumph over evil in the world. Of the medieval audience for Revelation, Eco, in his essay on the Beatus manuscript, asserts that "People die, of hunger, of wars, of pestilence; the Apocalypse with its horsemen seems, to the stunned populace who hear it narrated by monks and parish priests, a chronicle of the present time. The opening of each seal must have appeared to a medieval listener much as the front page of the morning paper appears to us. . . . The only consolation was that all those scourges, long-lasting, endemic, were the harbingers of a decisive event, a resolution."[4] Although most contemporary readers of Revelation no longer take literally its descriptions and predictions, as medieval believers surely did, *The Name of the Rose* nonetheless exploits the strong appeal apocalyptic images of chaos and eventual order still hold for contemporary readers. In his essay on the Beatus manuscript, Umberto Eco addresses precisely this point: "Revelation is a permanent model of waiting for the end; it is the permanent model of a hope of transformation; it is the permanent model of a conflictuality that runs through all of human history."[5]

The Beatus manuscript is referred to repeatedly in *The Name of the Rose* and pictured in Eco's *Postscript to "The Name of the Rose"* as a way of illustrating passages from John's Revelation that are cited in the novel.[6] The presence of several medieval Spanish apocalypse manuscripts in the abbey's library, presumably other examples of the many illustrated versions of Beatus of Liébana's commentary, provides William with an important clue to the identity of the murderer—this time, as it happens, a clue that enlightens rather than obscures his path to the identity of the murderers. Given Eco's embedding of medieval apocalyptic texts in his own apocalyptic novel, and his assertion that Revelation is a "permanent model" of historical consciousness, William's word *nowadays* is indeed highly charged. The illustration from a Gothic apocalypse manuscript on the dust jacket of the American edition of *The Name of the Rose* adds an extratextual layer to the novel's insistence on the complex contemporaneity of the biblical apocalyptic tradition.

The perennial interest of Revelation on which Eco insists does not mean that its significance and its uses have remained static over the centuries. In our own times, apocalyptic visions are likely to be less religious than historical; the imagery of Revelation is frequently applied to political events and situations to suggest their cataclysmic potential, with no explicit expectation of recuperation or renewal. Although the word *apocalypse* was not originally a synonym for disaster or catastrophe, nor does it literally mean the end of the world, we currently use it almost exclusively in this way. Our contemporary emphasis on the cataclymsic side of Revelation usually does not indicate hope because the end is near, as it did for medieval men and women; instead, it suggests our pessimism about historical potential and our awareness of our own capacity for self-destruction.[7] Adso of Melk's narration is surprisingly modern in its emphasis on the apocalyptic iconography of disaster rather than of triumph, in its resignation to the end of the world. Passive waiting for the Second Coming and the consequent kingdom of God on earth was the prescribed medieval stance vis-à-vis the end of the world, but medieval orthodoxy would have demanded of Adso a greater emphasis on the divinely conceived new world that was soon to supersede the old—a posture of faith rather than despair. In Adso's final, skeptical emphasis on the pessimistic side of apocalypse, and in the political uses of apocalyptic visions by the religious groups that populate the novel, Eco dramatizes the subversive uses of apocalyptic ideas which by 1327 had begun to propel the medieval world toward the modern age.

I have said that Jorge of Burgos is in his final, fatal gesture, linked ironically to John of Patmos. It is much more Adso than Jorge, however, who bears the stamp of apocalyptic textual tradition. Adso himself is an apocalyptist; because of the apocalyptist's particular temporal perspective on events, his narration, whether biblical or medieval or modern, assumes a characteristic narrative form. (Adso's name is certainly calculated by Eco to recall Adso of Montier-en-Der, who wrote an apocalyptic narrative, *Libellus de Antechristo*, in 954.[8]) The apocalyptist purports to speak from a point beyond the end of the history he narrates, his sweeping perspective relating its beginning to its end in the most conclusive of terms. Speaking from his comprehensive temporal vantage point in Revelation, John senses himself compelled to write his history, for God has ordered him: "Write the things which thou has seen, the things which are, and the things which shall be hereafter" (Rev. 1:19), a command Adso also hears. Thus the apocalyptic narrator seeks to identify and codify God's design behind the concretions of reality, the meaning behind the persecution of God's chosen people, the transcendent end which their suffering serves. Writing from his exile on the Greek island of Patmos, John's coded message to the seven churches of Asia is an early example of what has become one of the most familiar of modern narrative stances: notes from underground. The apocalyptic narrator is alienated from the mainstream; he protests the entrenched system and its abuses and predicts its end. He is always, in some sense, an exile, an outsider, perhaps even an outlaw, distanced from the world he describes yet possessing an urgent moral stake in that world and its collective end. Contemporary novels as different from Eco's as Walker Percy's *Lancelot* and William Faulkner's *Absalom, Absalom!*, Gabriel García Márquez's *One Hundred Years of Solitude* and Alan Paton's *Too Late the Phalarope* are also explicitly apocalyptic in their imagery and narrative perspectives.[9] Like Adso, the narrators of these novels render accounts of entire worlds destroyed; their tone, like that of Adso, is elegaic, combining nostalgia and violence to tell their tales of loss.

The biblical apocalyptist struggles to reveal to his audience what he believes has been revealed to him by God. He sees himself—and is meant to be seen by his readers—as both decipherer of God's veiled truths and creator of his own veiled text, as both observer and participant in the historical drama he must also narrate. Thus Adso is simultaneously reader (or, perhaps, listener) and writer, seer and poet, voyeur and voyant. This aesthetic ambiguity became conventional in medieval painting, sculpture, and tapestry and has remained so until the present. In some artistic portrayals, John is depicted with his eyes gazing heavenward, his stylus poised on his tablet, as if taking divine dictation; in others, he stands to the side of a scene from Revelation, holding one end of a scroll that wafts down to him from an angel above, as if reading from it what his own text also describes.[10] Often, books are around him on a table or on the ground at his feet, as if to emphasize the scribal

nature of the apocalyptist's calling and connect him iconographically to the
Judaic prophetic tradition, which his visionary text continues and in a sense
culminates.

Apocalyptic texts are as concerned with concealing meaning as with
revealing it. Because John and his audience were outlaws in the Roman
empire, to narrate at all was dangerous; communication required a language
inaccessible to outsiders. Hermetic symbols and numerical patterns were
essential to their security, as they had been for the Hebrews, suffering
persecution under the empires of Babylonia, Persia, and Greece. The desire
for textual secrecy, however, lies deeper than self-protection, a point Frank
Kermode has explored in his recent study, *The Genesis of Secrecy*.[11] Not only
because of their historical circumstances but also because of their visionary
assumptions, apocalyptic texts, more than most literary texts, call for
interpretation and completion in ways intended to strictly limit their audience. Eco's often-quoted comment about the calculated difficulty of the
first hundred pages of his novel, by which he aimed to create his own readers,
is perfectly consonant with apocalyptic narrative intention: because of their
symbolic secrecy, apocalyptic texts always create their own readers.

The exclusionary ethic and aesthetic of apocalyptic narration, when
combined with the conventions of modern detective fiction, serves doubly to
emphasize the processes of interpretation. Detection and apocalypse are
analogous modes. Both involve the inference of cause from effect; both
attempt to decipher meaning from the signs available in the present (though
detection points toward an actual past, apocalypse toward a projected future).
Semiotic studies often invoke such conjectural activities to figure the activity
of the discipline itself, which, of course, is the study of signs and how signs
generate meaning.[12] Umberto Eco—a semiotican long before he was a
novelist—recognizes in the detective his romanticized image and in the
apocalyptist his mythic image.

Surely it is this complex hermeneutic activity of the apocalyptist, as well
as the transitional character of his fourteenth-century setting, that attracts
Eco to the narrative strategies of apocalypse. In his text on the Beatus
apocalypse, he writes: "Read today, and by a reader obsessed with the problem
of communication, the text of Revelation gives the comforting impression of
a message written in code. Images abound . . . and assail the reader in a
whirlwind of signs open to every reading."[13] Again the reference to an
obsession with apocalyptic narration, this time to the author's own rather
than to his character's; again the emphasis on the apocalyptist's struggle to
decipher and communicate what he believes to be the truth about his times.

Adso is eighteen at the time of the events he narrates. He directly associates himself with John when he tells his reader that, upon entering the abbatial church, he hears a voice "mighty as a trumpet that said, 'Write in a book what you now see' (and this is what I am doing)" (45). More than sixty years later, Adso recalls that command; but it is a more obscure compulsion than simple obedience that moves him to record the destruction of the abbey and the demise of the world it represents. Indeed, a delay of sixty years in obeying God's command hardly constitutes obedience. The two halves of this sentence figure the disjunction between the two Adsos—ingenuous, young believer and disillusioned, older narrator—whom Eco places in ironic relation at the end of the novel.

In the epilogue to his story, Adso muses on the compulsions that moved him to return to the abbey as an old man, first in person then in words. Like John in Revelation, Adso sees Christendom beseiged on every side; hence, he feels an urgent need to record past and present disasters and to warn of future ones—"divine chastisements," as he calls the disasters that destroy the abbey. And whom does he hope to warn? In his epilogue, Adso refers only to an "unknown reader"—his fellow clerics, we assume, though we might expect a more brotherly form of address; "unknown reader" is another of the strikingly, even anachronistically, modern notes of the epilogue. The clergy were the only literate people of the time, a point which the novel, with its central focus on written texts, makes clear. Of course, Adso knows that apocalyptic visions are widely consumed by an illiterate audience but in visual or aural form rather than in books. As he looks at the carved images from Revelation on the tympanum above the door of the abbatial church, he thinks of the "silent speech" of the carved stone images—"the literature of the layman" (41). We must assume, then, that Adso's written text is directed to like-minded clergy, both present and future. Indeed, scarcely a monk in the entire abbey misses the opportunity to utter apocalyptic phrases like "the foul beast that is the Antichrist," "the world is teetering on the brink of the abyss," "the stink of the cities," "fires, sacks, earthquakes," "*mundus senescit*," and so on. I have extracted these formulations from the abbot's words of welcome (!) to William and Adso, but they are typical of those used constantly at every level of the monastic hierarchy. Thus, from the outset of Adso's story, we are reminded of the community of interest which, by definition, inheres in apocalyptic narration.

A more compelling motivation of Adso's narrative return to the abbey as an old man, however, is his need to explain to himself the disasters that occurred there, to try once again, this time in writing, to read God's signs in those events. The fragments he collects on his visit to the ruins of the abbey (his "lesser library") are a symbol of that effort. Thus, Adso's narration explicitly dramatizes the dual search implicit in all narration that can be accurately called apocalyptic: first, for the significant order behind historical events and experience, then for the means to narrate that order.

In the comments that frame his story Adso denies he has succeeded in either search. In the first two paragraphs of his narration he refers to his advanced age and to the remaining fragments ("alas, how illegible") of the past. And in his epilogue, as he looks back from beyond the end of the world he describes, he concludes (with, as I have said, modern rather than medieval emphasis) that there is no discernible historical design beyond "the natural sequence of the events and the times that connect them," that his narration merely reiterates that absence. As in his first paragraph, he refers to the "fragments, quotations, unfinished sentences, amputated stumps of books"—the remains of the abbey's library:

> The more I reread this list the more I am convinced it is the result of chance and contains no message. . . . [and] what I have written on these pages, which you will now read, unknown reader, is only a cento, a figured hymn, an immense acrostic that says and repeats nothing but what those fragments have suggested to me. . . . (501)

Echoing William's disillusionment with the inefficacy of his detective procedures when he realizes that only by chance has he solved the mystery of the murders, Adso ultimately abjures his ambitions as detective, explicitly abandoning his role as apocalyptic interpreter and narrator of God's eschatological intention. He describes his youthful enthusiasm as he remembers it, but he does not claim to have sustained it.

It is to his own end rather than to the end of the world that Adso attends in his epilogue—and to God's silence, not God's revelation. "I shall fall into the silent and uninhabited divinity where there is no work and no image" (501). The lyricism of this "last page" of Adso's narration is emotionally charged, as most of his preceding intellectual—and, often, expository—narration is not. The tone of the aged, disillusioned Adso/narrator is a far cry from that of the youthful Adso/character, who clearly operates according to the positive assumptions of apocalyptic narration. The young Adso still believes that historical meaning is comprehensible and communicable—precisely those assumptions rejected in the frame that the old Adso gives to his narration.

This ironic disjunction between historical potential, on the one hand, and historical hindsight, on the other, is to some degree continually present in apocalyptic narration. Although the apocalyptist narrates events in the hope that it is not too late to warn his audience, his vision nonetheless telescopes time, mocking intentionality by juxtaposing the youthful optimism of beginnings to the harsh reality of cataclysmic ends. Eco himself has addressed this disparity between the two Adsos in his *Postscript*; he writes of the aged Adso/narrator that he "chooses a flight into the divine nothingness, which was not what his master had taught him."[14] What his master had taught him—that events are accessible to interpretation—coincides with the primary epistemological premise of apocalyptic narration; Adso's youthful acceptance of this premise is figured in his constant recourse to apocalyptic types and tropes to explain the events in the abbey and his role in them.

To enumerate those types and tropes would be to reiterate the novel, for they appear on almost every page. Reference to an initial scene will suffice. Just after arriving at the abbey and hearing the abbot's apocalyptic formulas, Adso and William enter the abbatial church. Adso immediately sees the scene of the Last Judgment carved on the tympanum above the entrance, on the pillars supporting the entrance, and on the walls beside it—typical, he notes, of churches of the region.[15] Adso describes the sculpted Christ's ambivalent attitude of admonition and blessing, his dual promise of damnation and salvation, and the symbolic embodiment of that duality in the stone angels and monsters—"sainted limbs and infernal sinews." He is nearly overcome by the vivid satanic bestiary. It is in a kind of visionary delirium that he hears the trumpeted voice commanding him to write. Then, dropping his descriptive mode, Adso begins to enumerate passages and images from John's revelation without attribution, as if they were his own: the seven golden candlesticks, a figure with a golden girdle and white hair like wool, seven stars in his right hand and a two-edged sword in his mouth, and so on. When Adso comes to his senses, he tells his reader that his vision and the events in the abbey surely coincide:

> and how many times in the following days did I return to contemplate the doorway, convinced I was experiencing the very events that it narrated. And I knew we had made our way up there in order to witness a great and celestial massacre. (45)

Adso simultaneously refers to God's promised last judgment of evil and to the murders in the abbey, equating the images of Revelation to actual events and interpreting them in those terms.

We have already seen this tendency to seek a preconceived order in historical events in William's deductive procedures, and we will see it again in Eco's dramatization of the political apocalypticism of the early fourteenth century. What is interesting, however, is the philosophy of language implied by the young Adso's equation of apocalyptic images and historical experience. Adso unquestioningly accepts the synonymity of providential pattern and literary design: the world is a dialectic of tropes, and what exists is identified with what is said; language is the embodiment of ontological truth.[16] William, too, accepts this equation. Early in the novel, we see William depending on the identity of signifier and signified as he describes Brunellus, the horse he has not seen; and again, when Adso inadvertently discovers a way to enter the *finis Africae* (457–60). Both William and Adso eventually realize that their interpretive procedures are based on untenable assumptions of similitude, yet Adso also recognizes that words are what remain, even after the world they describe does not.

I have said that at the conclusion of his story, Adso is resigned to the irrevocability of the end of the world, that he does not look forward to the new world biblical apocalypse specifically envisions. Nevertheless, his narration does survive the end of his world, and it does in some sense recuperate the loss it also describes. Indeed, Adso's final Latin phrase suggests that it may be the simple staying power of language that ultimately compels his narration. In his *Postscript*, Eco discusses this final phrase from which the novel's title is derived: *Stat rosa pristina nomine, nomina nuda tenemus*—literally, "the rose stays fresh in name, we have only the name." The phrase is from Bernard of Morlay's *De contemptu mundi*, where he extends the *ubi sunt* convention of the rose as a symbol of the destructive power of time. His phrase aims to mitigate the assertion that the rose will fade and disappear by proposing that it can be preserved in words. Language can "speak of the non-existent and the destroyed"; the rose will die, its description will not.[17] Adso's narration is a monument to this capacity of language, a naming of the rose in Bernard's sense, as its title announces.

Adso's faith in language may be connected to his youthful apocalyptic zeal, despite his final rejection of apocalyptic patterns of historical significance. Revelation repeatedly symbolizes the power of language—in Christ's repeated self-characterization as alpha and omega, in the representation of Christ's word as a two-edged sword, in the words written in blood on Christ's vestments. The aged Adso would seem to have internalized the apocalyptist's hope that language may yet be viable even as he realizes that the apocalyptist's patterned vision of historical transcendence is not. Thus, he leaves to the reader the task he has himself resigned:

> I prepare to leave on this parchment my testimony . . . now repeating
> verbatim all I saw and heard, without venturing to seek a design, as if to
> leave to those who will come after (if the Antichrist has not come first) signs
> of signs, so that the prayer of deciphering may be exercised on them. (11)

Adso leaves the reader with his personal (and distinctly heretical) revelation that historical meaning, if not attainable in the world, may yet be discovered in the literary forms and fictions we ourselves create. Adso's dramatized narrative activity reminds us how precarious is our grasp on meaning in the world and how perpetual is our need—and our responsibility—to probe its language and its forms.

In *The Name of the Rose*, Adso's apocalyptic narrative form constantly reflects the content of his narration, for he describes a world full of apocalyptic visions and visionaries. Just as the evolution of Adso's apocalyptic attitudes suggests the transitional nature of the fourteenth century, so also the popular apocalyptic movements of the time, both orthodox and heretical, suggest its turbulent undercurrent of change. The spiritual Franciscans and their dissident offshoots, generally called Fraticelli or "Little Brothers," the Apostolic Brethren led by Fra Dolcino, the Minorites, and a number of other popular millenarian movements are used in the novel to embody the processes of secularization that by 1327 had begun seriously to undermine medieval structures and assumptions. Eco's concentration on the manifestations of the medieval apocalyptic tradition that oppose the institutions of medieval Christianity imbues *The Name of the Rose* with its rich background of ecclesiastical debate and factional tension and invests the novel with forebodings of prolonged political and social turmoil.

Norman Cohn, in a landmark study, has described the amorphous, popular, protorevolutionary movements Eco incorporates into his novel: the Cathars, the Waldensians, the Brethren of the Free Spirit, and, more centrally, the various radical offspring of the Franciscans.[18] These groups were often deemed heretical by the Catholic church and were therefore of necessity underground movements. Cohn labels them "millenarian," a word that implies a desire for immediate social change as the word *millennialist* does not. The descriptive term *political apocalyptic* has also been applied to these groups to emphasize their opposition to the monolithic medieval church. J.G.A. Pocock writes that medieval heretical movements almost invariably had recourse to apocalypticism in order to assert that redemption might be attained through social and historical processes and not just through the institutional operations of the timelessly based church.[19] For that reason, apocalypticism became a powerful instrument of change, depicting as it did redemption as potentially the extension or transformation of existing secular processes.

The heterodox apocalyptic groups Cohn and Pocock describe, and which

Eco integrates into *The Name of the Rose*, all look forward to the imminent end of the present age of corruption and the beginning of a new dispensation, of which they believed they would constitute the nucleus. These groups are unwilling or unable to accept things as they are—an aspect of apocalypticism which Eco explores in his study of mass cultural heroes and to which I have already referred. Such apocalyptic expectations have been a part of the Judeo-Christian tradition since the second century before Christ, but there is a crucial difference between earlier apocalyptic expectations and the heterodox apocalypticism that emerges during the late Middle Ages. Instead of waiting patiently for God's kingdom, as apocalyptic visionaries and their audiences had heretofore understood they must, these movements began to base their subversive activities on the conviction that they themselves might hasten the end of this corrupt age and the beginning of the next. Up to this time, apocalyptic preaching had been intended as an indictment of the existing system, but it had never aimed to incite active opposition to the system. I have already argued that Adso in his old age departs from this medieval apocalyptic orthodoxy of faithful expectation, assuming what is recognizably a modern stance. The departure of the apocalyptic groups Eco depicts is far more aggressive, more political, than Adso's.

The philosophical impetus for the new reading of apocalypse as a call to action can be found in the writings of a Cistercian abbot, Joachim of Fiore (1145–1202). Joachim's interpretation of Revelation, *Expositio in Apocalypsim*, provides the framework for challenging the Augustinian separation between secular and sacred history; this prophetic system Norman Cohn characterizes as the most influential in Europe until the appearance of Marxism.[20] Joachim found in Revelation a comment on the current world situation and a prediction of the future, as is consonant with the medieval attitude toward language mentioned above. His interpretation of Revelation, however, concluded with a new and revolutionary element. Joachim posited three stages of history, the third of which was to precede the end of the world and was to be led by a new order of "spiritual men." In other words, their earthly activity was to play a role in sacred history. Almost immediately, a variety of religious bands identified themselves with the spiritual leaders of the third age, thus establishing the transcendental justification for their own historical importance and the justification for their increasingly militant opposition to the institutional church.

The growth of apocalypticism as a revolutionary ideology is dramatized by Eco in his narrative focus on the heretical Fra Dolcino and his Apostolic Brethren. Fra Dolcino was perhaps the first to make the conceptual leap from preaching apocalyptic ideas to advocating armed insurgency.[21] The explosive potential of such preaching is concentrated in the characters Salvatore and Remigio. They are laymen who have found refuge in the abbey but whose seething hatred of the Benedictines, whose vulgar speech and seditious political activity are in stark contrast to the elegant philosophical discussions and ecclesiastic status of William, Adso, Jorge, and the other monks in the abbey. William immediately recognizes them as former members (or, more likely, current but underground members) of Fra Dolcino's Apostolic Brethren and explains to Adso that they are attracted to such groups for the same reason that apocalyptic visions have always been attractive to those suffering injustice or ostracism: apocalypse offers the hope of abrupt and radical change, of punishment for their oppressors and rewards for their own people.

But if this has always been so, why now the energetic repression of these apocalyptic groups by the Inquisition? William explains that these groups want social and economic changes that threaten the established hierarchy of the medieval church, and he implies that therein lies their heresy, not in doctrinal issues and errors, as the Inquisition pretends. Using St. Francis' metaphor of the leper, he says:

> All heresies are the banner of a reality, an exclusion. Scratch the heresy and you will find the leper. Every battle against heresy wants only this: to keep the leper as he is. As for the lepers, what can you ask of them? That they distinguish in the Trinitarian dogma or in the definition of the Eucharist how much is correct and how much is wrong? Come, Adso, these games are for us men of learning. The simple have other problems. (203)

Realizing that he is himself verging on heresy with such a statement, William adds hurriedly,

> And mind you, they solve them all in the wrong way. This is why they become heretics. (203)

Despite this disclaimer, William knows that heresy is based on the Greek root "to choose," and that freedom of choice is precisely what the monolithic medieval church cannot allow. The scene of the cellarer's trial by the Inquisition at the heart of *The Name of the Rose* makes palpable the connection between revelation and revolution and dramatizes the fervor of dissent that made these apocalyptic groups the necessary forerunners of the Reformation. It also confirms the suggestion implicit in William's comments—that inquisitors create heretics.

Apocalyptic programs are not always conceived by heretics. William reminds us that Saint Francis himself "wanted to call the outcast, ready to revolt, to be part of the people of God" (202). But because he had to work within the rigid confines of the institutional church, William laments, he did not succeed. Here, William refers to the church's refusal to accommodate the Spiritual Franciscans and their sympathizers. The principal leaders of the dissident Franciscans—Peter Olivi, Angelo of Clareno, Ubertino of Casale— are mentioned; but it is only Ubertino who is fully embodied in the novel.

In "Sext" on the first day, the important, early chapter where we see Adso overcome by apocalyptic images and voices, we are also introduced to Ubertino. Ubertino emerges from the dark of the church, himself seeming to be a figure from an apocalyptic scene Adso describes. The context for Ubertino's appearance is carefully calculated by Eco, for Ubertino was the essential source of the association of Saint Francis and the Franciscans with apocalyptic expectation. In *Arbor vitae crucifixae* (The Tree of the Crucified Life of Jesus, 1305), to which Adso refers in the novel, Ubertino engendered the potent myth that Saint Francis was the spiritual leader of the Joachimite third age; the fifth book of *Arbor vitae crucifixae* is, as one historian has said, "a complete Franciscanizing of the Apocalypse."[22] The special apocalyptic role assigned to Francis by Ubertino had its basis in the "apostolic poverty" that Francis revived. To the Spiritual Franciscans, poverty became the sign of their apocalyptic role as the "spiritual men" predicted by Joachim. The Spir- ituals—Beguines in Provence, Fraticelli in Tuscany—were vigorously per- secuted by Pope John XXII (1316–34), with the cooperation of the Michael of Cesena, the minister general of the Franciscan order, although Ubertino was saved by powerful friends who allowed him to transfer to the Benedictine order.[23] It is one of the many ironies of the theological politics in *The Name of the Rose* that this brilliant, influential leader finds himself in the Benedictine abbey for the same reasons as Remigio and Salvatore.

Umberto Eco, in his *Postscript to "The Name of the Rose"*, says that a novel about the fourteenth century cannot ignore the debate on poverty, a debate which, as the novel shows, was intricately intertwined with apocalyptic visions of radical transformation. Adso's narrative structure surely was de- vised to mirror—and hence, intensify—the presentation of the apocalyptic fervor of the time and give coherence to what might otherwise have been a diffuse, digressive, historical narration. In *The Name of the Rose* the her- menuetic concerns of apocalyptic narration and the political concerns of apocalyptic movements proceed in concert; indeed, it is the complementarity of its narrative mode and the history it tells which is, in my opinion, the novel's greatest structural attribute.

So we return to William's statement, "Everyone nowadays is obsessed with the book of John." Eco's best-seller depends on its adroit use of John's

Revelation, as well as the philosophical implications and political consequences of the Judeo-Christian apocalyptic tradition. Although William may overstate his case with the word *everyone*, there are a surprising number of important modern novelists (I have already mentioned four) who use the myth of apocalypse in both the form and the content of their fiction. I want to touch on just two more writers who use apocalyptic narratives and apocalyptic movements as explicitly as Eco does and for essentially the same purposes. The Mexican novelist Carlos Fuentes, in *Terra Nostra* (1975), investigates the historical and philosophical origins of Mexico. He makes two heretical apocalyptic sects, the Adamites and the Brethren of the Free Spirit, the moral loci of his novel, and invokes the symbolic systems of several medieval visionaries, whether clerics or statesmen or artists. Although Fuentes has no single apocalyptic narrator like Adso, the narrative structure of his novel is nonetheless apocalyptic in its own deconstructive and reconstructive aims and techniques. The Peruvian writer Mario Vargas Llosa, in *The War of the End of the World* (1981), also uses apocalyptic types and tropes, in this case to dramatize a millenialist uprising led by a figure known as the Counsellor in northern Brazil at the end of the nineteenth century. Like Eco, Vargas Llosa and Fuentes are concerned with the meaning of history and how historical meaning is narrated. It is the ancient, mythic mode of apocalypse that provides the means to dramatize these most contemporary of novelistic concerns.

Notes

This article had its beginnings in a review published in *Humanities in the South*; I am grateful for permission to use parts of that review here.

1. Umberto Eco, *The Name of the Rose*, trans. William Weaver (San Diego: Harcourt Brace Jovanovich, 1983), 255. Subsequent citations of this work appear in the text.

2. Most recently, Eco's comment from a recent interview in *Die Zeit* joins the fourteenth and the twentieth centuries in these terms. He states, "What joins the two epochs is exactly this: the feeling of living in a dangerous time of transition." *Time*, 23 December 1985, 32. For an extended treatment of the fourteenth century, which also posits similarities with the twentieth, see Barbara Tuchman, *The Distant Mirror: The Calamitous Fourteenth Century* (New York: Knopf, 1978).

3. Umberto Eco, *Beatus of Liébana* (Milano: Franco Maria Ricci, 1983); I am grateful to the author for sending me a copy of this beautiful book.

Eco discusses popular apocalyptic agents such as Superman in *Apocalittici e integrati* (Milano: Bompiani, 1968); and in his essay, "Il mito di Superman e la dissoluzione del tempo," in *Dimitizzazione e immagine*, ed. E. Castelli (Padua: Cedam,

1962). The second work has been translated by Natalie Chilton as "The Myth of Superman," in *The Role of the Reader: Explorations in the Semiotics of Texts* (Bloomington: Indiana University Press, 1979), 107–24.

4. Excerpts from Eco's book on the Beatus manuscript are published in *FMR* 2 (July 1984), 63–92, under the title, "Waiting for the Millennium." Because of its greater accessibility, I cite from the essay, pp. 72, 74.

5. Eco, *Beatus of Liébana*, p. 90.

6. Eco, *Postscript to "The Name of the Rose,"* trans. William Weaver (San Diego: Harcourt Brace Jovanovich, 1984), 21, 37, 43, 51.

7. In the United States, exceptions to this generalization are certain fundamentalist Protestant sects whose allegorical reading of current events in terms of the symbols of Revelation remains within the medieval hermeneutic tradition. The Jehovah's Witnesses are an example. It should also be noted that a number of the sects indigenous to the United States originated with an urgent apocalyptic expectation; among them, as their names suggest, are the Church of the Latter Day Saints and the Seventh Day Adventists. See Charles H. Lippy's essay on the apocalyptic strain in American religion, in *The Apocalyptic Vision in America: Interdisciplinary Essays on Myth and Culture*, ed. Lois Parkinson Zamora (Bowling Green, Ohio: Bowling Green State University Popular Press, 1982), 37–63.

8. Adso of Montier-en-Der is mentioned by Eco in "Waiting for the Millennium," 74; and by Jorge of Burgos in *The Name of the Rose*, 83.

9. See my article on the apocalyptic narrative vision in Faulkner and García Márquez, "The End of Innocence: Myth and Narrative Structure in Faulkner's *Absalom, Absalom!* and García Márquez's *Cien años de soledad*," *Hispanic Review*, 4 (1982): 23–40.

10. The wealth of visual treatments of Revelation is most completely catalogued in *Apocalypse: Visions from the Book of Revelation in Western Art* (New York: Alpine Fine Arts Collection, Ltd., 1978). See also Kathryn Henkel, *The Apocalypse* (College Park: University of Maryland Department of Art, 1973).

11. Kermode, *The Genesis of Secrecy* (Cambridge: Harvard University Press, 1979). Kermode examines the narrative implications of apocalyptic texts in *The Sense of an Ending* (New York: Oxford University Press, 1967).

12. See Carlo Ginsberg's essay on the related conjectural procedures of doctors, lawyers, detectives, and hunters, in Umberto Eco and Thomas Sebeok, eds., *The Sign of Three: Dupin, Holmes, Pierce* (Bloomington: Indiana University Press, 1983).

13. Eco, *Beatus of Liébana*, 66.

14. Eco, *Postscript*, 34.

15. The church at Moissac apparently is the model for the abbatial church in the novel, for pictures of its carved entrance are used in Eco's *Postscript* to illustrate passages from Adso's description. The churches at Vézelay and Autun are other splendid examples of French churches which present complex apocalyptic visions in stone.

16. Eco has written about medieval linguistic theory in ways that illuminate his

novel, in *The Aesthetics of Chaosmos: The Middle Ages of James Joyce*, trans. Ellen J. Esrock (1962; Tulsa, Oklahoma: University of Tulsa Press, 1982).

17. Eco, *Postscript*, p. 1.

18. Cohn, *The Pursuit of the Millennium* (1957; rev. ed., New York: Oxford University Press, 1970). See also, Bernard McGinn, *Visions of the End: Apocalyptic Traditions in the Middle Ages* (New York: Columbia University Press, 1979), 203–39; and *La Fin des temps: Terreurs et prophéties au Moyen Age*, ed. Georges Duby (Paris: Editions Stock, 1982), for useful collections of medieval apocalyptic texts and contexts.

19. Pocock, *The Machiavellian Moment* (Princeton: Princeton University Press, 1975), 45–46.

20. This assertion is made by Cohn at the beginning of Chapter 5 of his *Pursuit of the Millennium*. The definitive studies of Joachim's role in engendering the revolutionary apocalyptic of the period depicted in *The Name of the Rose* are by Marjorie Reeves, *The Influence of Prophecy in the Later Middle Ages* (Oxford: Clarendon Press, 1969); and *Joachim of Fiore and the Prophetic Future* (London: SPCK, 1976).

21. McGinn, *Visions*, 226–29. The Inquisition's persecution of apocalyptic groups such as Fra Dolcino's resulted in the destruction of most of their documents and treatises. Ironically, much of what remains of these heretical groups has been preserved by the Inquisition itself, in the transcriptions of its investigations, accusations, and judicial proceedings. Indeed, the only record of Fra Dolcino's dicta are two letters preserved by virtue of their inclusion in the inquisitorial manual of Bernard Gui, whom Eco makes the presiding inquisitor at the trial of the cellarer.

22. McGinn quotes this statement by G. Leff in *Visions*, 206.

23. McGinn, *Visions*, 207.

3 The Name of the Rose
as a Postmodern Novel

Mark Parker

We live in a decade of "post's": poststructuralism, postmodernism, and the teasingly paradoxical postcontemporary. Almost no one, however, seems happy with the term *postmodern*. It is most often used, as one critic puts it, "pis aller," as if it were a tool designed obsolete or a category always empty. [1] In his *Postscript to "The Name of the Rose,"* Eco slips by its insufficiencies with characteristic good humor, noting its ever-widening range and variety of application, and ultimately presenting it as "an ideal category—or better still, a Kunstwollen, a way of operating." [2] This tendency toward a functional, not a descriptive, definition is characteristic of his humor: Eco moves at once from the ambiguities of *what* to the palpabilities of *how*, treating the postmodern as an ironic "reply to the modern" (67). Despite some deprecating preliminaries, Eco takes pains to recast this term, redefining it with some of the irony he holds so central to a postmodern attitude. By the end of this section of the *Postscript*, perhaps the reader can say "postmodern" with the success that Eco's post-Cartland lovers can say "I love you."

To accept this "challenge of the past, of the already said, which cannot be eliminated" (67), one must, of course, know something about it. The term *postmodern* itself has a short but significant history; to see how Eco has inserted himself into the critical discussion of this movement or period or Kunstwollen, it is first necessary to take a short tour through some of the better-known discussions of it.

The term gets off to an inauspicious start in two early articles, Irving Howe's "Mass Society and Postmodern Fiction" and Alfred Kazin's "Psychoanalysis and Literary Criticism Today." Both articles fix upon a consistent problem for postmodern fiction: the lack of an authoritative system of values or tradition to criticize or rebel against. Kazin sees desperation in the attempts of Britain's "angry young men" to find suitable objects for their emotions and in Norman Mailer's celebration of the murderous assaults of two eighteen-year-olds on a candy-store keeper as a daring, revolutionary act. Howe sees "a world increasingly shapeless and an experience increasingly fluid," a world and an experience that resist the attempts of novelists to embody through them values and moral judgments.[3] Criticism of bourgeois values and society forms the backbone of modernist writing. Even the less analytic of modernists could easily snatch up and successfully employ the systematic, radical criticisms of nineteenth-century society provided by Marx, Freud, Nietzsche, and others. Novelists could count on this stable core of assumptions to provide them with "symbolic economies and dramatic conveniences."[4] There was a live consensus to which modernists had access, which they exploited by employing characters in conscious rebellion against society (perhaps given clearest expression in the youthful protagonists of Joyce and Lawrence). The postmoderns, however, lacking this coherent value system or authoritative moral tradition to rebel against, face a problem of self- definition. One can hardly criticize a social order so chaotic and elusive; it is necessary instead to project a moral order. According to Alfred Kazin, what is required "is no longer the rebel" but "the stranger—who seeks not to destroy the moral order, but to create one that will give back to him the idea of humanity."[5] Howe—and, by implication, Kazin—blame this sad situation on "mass society." Howe registers his objections in the form of a jeremiad:

> By the mass society we mean a relatively comfortable, half welfare and half-garrison society in which the population grows passive, indifferent, and atomized; in which traditional loyalties, ties, and associations become lax or dissolve entirely; in which coherent publics based on definite interests and opinions gradually fall apart; and in which man becomes a consumer, himself mass-produced like the products, diversions, and values he absorbs.

For Kazin and Howe, postmodern fiction is full of "distinctive failures" and should be accorded "patience and charity."[6]

These early assessments of the postmodern, made before the bulk of the novels deemed postmodern were written, seem cannily prophetic when considered in the light of Gerald Graff's later investigation of contemporary fiction, "Babbitt at the Abyss." Graff, through an extensive survey of recent fiction, reaffirms and extends their conclusions. To his mind, postmodernist fiction "has often been weakened by its inability or refusal to retain any moorings in social reality."[7] The modernist attack on bourgeois values has become an empty gesture in the hands of many postmoderns; since this culture no longer exists, "such demolition is needless."[8] It is as though the moderns had sunk all the ships, leaving to the postmoderns the barren joy of shelling the wreckage. Like Howe and Kazin, Graff attributes the failures of postmodern fiction to mass society:

> If this deficiency exists, then one reason for it may be that in the kind of mass society which has grown up in the last three decades, our personal relationships, public values, and the connections between the two have become so disoriented, scrambled, and confused that writers, as well as everyone else, have found it peculiarly difficult to arrive at clear, coherent, and convincing generalizations.[9]

Such pessimism features strongly in this strain of postmodern criticism, a strain that Graff, in another article, brands as "apocalyptic."[10]

Against this gloomy assessment stands a strain of postmodern criticism far more optimistic, at times even celebratory, one practiced by a determined Susan Sontag, by a puckish Leslie Fiedler, and in a "visionary" (Graff's term) mode by Ihab Hassan.[11] This strain tends to embrace mass culture, or at least portions of it, as a kind of revolutionary gesture toward liberation. According to Sontag, faced with a technique of interpretation and a corresponding set of interpretations so encrusted, so deadening, and so repressive, "What is important now is to recover our senses. We must learn to *see* more, to *hear* more, to *feel* more."[12] Fiedler, noting that an element of science fiction has passed into postmodern fiction, welcomes "the prospect of radical trans-formation" of man into "something else" and hails the coming of "the new mutants" who will disengage utterly from the humanist, bourgeois, Marxist, "cult of reason" traditions.[13] Hassan sees postmodernism as a reaction to "the unimaginable . . . extermination and totalitarianism," as a response that has "tended toward artistic Anarchy in deeper complicity with things falling apart—or has tended toward Pop," and as an open embracement of radical transformation: "Who knows but that our only alternative may be to our 'human' consciousness."[14] In their discussions of critical values and strat-egies, these critics lean toward a more popular aesthetic and an embrace of the mass society Kazin, Howe, and Graff by turns find so disturbing and depressing.

Eco inserts himself deftly into this critical debate in his 1964 analysis of mass culture, *Apocalittici e integrati* (Apocalyptic and Integrated Intellec-tuals).[15] Building on Dwight MacDonald's categories of mass-cult and mid-cult and on Clement Greenberg's insistence on the economic and political bases for mass culture, Eco locates part of the problem of defining and describing mass culture in the critics themselves. According to Eco, they tend to ask the wrong question. Implicitly or explicitly, these critics ask, "Is mass culture good or bad?" when the real question is somewhat different. As Eco himself puts it, "When the present situation of an industrial society makes mass communication a fact, what can be done to render these means of communication capable of transmitting cultural values?"[16] In other words, mass culture is controlled by economics. It moves to the logic of profit, and it is prepared without the benefit of intellectuals. Intellectuals, in fact, tend to adopt an attitude of protest and reservation toward mass culture. To withdraw, however, is to say that this sytem is so extensive and pervasive an order that no isolated act of modification would be able to affect it, in fact, that such acts are futile gestures. Although reform in politics or economics often suggests complicity between opposed groups (wages are raised, strikers appeased; but the fundamental relation between the two groups is unchanged, and basic inequalities are not addressed), in culture it has no such ramifications. (Put another way, culture is part of the superstructure of society, not the socioeconomic base. The same caution does not apply in this realm.) Slight reforms in these other spheres may attenuate contradictions and avoid violent change for a long time, ultimately becoming complicity, but this never happens in the realm of ideas. Ideas never become an unequivocal point of reference that brings about pacification; the level of discourse is always raised. If you raise the pay of striking workers, you may keep the same system; nothing changes. If you teach illiterates to read—even if only to stuff them with propaganda—you have changed things fundamentally: they may read other books tomorrow. Thus, the proper attitude for the intellectual toward mass culture is one of acceptance and intervention. Mass culture is a fact, a certainty; its ramifications require that the intellectual steer between the disgust and withdrawal displayed by those Eco calls "the apocalyptic" and the flaccid, unqualified acceptance of those he calls "the integrated." Mass culture deserves serious attention because of its apparent dangers and its often forgotten benefits. We need forget neither its atrocities of taste nor its facilitation of cultural access. According to Eco, the intellectual must analyze carefully the nature of these means of communication, their effects on people as well as the reciprocal effects of people on mass culture. To do this, a thoroughgoing investigation must be directed at such phenomena as comic strips, popular songs, and television programs. What Eco, after doing some exemplary investigations in the book, suggests is that these media all have the tendency to promote complacency in the spectator. Their messages tend to be consoling ones, promoting the sense that the world present to the spectator is a good one, or at least the best one possible, even that it is justified and permanent. Media often provide this consolation by omission; Superman comic strips exclude politics by concentrating on the righting of private wrongs. The virtues promulgated and issues examined by the comics are civic, not political; they never suggest that the system itself is capable of improvement, much less that it may be culpable. The great defect of mass culture is "to convey a standardized, oversimplified, static and complacent vision that masks the real complexity of things and implicitly denies the possibility of change." Eco suggests that what mass culture needs is instructions for use. According to him, nothing is wrong with the distraction and diversion it affords. The difficulty lies in the fact that, for most people, such offerings alone constitute culture and exert a strongly reactionary force in society. Eco is not, however, like those liberals whom Dwight MacDonald criticizes; he does not suggest that mass culture be raised wholesale to High Culture. Instead, Eco argues for what he calls "honest" works, works that do not belie the complexity of society, that admit to the historical circumstances in which we find ourselves, that promote thought instead of predigested opinion, that do not have artistic pretensions like those of kitsch. [17]

This kind of analysis emphasizes the instrumental nature of mass media and mass culture. By shifting the discussion from the dead-end dichotomy of "Is mass culture good or bad?" Eco has managed to avoid both the pointless jeremiads against and the mindless celebrations of mass culture, which only muddy the issue. Eco suggests that we examine mass media and mass culture as we would any other system, focusing on the way it functions. We might do well to think of it as if it were a perceptual tool, a way of knowing the world. Mass culture, according to Eco, is a fact; it can neither be eradicated nor ignored; it is necessary to engage it.

At the end of his theoretical treatment of mass culture, Eco makes what in retrospect is a wryly proleptic comment: "I believe that there can be a novel intended at once as a work of entertainment, a consumer item, and an aesthetically valid work capable of providing original, not kitsch, values." [18] This double intention fits well *The Name of the Rose*. Couched as a mystery in a fourteenth-century monastery replete with grisly (or witty) murders, sprinkled with a generous dose of latinate obscurity, offering historical accuracy for the plausibility-hounds in the audience, hinting at less than celestial relations among the monks, and providing a steamy sexual encounter for the narrator—the novel features many of the tricks of the potboiler trade. Alongside these devices, however, Eco places William of Baskerville, whose views, though carefully attuned to the historical moment in the novel, are much akin to Eco's own. William offers us the spectacle of the intellectual in confrontation with the mass culture of his own day. William's remarks on the people, whom he calls with a wonderfully bifurcated attitude "the simple," serve to remind us of the importance of this confrontation and the difficulties involved in it.

The gist of Eco's attitude is clearly seen in a conversation William has with Adso, his young naive assistant, who plays a kind of medieval, youthful

Watson to William's Holmes. Adso, confused about the distinctions among heretical sects, asks William to clarify them. William responds by offering up several analogies—first, a comparison of the body of the church to a river which, over the centuries, has begun to meander and form a crisscrossing delta because of its sheer size. Characteristically, as he pursues this analogy, William becomes dissatisfied with it, finally urging Adso: "Forget this story of the river."[19] For William, analogizing is simply one intellectual tool among others; when its efficacy becomes questionable, he discards it. William then serves up another analogy, which, to Adso's bewilderment, he subsequently discards as well. Then he begins to analyze the situation of the masses (the simple). It is at this point that we can see Eco's own appraisal of mass culture and mass media, for he moves from doctrinal matters, which tend to change according to the desires of those in power, to social theory. The simple have "no subtlety of doctrine" (234). They "cannot choose their personal heresy" (235); they are caught up in current movements which happen to include some of what they recall from other movements already abandoned. William then begins to speculate on the meaning of the simple; he concludes that the condition of being simple, of being in the masses, is of greater moment than the particular heresy—that, in fact, the heresy is (in Aristotle's terms) accidental rather than essential. What creates social unrest is the tendency on the part of those in power to leave part of the flock outside, to push some people to the margins of society—without land, guild, or corporation. The sign of this exclusion is leprosy, not on the physical but on the semiotic level. As William says, "All heresies are the banner of a reality, an exclusion. Scratch the heresy and you will find the leper. Every battle against heresy wants only this: to keep the leper as he is" (239). Adso, confused by William's refusal to assign blame to the heretics, the lepers, or the overseers, presses him to take a stand: "But who was right, who is right, who was wrong?" (240). William answers in Eco's own instrumental terms; what his explanation provides is not truth but a closer look at the situation. It is like looking at a tool closely and then more closely. What comes of the two examinations is not some ultimate, final certainty but skill in manipulating the conceptual tools one employs. This, despite William's insistence that he is saying more than Adso is willing to recognize, isn't enough for Adso. William then looks more closely at the concept and category of the simple. He proposes, in an axiomatic way, that the simple, both in themselves and as a sign, have something to tell the intellectual. Their message goes beyond the traditional belief that God often chooses to speak through them. According to William,

The simple have something more than do learned doctors, who often become
lost in their search for broad, general laws. The simple have a sense of the
individual, but this sense, by itself, is not enough. The simple grasp a truth
of their own, perhaps truer than that of the doctors of the church, but then
they destroy it in unthinking actions. What must be done? Give learning to
the simple? Too easy, or too difficult. The Franciscan teachers considered this
problem. The great Bonaventure said that the wise must enhance conceptual
clarity with the truth implicit in the action of the simple. . . . (241)

Eco's own theory of mass culture is sufficiently evident in this passage. In
Apocalittici e integrati, Eco calls for a dialectic between the intellectuals who
insert themselves into the machinery of mass media and the consumers of
mass culture. He insists that the situation change from the present one, in
which the technicians of mass culture situate themselves in and exploit a
paternalistic, self-serving relation to the masses. There must be a dialectical
relation between the engaged intellectual—who has the benefits of the
compression provided by broad, general laws and conceptual categories—and
the masses, with their sense of the individual. William continues in this vein:
"How are we to remain close to the experience of the simple, maintaining, so
to speak, their operative virtue, the capacity [for] working toward the
transformation and betterment of their world?" (242). Eco's picture of
William confronting the new world of mass culture dramatizes the predica-
ment of the intellectual, consciously hindered by the exasperating limits to
the tools of his investigation, the broad, general laws and conceptual categories which by their very nature, their own truth, obscure the truth of the
experience of the simple. For Eco, the simple have a less mediated—perhaps,
in some cases, relatively unmediated—view of the world which the intellectual, because of the conceptual apparatus that makes him an intellectual,
cannot see. The only possibility of bridging this gap lies in cultivating a
dialectical relation between the two groups, for each is, fundamentally and
possibly irrevocably, outside the other's truth.

The *Postscript* reaffirms this activist stance toward mass society in its
division of novels into two kinds: "the text that seeks to produce a new reader
and the text that tries to fulfill the wishes of the readers already to be found in
the street."[20] Clearly, Eco prefers the former, describing the kind of novelist
who "wants to reveal to his public what it *should* want, even if it does not
know it" and even going so far as to suggest that the "text is meant to be an
experience of transformation for its reader."[21] Despite the withdrawal from
social action described by the fictive transcriber of Adso's manuscript, who,
in the preface to *The Name of the Rose*, claims to write "out of pure love of

writing" and "for sheer narrative pleasure," the *Postscript* takes on a limited
"commitment to the present, in order to change the world."[22]

As vexed as the question of mass society in postmodern critical discussions may be, it pales by comparison with the question of the relation of
postmodernism to modernism. Periodization is a dubious activity under the
best of circumstances, and these are, critically speaking, most unpropitious
times. In an article written in 1971, Michael Holquist proposes a view of
postmodernism as a response to a vivid split between high and low in
modernism itself. What myth and depth psychology are to the modern
period, the detective story—"radically anti-mythical" and "militantly anti-
psychological"—is to postmodernism.[23] Holquist provides a picture of
modernism's caste of professional exegetes devoted to unraveling the unset-
tling complexities of Joyce, Pound, and Woolf by day and soothing their
troubled minds with a bit of reassuring detective fiction by night. The two
realms of modernism are linked by intellectuals who not only read both high
and low but in many cases (Michael Innes, C. Day Lewis, Dorothy Sayers)
wrote detective novels. In postmodernism, high modernism's world, one in
which "dangerous questions are raised . . . a threatening, unfamiliar place,
inimical more often than not to reason" is expressed through the medium of
detective fiction, producing variants of the old form which, instead of
reassuring the reader, give "a strangeness which is more often than not the
result of jumbling the well-known patterns of classical detective stories."
Postmodern narratives defeat the "syllogistic order" of their detective pro-
genitors and in doing so, "dramatize the void."[24]

Eco's participation in this aspect of the postmodern venture is clear; his
remarks in the *Postscript*, if anything, abruptly deflate any argument celebrating the reassuring nature of the use of the detective story in his novel: "this is a
mystery in which very little is discovered and the detective is defeated."[25] Yet
he differs from Holquist in describing the aims of this technique. Rather than
discussing the novel as yet another performance of the abyss-story, Eco
stresses the fundamental element of conjecture, of structuring, in the detective genre and its consequent connection to many other stories. Holquist's
interpretation of the postmodern use of the detective story, which implies
many routes to the sight of the void, ultimately is reductive; Eco's displays a
centrifugal tendency.

Hassan, in his essay "POSTmodernISM," views the relation between
modern and postmodern somewhat differently. He cites such critics as
Richard Poirier who, perhaps unwittingly, "revalue Modernism in terms of
Postmodernism"; that is, they tend not simply to revise modernism but to

read it through a postmodern aesthetic.[26] Although Hassan's gnomic, "paracritical" style omits specific instances, they are not difficult to find. For instance, in a review of a collection of articles on Eliot, Richard Poirier stresses Eliot's tendency "to devalue literature in the interests of the preeminent values of language," a position that echoes Barthes' insistence in *Writing Degree Zero* that "the whole of literature" since Flaubert has become "the problematics of language."[27] For Poirier, Eliot is at his most impressive when he is "de-creative," when he de-authorizes part of his past, "when his language challenges the conceptual and poetic schemas on which he seems to depend."[28] At his best, Eliot refuses to "pacify" experience. He stubbornly refuses to give final significance to or to totalize what is given. Poirier's critical practice is Hassan's point: "Modernism does not suddenly cease so that Postmodernism may begin: they now coexist."[30]

In his "Myth of the Postmodernist Breakthrough," Gerald Graff arrives at a similar conclusion to that of Hassan and Poirier but adopts a decidedly more pessimistic attitude.[31] Graff, in response to celebrations of a postmodern "breakthrough," argues that the movement is, rather, "the logical culmination of the premises of these earlier movements," namely, romantic and modernist.[32] He defines postmodernism as "that movement within contemporary literature and criticism which calls into question the claims of literature and art to truth and human value," then argues that this is precisely what earlier authors did: Wordsworth's doubts about whether the "significant external reality" of nature was perceived or created are carried over in modernism's obsession with ritual, myth, provisional order, and frames of reference. Romanticism included a strong component of doubt of the authority of their productions, and the moderns have continued this ambiguous attitude. The New Critics, according to Graff, have a part in this sequence of doubt; they were "masters of interpretation who had a profound skepticism of interpretation," and their postmodern successors simply turn their own skepticism upon them.[33] Like Hassan, Graff suggests a certain coexistence between modernism and postmodernism; but his coexistence is far less benign. In a sharp critique of social and critical pluralism, Graff provides a picture of postmodernism as a "reactionary" ideology, one that "is the reigning philosophy of the establishment."[34] Far from being a breakthrough, postmodernism offers an avant-garde that is merely a weak copy of the status quo: "Advanced industrial society has outstripped the avant-garde by incorporating in its own form the avant-garde's main values—the worship of change, dynamic energy, and autonomous process, the contempt for tradition and critical norms."[35] He advocates a careful reassessment of humanist values, one that recognizes their foundation in a particular social class but that does not banish them simply for that reason.

Eco's solution to the nature of the modern-postmodern relationship is to leave out history altogether, at least for the time being. Characteristically, he defines postmodernism in terms of a "way of operating," a position that allows him to posit a relation between the two based on function, not some elusive essence: "We could say that every period has its own postmodernism, just as every period would have its own mannerism." This scheme helps explain the puzzling heterogeneity of the literary scene: "in the same artist the modern moment and the postmodern moment can coexist, or alternate, or follow each other closely."[36] By choosing the term *coexist* ("convivere," in the original), Eco shows affinities for the assessments worked out by Hassan and Graff; but Eco wears his term with a difference.[37]

Much closer to Eco's remarks in the *Postscript* are the ideas of postmodern novelist and critic William Gass, in his essay "Tropes of the Text."[38] Gass traces the tendency of English novelists to think of their work in terms of some trope. The early choices were made based on an innocent pragmatism, a desire to relax the reader's (and perhaps even the author's) strictures against the frivolity of novel-reading. Richardson, for example, chose the letter as a trope for his novels not because he had some deep interest in the letter as a form but because "it offered itself as the only way his tale could be told."[39] Postmodern novelists show a far deeper commitment to their tropes, even to difficult burdensome ones. Such tropes are fundamental to the moment, despite the fact that they bring "nothing but confusion, nothing but postmodernism, nothing but grief."[40]

Stripped of its agon, this version of postmodernism as a deepening, even self-conscious, commitment to the trope of the text has vivid parallels in the *Postscript*. Eco's discussion of labyrinths reveals how deeply this trope structures *The Name of the Rose*. The novel seems to be controlled not by the genre of detective fiction (an example of "conjecture") but the trope of the labyrinth, "an abstract model of conjecturality."[41] Both the genre and the trope have a built-in metaphysical dimension, but the trope offers added possibilities. Eco goes into some detail on these, positing three types of labyrinths: the Greek or classical, the mannerist, and the rhizome. It is through the possibilities of the trope that Eco can describe William's world, "a rhizome structure" that "can be structured but is never structured definitively."[42] This goes far beyond the idea of postmodernism as a failed detective metaphysic, or what Holquist suggested was a dramatization of the void. In this discussion of labyrinths, Eco hints at another view of the postmodern phenomenon. Later in the *Postscript*, Eco suggests that "we could say that every period has its own postmodernism, just as every period has its own mannerism (and, in fact, I wonder if postmodernism is not the modern name for mannerism as a metahistorical category)."[43] If we apply this bit of conjecture to the three types of labyrinths Eco posits, we find a slight bit of slippage between definitions. The labyrinths are presented so as to invite interpretation along the lines of literary movements. First, there is the Thesean or Greek version, with a definite center and no possibility for losing oneself. The mannerist maze follows, with its blind alleys which provide for losing oneself. Last comes the rhizome, with its decentered space. Given that Eco comments explicitly on the parallel between mannerism and postmodernism as metahistorical categories, it is not hard to see the Greek labyrinth as figuring modernism, that movement so intensely given to the search for authoritative centers in the deep structures of myth or psychology. Where, then, does that leave William—not lost, since being lost implies at least the possibility of finding one's way—but simply existing in his decentered rhizome space?

All of these aspects of the *Postscript*—its stand on the issue of mass society, its participation in the critical debate on the relation of postmodern to modern, and its self-conscious discussion of tropes—mark *The Name of the Rose* as postmodern. It is in the debts that Eco consciously pays, in those tips of the hat to Borges and, perhaps even more obviously, to John Barth that the postmodern quality of revisiting the past "with irony, not innocently" is most visible.[44] In the *Postscript*, Eco sends the reader to two of Barth's articles on postmodern fiction, mentioning the titles of both and quoting a long passage from one of them.

A quick look at the earlier of these two articles shows the nature and depth of Eco's obligation. Barth's "The Literature of Exhaustion" contains two foci that are relevant here. It introduces Borges as an exemplary contemporary writer, and it explores what Barth terms "the literature of exhausted possibility."[45] Not surprisingly, the two are related. Exhaustion, in Barth's sense, has to do not with "physical, moral or intellectual decadence" but "with the used-upness of certain forms or exhaustion of certain possibilities."[46] This burden of the past—more specifically, the past successes of writers—poses great difficulty for writers of the present. Rather than bewail the impossibility of the situation, however, Barth, much as Eco does in the *Postscript* and in *Apocalittici e integrati*, rephrases the question along functional lines: "What it comes to is that an artist doesn't merely exemplify an ultimacy; he employs it."[47] The "technically up-to-date artist" can use exhausted forms without embarassment "if done with ironic intent by a composer quite aware of where we've been and where we are." As far as form is concerned, a writer can't put his foot in the same form twice, because, as time goes by, the same form isn't the same form—the context changes. As with Eco's post-Cartland lovers, recognition of "used-upness" provides an unexpected, almost paradoxical range of possibilities. Barth then introduces a definition of the Baroque by Borges: "that style which deliberately exhausts (or tries to exhaust) its possibilities and borders on its own caricature."[48] He then discusses images favored by Borges, ending with his most favored image, that of the labyrinth. For Barth, this "is a place in which, ideally, all the possibilities of choice (of direction, in this case) are embodied, and—barring special dispensation like Theseus'—must be exhausted before one reaches the heart."[49] Waiting at the heart is the Minotaur, representing "defeat and death, or victory and freedom." Barth, however, is not content to simply serve up Borges, no matter how apt or, in 1967 terms, new. He rejects the labyrinth, at least the Theseus version of it, as "non-Baroque," because here the hero has access to the "shortcut" of Ariadne's thread, and he offers the image of Menelaus holding fast to Proteus on the beach at Pharos as "genuinely Baroque in the Borgesian spirit."[50] Barth visits the past of Borges, with irony, and puts it to his own use, teasing out from this visit an allegory of "the positive artistic morality in the literature of exhaustion." Menelaus is truly in the labyrinth, for he

> is lost, in the larger labyrinth of the world, and has got to hold fast while the Old Man of the Sea exhausts reality's frightening guises so that he may extort direction from him when Proteus returns to his "true" self.[51]

From Borges' success, Barth plucks his own victory, turning the burden of Borges' achievement to an opportunity of his own. He closes by celebrating the heroic nature of this move, how it requires virtuosity, not simply competence, and how it requires "the aid of very special gifts." Barth structures the encounter with the strong writer by his successor as a quest, including all the basic Proppian elements of hero, donor, villain, and agon.

The presence of Barth, even of his terminology, throughout the pages of the *Postscript* is unmistakable. The question is, of course, an obvious one: With what ironic intent has Eco echoed Barth echoing Borges? Truly, as Eco notes at the end of his remarks, "there exist obsessive ideas, they are never personal; books talk among themselves, and any detection should prove that we are the guilty party."[52] Criticism, as Eco's own story ramifies into other stories, ramifies into other criticism.

Notes

1. David Perkins, *A History of Modern Poetry: Modernism and After* (Cambridge: Harvard University Press, 1987), p. 393.

2. Umberto Eco, *Postscript to "The Name of the Rose,"* trans. William Weaver (San Diego: Harcourt Brace Jovanovich, 1984), 66. Future references are followed by page numbers in parentheses.

3. Howe, "Mass Society and Postmodern Fiction," in *Decline of the New* (New York: Harcourt Brace, 1970), p. 198.

4. Howe, "Mass Society," 196.

5. Kazin, "Psychoanalysis and Literary Culture Today," in *Contemporaries* (Boston: Atlantic Monthly Press, 1962), 373.

6. Howe, "Mass Society," 196, 192.

7. Graff, "Babbitt at the Abyss: The Social Context of Postmodern American Fiction," *Tri-Quarterly* 33 (1975): 307.

8. Graff, "Babbitt," 308.

9. Graff, "Babbitt," 307.

10. Gerald Graff, "The Myth of the Postmodern Breakthrough," *Tri-Quarterly* 26 (1975): 384. Graff's terms for the two strains of postmodernism he perceives are almost identical to those Eco chooses in his 1964 *Apocalittici e integrati*, which translate roughly as "apocalyptic" and "integrated" (that is, happily ensconced in the mass culture) intellectuals.

11. Susan Sontag, *Against Interpretation* (New York: Farrar, Strauss & Giroux, 1966). Leslie Fiedler, "The New Mutants," *Partisan Review* 32 (1965): 502–25. Ihab Hassan, "POSTmodernISM: A Paracritical Bibliography," in *Paracriticisms* (Urbana: University of Illinois Press, 1975).

12. Sontag, *Against Interpretation*, 14.

13. Fiedler, "New Mutants," 508.

14. Hassan, "POSTmodernISM," 59.

15. Umberto Eco, *Apocalittici e integrati* (Milano: Gruppo Editoriale Fabbri-Bompiani, 1985). To my knowledge, there is no English translation; the translations here are my own.

16. Eco, *Apocalittici*, 47.

17. David Robey, "Umberto Eco," in *Writers and Society in Contemporary Italy*, ed. Michael Caesar and Peter Hainsworth (New York: St. Martin's Press, 1984), 71.

18. Eco, *Apocalittici*, 53–54.

19. Eco, *The Name of the Rose*, trans. William Weaver (New York: Warner Books, 1983). Further references are followed by page numbers in parentheses.

20. Eco, *Postscript*, 48–49.

21. Eco, *Postscript*, 49, 53.

22. Eco, *Postscript*, xviii.

23. Holquist, "Whodunit and Other Questions: Metaphysical Detective Stories in Post-War Fiction," *New Literary History* 3 (1971): 135–56.

24. Holquist, "Whodunit," 147, 155.

25. Eco, *Postscript*, 54.

26. Hassan, POSTmodernISM," 47.

27. Poirier, "T. S. Eliot and the Literature of Waste," *New Republic* 156 (1967): 20. Roland Barthes, *Writing Degree Zero*, trans. Annette Lavers and Colin Smith (London: Jonathan Cape, 1967), 9.

28. Poirier, "T. S. Eliot," 20.

29. Poirier, "T. S. Eliot," 25.

30. Hassan, "POSTmodernISM," 47.

31. Graff, "Myth."

32. Graff, "Myth," 385.

33. Graff, "Myth," 400.

34. Graff, "Myth," 410.

35. Graff, "Myth," 415.

36. Eco, *Postscript*, 66, 68.

37. Umberto Eco, "Postillo a *Il nome della rosa*, in appendice a *Il nome della rosa*" (Milano: Gruppo Editoriale Fabbri, Bomiani, Sonzogno, 1986), 530.

38. Gass, "Tropes of the Text," in *Habitations of the Word* (New York: Simon and Schuster, 1985).

39. Gass, "Tropes," 145.

40. Gass, "Tropes," 159.

41. Eco, *Postscript*, 57.

42. Eco, *Postscript*, 58.

43. Eco, *Postscript*, 66.

44. Eco, *Postscript*, 67.

45. John Barth, "The Literature of Exhaustion," *Atlantic Monthly* 220 (1967): 29.

46. Barth, "Literature of Exhaustion," 29.

47. Barth, "Literature of Exhaustion," 31.

48. Barth, "Literature of Exhaustion," 34.

49. Barth, "Literature of Exhaustion," 34.

50. Barth, "Literature of Exhaustion," 34.

51. Barth, "Literature of Exhaustion," 34.

52. Eco, *Postscript*, p. 81.

DETECTIVES

4 The Hounding of Baskerville: Allusion and Apocalypse in Eco's *The Name of the Rose*

Michael Cohen

Let me adopt the method of the inverted detective story, rather than the more traditional variety, and give you my solution at the beginning: I believe that when William of Baskerville and Adso visit the abbey "di cui è bene e pio si taccia ormai anche il nome" ("whose name it is only right and pious now to omit"; 19/11), their seven days there constitute a kind of recapitulation of mystery fiction.[1] Eco's survey of the genre begins with ratiocination considered by the detective's audience as something more than natural, some form of powerful wizardry; it moves to a middle phase in which deduction comes into its own as an accepted method of arriving at truth (though not without opposition from other approaches); and it ends in failure, disillusionment, and epistemological doubt about the empirical results of this way of proceeding as well as about its philosophical basis.

Thus Eco's allusions to particular detectives, detective writers, and stories in *The Name of the Rose* are not merely homage or creative borrowing, though they are both these things. What Eco is doing amounts to a *novel* form of literary history. He alludes to a kind of prehistory of the genre by borrowing from Voltaire's *Zadig*. His main sources of reference are Arthur Conan Doyle's Sherlock Holmes stories. At the end his references are to Jorge Luis Borges' stories of labyrinths, solipsistic reasoning, and mirrored and defeated detectives. Along the way he alludes to other mileposts like the "fair play" school and hard-boiled detective stories. All this is set within a fourteenth-century Benedictine monastery, and especially within its peculiar library whose most prized volumes are apocalyptic texts. Within an apocalyptic library, Eco traces the apocalypse of the detective.

Baskerville and Adso are types of Holmes and Watson, but they are living in the fourteenth century rather than the nineteenth, and they are surrounded by superstition and ignorance. In "A Scandal in Bohemia," Watson says of Holmes's methods, "You would certainly have been burned, had you lived a few centuries ago."[2] Baskerville does not face being burned, but he is discreet, and the suggestion is always there that if he were on the wrong side of the inquisitors, he would quickly find himself accused of witchcraft. Even Adso says of Baskerville's use of a sextant, "all'inizio temetti che si trattasse di stregoneria" ("at the beginning I feared it was witchcraft"; 25/17). Baskerville's instruments (sextant, astrolabe, eyeglasses) have to do with direct observation or with inferential seeing (magnet, clock), and for his contemporaries all potentially are suspect. The fairly enlightened artisan Nicholas of Morimondo tries to comprehend William's simple eyeglasses but says that many people would say they were a product of witchcraft or of diabolical machination. Any behavior of machine, mind, or passion that is not understood by this society (because of ignorance of science or of psychology or because of failure of compassion) is deemed diabolical. This is the attitude Baskerville struggles against and that ultimately contributes to his defeat.

William's first exploit, the incident of the abbot's horse, is taken not from Doyle but from the episode of the king's horse in Voltaire's *Zadig* (1747). This episode of Voltaire's novelette was, because of the deductive methods of the hero, considered by early historians of detective fiction and by such writers as H. Douglas Thomson and Dorothy Sayers to constitute a kind of protodetective story. William adopts Zadig's dramatic way of announcing minute details concerning a horse he has never seen:

> C'est, répondit Zadig, le cheval qui galope le mieux; il a cinq pieds de haut, le sabot fort petit, il porte une queue de trois pieds et demi de long. . . . — Quel chemin a-t-il pris? Où est-il? demanda le grand veneur. —Je ne l'ai point vu, répondit Zadig, et je n'en ai jamais entendu parler.[3]

> Zadig replied, "It is your best galloper. It is fifteen hands high, and has very dainty hooves. Its tail is three and a half feet long. . . ." "Which way did it go? Where is it? asked the master of the hunt. "I have not seen the animal," replied Zadig. "I have never even heard of it before."[4]

> ". . . il cavallo è passatto di qua e si è diretto per il sentiero di destra. . . ."
> "Quando lo avete visto?" domandò il cellario.
> "Non l'abbiamo visto affatto, non è vero Adso?" disse Guglielmo, volgendosi verso di me con aria divertita. "Ma . . . è evidente che state cercando Brunello, il cavallo preferito dall'Abate, il miglior galoppatore della vostra scuderia, nero di pelo, alto cinque piedi, dalla coda sontuosa, dallo zoccolo piccolo e rotondo ma dal galoppo assai regolare; capo minuto, orecchie sottili ma occhi grandi."

> *(Il nome,* 31)

The horse came this way and took the path to the right. . . ."

"When did you see him?" the cellarer asked.

"We haven't seen him at all, have we, Adso?" William said, turning toward me with an amused look. "But . . . it is obvious you are hunting for Brunellus, the abbot's favorite horse, fifteen hands, the fastest in your stables, with a dark coat, a full tail, small round hoofs, but a very steady gait; small head, sharp ears, big eyes."

(Weaver trans., 23)

The evidence for both men's deductions is the same—spacing of hoof marks, trees disturbed at the height of five feet, and so on. William goes beyond his model to name the horse and give it features he could not have deduced, knowing as he does that the monks' minds work in certain predictable ways. They will believe, whether it is true or not, that this horse has certain features because they are the features which a noted church authority has said an excellent horse must possess, and since they believe this horse to be excellent, it must possess them.

In *Zadig*, however, the hero's deductions cost him four hundred ounces of gold, as well as the threat of being burned alive as a sorcerer. "Zadig vit combien il était dangereux quelquefois d'être trop savant, et se promit bien, à la première occasion, de ne point dire ce qu'il avait vu" ("Zadig realized how dangerous it could be to know too much, and made up his mind that next time he would tell nothing of what he saw"; 9/11). Even Zadig's pretended ignorance gets him into trouble. In *The Name of the Rose*, however, Eco introduces no suspicion this early in the story that the detective's talents for deduction may do him and those around him more harm than good. Yet the suggestion is there, buried in the allusion to Voltaire.

Like Watson, Adso is the chronicler of the detective-hero's adventures, the somewhat naive assistant who marvels at his master's displays of skill. Also like Watson, he is a character with interest and a life of his own, before and after his association with the hero. During the adventure, too, he provides his own romantic episode, one much steamier than Watson's romance with Mary Morstan. Not stupid, he helps the master see, giving him clues about the *u* in *equus* and about the dream of the *Coena Cypriani*, which lead directly to revelations about the mysterious library and its contents. As Holmes himself writes with little irony (in one of the adventures where Watson does not appear), "A confederate who foresees your conclusions and course of action is always dangerous, but one to whom each development comes as a perpetual surprise, and to whom the future is always a closed book, is, indeed, an ideal helpmate." (Doyle, p. 1000).

William of Baskerville shares many features with Sherlock Holmes. He is tall and beak-nosed; he rubs his hands when pleased, is energetic, but has occasional bouts of sluggishness, of which Adso says, echoing Doyle's Watson on Sherlock Holmes's lethargy:

> In quelle occasioni appariva nei suoi occhi un'espressione vacua e assente, e avrei sospettato che fosse sotto l'impero di qualche sostanze vegetale capace di dar visioni, se la palese temperanza che regolava la sua vita non mi avesse indotto a respingere questo pensiero.
>
> *(Il nome*, 24)

> On those occasions a vacant, absent expression appeared in his eyes, and I would have suspected he was in the power of some vegetal substance capable of producing visions if the obvious temperance of his life had not led me to reject this thought.
>
> (Weaver trans., 16)

> On these occasions I have noticed such a dreamy, vacant expression in his eyes, that I might have suspected him of being addicted to the use of some narcotic, had not the temperance and cleanliness of his whole life forbidden such a notion.
>
> (Doyle, 20)

Both detectives have a delicate touch with their philosophic—that is, their scientific—instruments. They employ the most modern such instruments. For Holmes, this means the best chemical equipment and a powerful microscope; for Baskerville, it means a clock, an astrolabe, a magnet, and a pair of spectacles. Both men study those aspects of the natural world that are likely to be useful to them. Holmes can distinguish 140 varieties of tobacco and has what Watson, who ought to know, calls a "profound" knowledge of chemistry; William knows the medieval pharmacopoeia better than the abbey's herbalist Severinus. Both men have more than a little vanity and a taste for the dramatic.

This mining of the Holmes stories gives Eco an entire series of ready-made associations for Baskerville and Adso. Primarily, it brings Baskerville the esteem attaching to fiction's most famous and most successful of detectives. Moreover, the light of Holmes's reputation gives Baskerville some reflected gleams as upholder of reason in a dark age of authoritarianism. Both Holmes and Baskerville stand in a special relation to authority and their respective establishments that, sometimes grudgingly, harbor them and allow them to do their work. Though not a former policeman, Holmes is certainly one who knows police methods. He is occasionally consulted by them but makes it clear that he feels no obligation to correct their mistakes or "supply their deficiencies" (Doyle, p. 257). In "The Blue Carbuncle," Holmes allows a jewel thief to escape, and in "Charles Augustus Milverton," he keeps quiet about the identity of a murderess who killed a blackmailer while the detective secretly watched. He has his own standards of justice, is of the opinion that the mere bringing to light of criminal activity can sometimes do harm rather than good, and is more willing to "play tricks with the law of England" than with his own conscience (Doyle, p. 646).

Baskerville is a churchman, of course, as practically any man of learning must have been in his century; but his ties to the church are almost as equivocal as Holmes's are to the law-enforcement establishment. He has been an inquisitor; but his notions of what an inquisitor is supposed to do have been far from orthodox, since he has condemned only those who committed serious crimes that made them liable "al braccio secolare" ("to the secular arm"; 38/30). He separates criminal acts from the diabolical causes to which the abbot and others wish to ascribe them. Both Holmes and Baskerville feel themselves outsiders in a world incapable of valuing their peculiar talents, except for the wrong reasons. Their own views of what is right are often at odds with the official establishment views. Both are compromisers, however; to a degree, both are willing to go along with institutional lunacy. They are not overt rebels; both know they cannot exist outside of the institutions whose very philosophies are called into question by the detectives' methods and results.

Not all Baskerville's methods are those of Holmes, however. Even when he seems to be reproducing the great detective's exploits, he may be seen to be doing something subtly or strikingly different, something more likely to be found in Holmes's successors of the twentieth century, not necessarily of the ratiocinative type. A notable example is the case of Venantius' secret message. At first glance, the circumstances look like Doyle's "Adventure of the Dancing Men." A message using a simple substitution code (in Holmes's case, stick men in different attitudes; in William's case, zodiacal symbols) falls into the detective's hands. Holmes uses rules of letter frequency to decipher the message and proceeds to act on the information he learns. Baskerville, though, has no hint there is secret writing on Venantius' notes until Adso accidentally holds the lamp too close, so that the heat brings out a few of the code characters. Once he has brought out the rest of the code letters, Baskerville is unable to act because he has lost his glasses. His starting method is as far from Holmes's as possible, an intuitive approach involving, as he explains to Adso, *guessing what the message means* before attempting to decipher it. Then he extends his intuitive method to an attempt at divining the message's rhythm and divides the first group of eight signs by two, coming up with three for an answer!

> Prova a guardare le prime tre parole, non considerare le lettere, considera solo il numero dei segni . . . IIIIIII IIIII IIIIIII . . . Ora prova a dividere in sillabe di almeno due segni ciascuna, e recita ad alta voce: ta-ta-ta, ta-ta, ta-ta-ta . . .
>
> *(Il nome,* p. 171)

> Try looking at the first three words, not considering the letters, but the number of the signs . . . IIIIIII IIIII IIIIIII. . . . Now try dividing them into syllables of at least two signs each, and recite aloud: ta-ta-ta, ta-ta, ta-ta-ta. . . .
>
> (Weaver trans., p. 166)

On this false ground Baskerville correctly guesses the first three words of the message, thereby giving him no fewer than twelve letters of the code (only five different letters remain). Then he stops cold, saying the deciphering could cost him a whole day. More than a hundred pages later, he comes to Adso with the message, which still cannot be understood even though it has been deciphered.

Another example occurs at Prime on the fourth day and causes William to exclaim to Adso, "Dio sia lodato . . . Abbiamo risolto due problemi!" ("God be praised. . . . We've solved two problems"; 278/275). The two problems are the recovery of his lenses and the question of who robbed him in the scriptorium. But the glasses are merely found by Severinus in the habit of the monk (now dead) who stole them; there is no solving on William's part at all. Moreover, the methods William has been using to get information are those of the hard-boiled dick who roughs up or threatens people, rather than of the ratiocinative detective who makes deductions from evidence no one else could interpret. William has just threatened both Salvatore and Remigio to get the stories of their pasts and their doings during the last few nights. Like the hard-boiled detective, William here leaves deductive methods and fits together information that he discovers by chance or that he extorts by threats of violence.

More disturbing, perhaps, from the point of view of traditional detective work, is the discussion William and Adso have about deductive syllogisms and the fallacy of the undistributed middle. They are speaking of the blackened fingers of both Venantius and Berengar. William posits a substance that turns the fingers black when touched.

Terminai trionfante il sillogismo: " . . . Venanzio e Berengario hanno le dita annerite, ergo hanno toccato questa sostanza!"

"Bravo Adso," disse Guglielmo, "peccato che il tuo sillogismo non sia valido, perché aut semel aut iterum medium generaliter esto, e in questo sillogismo il termine medio non appare mai come generale. Segno che abbiamo scelto male la premessa maggiore.

(*Il nome*, p. 265)

Triumphantly, I completed the syllogism: " . . . Venantius and Berengar have blackened fingers, ergo they touched the substance!"

"Good, Adso," William said, "a pity your syllogism is not valid, because *aut semel aut iterum medium generaliter esto*, and in this syllogism the middle term never appears as general. A sign that we haven't chosen the major premise well.

(Weaver trans., p. 261)

William tells Adso that he places too much faith in syllogisms; but the charge might be made of the detective as well. The problem of the undistributed middle plagues any deductive worker. Much more than that, it plagues the detective storywriter. The fallacy of the undistributed middle is the source of the disbelief the reader must suspend if the overall story is not to collapse. How does Sherlock Holmes know Jabez Wilson, of "The Red-Headed League," got his Chinese coin in China rather than in Limehouse? Maybe the dog did nothing during the night because he knew the intruder, but maybe he was drugged or on the prowl at the next farm ("Silver Blaze"). Once the writer brings up the problem of the undistributed middle, as Eco does here, we know we are in a different realm of fiction, one in which the detective may fail and in which the appropriate allusions are not to Doyle's work or the crude but effective sleuths of the hard-boiled school but to the futile and enigmatic detectives of Borges.

William does fail—and on an impressive scale. Failure itself, though, is not a sign of anything particularly "modern" in the detective story. The detectives in Wilkie Collins' *The Moonstone* (1867) fail, and Holmes himself admitted to having been beaten "four times, three times by men, and once by a woman" (Doyle, p. 219). William of Baskerville fails in large and small ways throughout the book, ultimately failing to establish any rule of order in any of the senses of the word. He arrives too late to save victim after victim; he does not realize the importance of the Aristotle manuscript when it is in his hands in Severinus's laboratory; he fails to pursue Benno, who took the manuscript; he is defeated by Bernard Gui (a defeat for rational and humane ways of acting, as well as a defeat for his religious order's principle of poverty). William fails to save the manuscript, the library, or the abbey. All these failures, however, are in some way secondary to William's defeat by Jorge of Burgos. What Jorge represents is the antithesis of the experimental, tentative way of knowledge William pursues; in his mad sermon Jorge says that "è proprio del sapere, cosa divina, essere completo" ("the property of knowledge, as a divine thing, is that it is complete"; 402/399).

William begins by believing in the truth of signs even in the absence of a larger order in the world; but before he leaves the abbey, even Adso takes him to the logical conclusions of his notions about order and God:

> Affermare l'assoluta onnipotenza di Dio e la sua assoluta disponibilità rispetto alle sue stesse scelte, non equivale a dimonstrare che Dio non esiste?
>
> (*Il nome*, 496)

> Isn't affirming God's absolute omnipotence and His absolute freedom with regard to His own choices tantamount to demonstrating that God does not exist?
>
> (Weaver trans., 493)

Although William will not affirm the truth of Adso's theological speculation, we realize that this is, in fact, the doubt with which he lives. William tries to stave off ultimate doubt with local certainties, but Jorge of Burgos has proved to him that any speculation about causes beyond the most obvious (and, therefore, useless) causal relationship is futile. In *The Name of the Rose* epistemological doubt is connected to theological doubt; a failure in detection implies a failure of faith.

William of Baskerville's nemesis is the blind Spaniard, Jorge of Burgos, who is meant to bring to mind the blind Argentinian Jorge Luis Borges. Borges' works furnish the perfect allusions for the kinds of doubt with which Eco surrounds his detective as *The Name of the Rose* progresses. When Eco alludes to Borges' labyrinthine libraries and compromised detectives, he signals the inadequacy of Baskerville's methods in a world unlike the assured Holmesian one. Blind and lost, the detective shows us detection as solipsism and detection that becomes part of the criminal plan. He finds himself faced not with a Moriarty but a criminal who is a reflection of himself, using his own thoughts and unattackable partly because of the detective's own doubts.

The two Borges stories to which Eco alludes are "La Biblioteca de Babel" (The Library of Babel) and "La muerte y la brújula" (Death and the Compass). In the first story the world is the library and the library is a labyrinth:

El universo (que otros llaman la Biblioteca) se compone de un número indefinido, y tal vez infinito, de galerías hexagonales. . . . Una de las caras [de cualquier hexágono] da a un angosto zaguán. . . . En el zaguán hay un espejo, que fielmente duplica las apariencias. Los hombres suelen inferir de ese espejo que la Biblioteca no es infinita (sí lo fuera realmente ¿a qué esa duplicación ilusoria?); yo prefiero soñar que las superficies bruñidas figuran y prometen el infinito. . . .⁵

The universe (which others call the Library) is composed of an indefinite and perhaps infinite number of hexagonal galleries. . . . One of the sides [of any hexagon] leads to a narrow hallway. . . . In the hallway there is a mirror which faithfully duplicates all appearances. Men usually infer from this mirror that the Library is not infinite (if it really were, why this illusory duplication?); I prefer to dream that its polished surfaces represent and promise the infinite. . . .⁶

Eco's abbey library is also "un gran labirinto, segno del labirinto del mondo," (a great labyrinth, sign of the labyrinth of the world; 163/158). It contains multisided chambers and illusory mirrors. The plan of the library reproduces the map of the world (to the extent that it was known in the fourteenth century), and in the tradition of the "fair play" or "Golden Age" detective stories, Eco provides a map of the abbey's grounds and, once Adso and William have worked it out, a map of the library.

One's inferences in Borges' library/world do not lead to any absolute truths. The inhabitants (librarians) of the library have been able to infer that the library contains all possible books; but this discovery leads not to knowledge but to paradox. The librarians search among the books, theorize about them, and believe things of them. Their attitudes constitute religious faiths and heresies, philosophical speculation, and superstition. There are even "buscadores oficiales, *inquisidores*," (official searchers, *inquisitors*; 91/55). Martin Stabb, in his monograph on Borges, notes that the story's primary symbols—library, book, and word—by their very nature point to another, more realistic world outside themselves.⁷ The dualism suggested here, however, may be specious and the other reality illusory; at least the other world is unreachable by those in the labyrinth. Eco uses the book to represent both knowledge itself and rational speculation, both of which are lost in the defeats Baskerville suffers at the abbey. The library burns—the Aristotle work on comedy along with all the other books. In addition, Eco is concerned with the reality beyond themselves that the signs, books, and library point to. He playfully hints at dualism when describing the style of manuscript illumination known as Babewyn:

Si trattava di un salterio ai margini del quale si delineava un mondo rovesciato rispetto a quello cui ci hanno abituati i nostri sensi. Come se al limine di un discorso che per definizione è il discorso della verità, si svolgesse profondamente legato a quello, per mirabili allusioni in aenigmate, un discorso menzognero su un universo posto a testa in giù, dove i cani fuggono davanti alla lepre e i cervi cacciano il leone.

(Il nome, 84)

This was a psalter in whose margins was delineated a world reversed with respect to the one to which our senses have accustomed us. As if at the border of a discourse that is by definition the discourse of truth, there proceeded, closely linked to it, through wondrous allusions in aenigmate, a discourse of falsehood on a topsy-turvy universe, in which dogs flee before the hare, and deer hunt the lion.

(Weaver trans., 76)

Eco suggests that the signs of words and books, as well as the signs in nature, may be equivocally connected, if connected at all, to some further reality. Baskerville begins his investigation with considerably more assurance about the coherence of things. At the beginning he tells Adso that the world can be read like a great book and quotes Alanus de Insulis:

omnis mundi creatura
quasi liber et pictura
nobis est in speculum
(32/23)

Before we have reached the middle of the story, though, Baskerville is voicing doubts about what we can know of the world's form. He speaks in response to Adso, who, in his innocence, wonders whether a particular kind of religious conviction can preserve one from sin:

"Se questa abbazia fosse uno speculum mundi, avresti già la risposta."
"Ma lo è?" chiesi.
"Perché vi sia specchio del mondo occorre che il mondo abbia una forma," concluse Guglielmo, che era troppo filosofo per la mia mente adolescente.

(Il nome, 127)

"If this abbey were a speculum mundi, you would already have the answer."
"But is it?" I asked.
"In order for there to be a mirror of the world, it is necessary that the world have a form," concluded William, who was too much of a philosopher for my adolescent mind.

(Weaver trans., 120)

Near the end of the novel, Baskerville is explicit about his doubt that "il mondo abbia un ordine" (the world has an order) and is content to try to find "almeno una serie di connessioni in piccole porzioni degli affari del mondo" (at least a series of connections in small areas of the world's affairs; 397/394). What William discovers is that the connections he makes among the "facts" of his investigation are connections only in his own mind. When he tries to link murders that are actually unrelated, the structure he makes helps his adversary Jorge of Burgos lead him astray and trap him.

The villain's use of the detective's own thought processes to trap and destroy him is the plot of Borges' "La muerte y la brújula" (Death and the Compass). In this story the detective, Erik Lönnrot, is lured into projecting a pattern for a series of murders and thus trying to anticipate a last one—which turns out to be a trap for him. The first three murders occur at locations which, when mapped, describe an equilateral triangle; but the triangle can be extended to form a diamond. The murder sites correspond to three points of the compass; the detective projects a fourth location. In the story, the diamonds of a harlequin's costume and the Tetragrammaton suggest patterns of four. All sorts of signs point to the reasoner's conclusions, but all of them are either false (supplied by the villain) or arbitrary (the first murder, for example, is the casual crime of a drunken bully). At the end of the story the detective meets his mirrored adversary, Red Sharlach (the detective's name means *red*), in a labyrinth with mirrors, and is there defeated (and presumably killed) by him.

Eco's story, too, begins with an arbitrary death, a suicide that looks as if it were connected to everything else that happens. But it is not. Baskerville also projects from the occurrences in the abbey a pattern derived from the last seven days of the Apocalypse. His adversary, Jorge, feeds and encourages the detective's false projection. Jorge waits for Baskerville in the library's labyrinth and, though he does not kill him, destroys the collected monuments of the past's reason and sanity—the lost section of Aristotle's *Poetics* that deals with comedy and the rest of the library's books. Within the labyrinth—which in the final analysis, represents not the world but the *mind* and all it can solipsistically know of the world—the detective is caught and defeated.

In *The Name of the Rose* the detective is a searcher whose defeat signals the defeat of a way of thinking and knowing for two ages—his own and ours. Through Jorge and the inquisitor Bernard Gui, Eco suggests that authoritarianism threatens rational inquiry and faith. A worse failure of reason comes from within, however. In his confrontation with Jorge, Baskerville finds that they are both only manipulating counters in the mind. Like Lönnrot in Borges' story, Baskerville meets a mirrored adversary whose thoughts are so close to the detective's that one can easily anticipate the other. The real casualty in Eco's story (represented by the library) and in Borges' story (represented by the detective himself) is the conviction that the world of signs points to something else beyond signs. In Eco's book, even Adso finally loses his faith in the correspondence of signs to a knowable reality; at the end he writes that, although the rose remains as it was in name, we have only names, *nomina nuda tenemus*.

Notes

1. Quotations from Umberto Eco, *Il nome della rosa* (*Milano: Bompiani, 1980*) are followed immediately by their English versions from the William Weaver translation, *The Name of the Rose* (San Diego: Harcourt Brace Jovanovich, 1983). After short quotations in the text, page citations in parentheses give the page number of the Italian edition, a slash mark, and the page number of the Weaver translation. The double notation with the slash mark is also followed in citing the texts and translations of Voltaire and Borges.

2. Sir Arthur Conan Doyle, *The Complete Sherlock Holmes* (Garden City, NY: Doubleday, 1930), 162.

3. Voltaire (François-Marie Arouet), "Zadig ou la destinée," *Romans et contes* (Paris: Garnier, 1959), 7–8.

4. Voltaire, "Zadig, or Destiny," *Candide and Other Stories*, trans. Joan Spencer (London: Oxford University Press, 1966), 9.

5. Jorge Luis Borges, *Ficciones* (Buenos Aires: Emece, 1956), 85.

6. Jorge Luis Borges, *Labyrinths: Selected Stories and Other Writings*, trans. Donald A. Yates and James E. Irby (New York: New Directions, 1964), 51.

7. Martin S. Stabb, *Jorge Luis Borges* (New York: Twayne, 1970), 112.

5   Eco's Conflation of Theology and Detection in *The Name of the Rose*

Joan DelFattore

A mystery story on two levels, *The Name of the Rose* presents a series of murders by unknown perpetrators and a series of debates about God, Christ, and the created world. Each series is a coherent sequence of related events—in Eco's vocabulary, a text—and the two series combine to form a more comprehensive, more complex text. In the novel's protagonist, William of Baskerville, Eco combines Holmesian detective methodology with the philosophical and theological methodologies of Roger Bacon and William of Occam. The result is a murder mystery that, like its accompanying theopolitical debate, is based on the relationships among universals, particulars, and reality. Having attempted to apply his theological convictions to the detection of a murderer, William labels himself a failure as a theologian and as a detective because of what he perceives as an insufficiency of method. However, the novel's interplay of detection and theology, of universals and individuals, and of cerebration and reality supports another conclusion: it is not William's method that fails him, but he who, finally, fails his method.

Beginning with the earliest reviews of *The Name of the Rose*, critics have noted the Holmesian significance of William's name and the physical resemblance between William of Baskerville and Sherlock Holmes. Adso, the novel's narrator, states:

> "[William's] height surpassed that of a normal man and he was so thin that he seemed still taller. His eyes were sharp and penetrating; his thin and slightly beaky nose gave his countenance the expression of a man on the lookout, save in certain moments of sluggishness of which I shall speak. [1]

Like his appearance, William's behavior resembles that of Holmes: he alternates between intense activity and profound inactivity, laments the destruction of evidence by inexperienced investigators, treats Adso as Holmes treats Watson, and occasionally indulges in drugs. All of this, however, points to the obvious conclusion that William is based on Holmes.

The more important question is, Why is William based on Holmes? The answer lies in Eco's evaluation of Holmes's methodology.

In his essay "Horns, Hooves, Insteps: Some Hypotheses on Three Types of Abduction," Eco refines Charles Sanders Peirce's definition of abduction and relates it to Holmes's detective method. Eco summarizes Peirce's notion of abduction as "the provisional entertainment of an explanatory inference, for the sake of further testing . . . which aims at isolating, along with the case, also the rule."[2] In refining this definition Eco suggests three levels of abduction based on the degree of uncertainty involved in inferring the rule, quoting an incident in Voltaire's *Zadig* as an example:

> Just at this moment, by one of the usual freaks of fortune, the finest horse in the king's stables escaped from a groom's hands and fled into the plains of Babylon. The Master of the King's Hounds and all the other officials rushed after it. . . . The Master of the King's Hounds came up to Zadig and asked if he had not seen the king's horse pass by.
> "The horse you are looking for is the best galloper in the stable," answered Zadig. "It is fifteen hands high, and has a very small hoof. Its tail is three and a half feet long. The studs on its bit are of twenty-three carat gold, and its shoes of eleven scruple silver."
> "Which road did it take?" asked the Master of the King's Hounds. "Where is it?"
> "I have not seen the horse," answered Zadig, "and I have never heard speak of it."[3]

Zadig later explains his conclusions:

> "As regards the king of kings' horse, you may know that as I walked along the road in this wood I saw the marks of horse-shoes, all equal distances apart. That horse, said I, gallops perfectly. The dust on the trees in this narrow road only seven feet wide was raised a little right and left, three and a half feet from the middle of the road. This horse, said I, has a tail three and a half feet long, and its movement right and left has swept up this dust. I saw beneath the trees, which made a cradle five feet high, some leaves newly fallen from the branches, and I recognized that this horse had touched there and was hence fifteen hands high. As regards his bit, it must be of twenty-three carat gold, for he rubbed the studs against a stone which I knew to be a touchstone and tested. From the marks his hoofs made on certain pebbles I knew the horse was shod with eleven scruple silver."[4]

According to Eco, Zadig engages in "hypothesis" or "overcoded abduction" when he infers a rule that is comparatively obvious, for example, when he interprets a particular type of imprint as evidence of the passage of a horse.

In "undercoded abduction," the thinker opts for the interpretation that offers the most economical explanation which fits all of the facts available, even if this explanation is only probable. Zadig thus concludes that the hoof marks, broken branches, raised dust, silvered pebbles, and gilded touchstone all proceed from a single cause: the passage of a horse fifteen hands high, with a tail three and a half feet long, wearing silver shoes and a gold bit. In defining the third level of abduction, Eco distinguishes between the methodology of Zadig and that of Sherlock Holmes. Unlike Zadig, Holmes engages in "creative abduction," in which the thinker invents an explanation that fits all of the facts but is so tenuous, and is one of so many probable explanations, that any correlation between the invention and reality seems almost coincidental. As an example, Eco cites the "mind-reading" episode in "The Cardboard Box," in which Holmes reproduces Watson's train of thought by hypothesizing from Watson's eye movements and facial expressions. In commenting on this episode, Eco observes:

> Holmes is certainly trying to imitate the way Watson should have thought (*ars imitatur naturam in sua operatione!*) but he was obliged to choose, among many of Watson's possible mental courses (that he probably figured out all together at the same time), the one which displayed more aesthetic coherence, or more 'elegance.' Holmes invented a story. It simply happened that that possible story was analogous to the actual one.[5]

Having distinguished between the levels of abduction on this basis, Eco introduces the concept of meta-abduction, in which the thinker acts as though inferences based on various levels of abduction were true, without any intermediate verification. For example, when Holmes breaks into Watson's reverie in "The Cardboard Box," it is not to question his train of thought but to offer a logical reply to it. In other words, Holmes behaves exactly as he would have if his untested conjecture had already been proved true. It is at the level of creative abduction and meta-abduction that William of Baskerville most closely resembles Holmes, and it is because of Holmes's association with this methodology that Eco based his detective persona on him.

The significance of "Horns, Hooves, Insteps" to *The Name of the Rose* becomes evident early in the novel, in a scene that raises Zadig's inferences about the king's horse to the level of creative abduction and meta-abduction. As William and Adso approach the abbey in which most of the novel's action takes place, they are greeted by a delegation of monks headed by the cellarer. The monks do not mention that they are looking for the abbot's horse, which has escaped from the abbey stables. Thus, they are startled when William replies to their greeting with a meta-abduction:

"The horse came this way and took the path to the right. He will not get far, because he will have to stop when he reaches the dungheap. He is too intelligent to plunge down that precipitous slope." (23)

William thus outdoes Zadig by voicing the inferences he has reached by observing the physical evidence, such as hoofprints and horsehairs, before the searchers tell him that they are looking for a horse. Nor does he fail, as Zadig does, to infer the horse's present location. Further, while Zadig's description of the king's horse is confined to what the physical evidence suggests, William's description of the abbot's horse includes a creative abduction based on his knowledge of how various authorities describe the ideal horse and on his belief that monks rely more heavily on authority than on the evidence of their own senses. Thus William states that the horse has a small head, large eyes, and pointed ears—not because he has found physical evidence to suggest that the horse has these qualities but because he invents a horse based on what he guesses the monks believe about it.

William's creative abduction regarding the monks' view of the abbot's horse is an early example of Eco's conflation of the detective tradition with theological issues. With regard to the detective tradition, William follows Holmes in establishing his credibility as a detective by means of a startling meta-abduction early in his relationship with his "clients." His tour de force regarding the abbot's horse serves the same function as Holmes's observation on first meeting his client in "The Adventure of the Norwood Builder": "I assure you that, beyond the obvious facts that you are a bachelor, a solicitor, a Freemason, and an asthmatic, I know nothing whatever about you."[6] With regard to theological issues, William, a British Franciscan, follows the British Franciscan Roger Bacon in preferring empirical experimentation to the reliance on authority that is characteristic of the scholastic theologians. William's Baconian empiricism is evident in the irony of his remarks to Adso:

"I am not sure [the abbot's horse] has those features, but no doubt the monks firmly believe he does. As Isidore of Seville said, the beauty of a horse requires 'that the head be small, siccum prope pelle ossibus adhaerente, short and pointed ears, big eyes, flaring nostrils, erect neck, thick mane and tail, round and solid hoofs.' If the horse whose passing I inferred had not really been the finest of the stables, stableboys would have been out chasing him, but instead, the cellarer in person had undertaken the search. And a monk who considers a horse excellent, whatever his natural forms, can only see him as the auctoritates have described him, especially if'—and here he smiled slyly in my direction—"the describer is a learned Benedictine."[24]

Similarly, William's protracted explanation of the episode of the horse includes a discussion of universals and individuals that both establishes his Occamite theological orientation and clarifies his detective methodology. Like William of Occam, another British Franciscan, William believes that universals have no reality. In this, he differs from Thomas Aquinas and other scholastic theologians who taught that universals have actual, if immaterial, existence. According to the scholastic theologians, each universal is unitary but exists in a formal sense in every individual of its type. The mind, itself immaterial, can comprehend only universals; it cannot comprehend individuals directly but abstracts an understanding of them through its perception of universals. Occam, on the other hand, taught that the individual is directly accessible to the intellect, that the individual alone is real, and that the individual is always the first object known. To Occam, universals are not the means by which the intellect perceives individuals but, rather, signs conceived by the intellect from the perception of individuals. Universals, a quality of the thought process, exist as part of the form of discourse, but only individuals have actual existence outside the mind itself. In defining his methodology to Adso, William asserts:

> "So I found myself halfway between the perception of the concept 'horse' and the knowledge of an individual horse. And in any case, what I knew of the universal horse had been given me by those traces, which were singular. I could say I was caught at that moment between the singularity of the traces and my ignorance, which assumed the quite diaphanous form of a universal idea. . . . So an hour ago I could expect all horses, but not because of the vastness of my intellect, but because of the paucity of my deduction. And my intellect's hunger was sated only when I saw the single horse that the monks were leading by the halter. Only then did I truly know that my previous reasoning had brought me close to the truth. And so the ideas, which I was using earlier to imagine a horse I had not yet seen, were pure signs, as the hoofprints in the snow were signs of the idea of 'horse'; and signs and the signs of signs are used only when we are lacking things." (28)

William's combination of Baconian empiricism with Occamite philosophy is further clarified when the abbot asks him to investigate the death of a young monk whose body has been found at the foot of a precipice. In explaining his preference for the hypothesis that the monk committed suicide, William interprets carefully collected empirical data in terms of Occam's razor, which corresponds to the methodology that Peirce later defined as "undercoded abduction":

"Dear Adso, one should not multiply explanations and causes unless it is strictly necessary. If Adelmo fell from the east tower, he must have got into the library, someone must have first struck him so he would offer no resistance, and then this person must have found a way of climbing up to the window with a lifeless body on his back, opening it, and pitching the hapless monk down. But with my hypothesis we need only Adelmo, his decision, and a shift of some land. Everything is explained, using a smaller number of causes." (91)

The method that William defines in these early episodes continues to work effectively throughout most of the novel. He uses it successfully, for example, in identifying the pattern of the library's labyrinthine maze and in inferring the abbey's ownership of a copy of Aristotle's long-lost treatise on comedy. Nevertheless, his ability to interpret the results of his abductive method is flawed because he never resolves the inconsistencies between Baconian empiricism and Occamite nominalism in defining the relationship between universals and individuals. He recognizes that Bacon's empirical approach to ascertaining natural laws depends on the assumption that all entities of the same type will behave in similar ways under similar conditions, and he recognizes that his own detective methodology depends on the same assumption. His early abduction regarding the monks' view of the abbot's horse, for example, is based on his belief that, having observed the behavior of representatives of a type (monk) under given conditions, he can predict what other representatives of that type will do under similar conditions. He has therefore associated himself with a method that presupposes the existence of universal characteristics that inhere in each individual of a given type, a presupposition he views as a contradiction of his belief that universals have existence only as signs and forms of discourse. Moreover, William's definition of God precludes belief in the existence of universals, which, in William's view, would limit the free will of God by preventing Him from causing the terms of an individual's existence to deviate from the relevant universals. This conflict places William in the paradoxical position of acting on a functional belief in assumptions whose philosophical validity he denies. He refuses to examine this position in more than a superficial way because he fears that he might find himself morally obligated to abandon the empirical methodology on which his professional success and personal vanity depend; or, on the other hand, that he might find himself involved in a frightening redefinition of his concept of God. Because he never resolves, and partially suppresses, his perplexity over the relationship of universals and particulars to his detective method, he repeatedly errs in interpreting the data furnished him by his successful abductions.

William's first major error of this type occurs when, having discovered a secret message written in zodiacal code, he deciphers it by means of Holmesian abduction.[7] He thus discovers the clue to the *finis Africae*, the secret center of the library labyrinth: " 'Secretum finis Africae manus supra idolum age primum et septimum de quatuor.' . . . 'The hand over the idol works on the first and the seventh of the four . . .' " (209) To enter the hidden room he must still learn what the idol is, what "the first and the seventh of the four" means, and what to do with the four when he has located it. In general terms, he has progressed from one level of signs to another without having reached the referent. Without consciously formulating what he is doing, he tries to interpret the results of his abduction by finding the common feature—the universal—that reveals the truth, as his assumption about the common feature of the monkish mentality revealed the truth about the monks' view of the abbot's horse. He thus looks for some manifestation of fourness as a universal rather than looking for the existence of the word *quatuor* as a concrete individual, which would be more in keeping with his philosophical, as opposed to his detective, orientation. It is not until near the end of the novel that he makes practical use of the tenet that " 'suppositio materialis, the discourse is presumed de dicto [relating to the word] and not de re [relating to the thing]' " (457). Applying this dictum to his abductive method, William realizes that "the first and the seventh of the four" refers not to some manifestation of fourness but to the first and seventh letters of the word *quatuor* as it appears above a distorted mirror at the heart of the library labyrinth.

William's initial failure to comprehend the significance of the word *quatuor* is paralleled by his initial failure to comprehend the significance of the distorted mirror above which the word appears. Just as he first thinks of *quatuor* in terms of evanescent manifestations of fourness rather than in terms of its concrete existence as a word, so he first thinks of the mirror in terms of the evanescent images on its surface rather than in terms of its concrete identity as a mirror. The nature of William's error is indirectly defined in Eco's *Semiotics and the Philosophy of Language*, published two years after the Italian edition of *The Name of the Rose*. Following a discussion that compares and contrasts mirror images with signs, Eco concludes that the essential identity of a mirror is not to produce signs but to act as a channel, giving viewers visual access to the front of their own bodies or, in the case of a slanted mirror, to locations that would otherwise have been outside their line of vision. Eco's identification of mirrors as channels is the point of the secret William discovers in *The Name of the Rose*: the mirror itself is the channel, the means of access, to the secret room at the heart of the library labyrinth. Just as the referent of *quatuor* in the riddle is the written word itself and not one of the potentially infinite number of manifestations of fourness, so the significance of the mirror to the riddle is its mirrorness, its essential nature as a channel, and not any of the potentially infinite number of images on its surface.[8]

The philosophical-methodological confusion that interferes with William's understanding of *quatuor* and the mirror also affects his most important abduction: that the Apocalypse is the controlling metaphor of the deaths that take place in the abbey; thus the identification of the murderer hinges on his association with the *Apocalypse*. Throughout the novel William is surrounded by apocalyptic imagery. Apocalyptic figures are carved on the tympanum of the abbey church, and the monks comment on them repeatedly and at length. Apocalyptic verses surmount the doorways in the library labyrinth, and one room of the library contains editions of the *Apocalypse* from all over the world. Moreover, William recognizes that the effect of all this apocalyptic imagery is organizational rather than merely cumulative. For example, the verses over the library doorways are not merely decorative; they define the labyrinth's overall construction and contain the secret of its hidden room. Having determined that the *Apocalypse* is the controlling metaphor or principle of order of the labyrinth, William gradually becomes convinced that it bears a similar relationship to the deaths. He senses from the beginning that the deaths are associated with the library, and he assumes that this connection gives the murderer some motive, metaphorical or actual, for employing the apocalyptic motif. Further, Alinardo, the oldest monk, mentions the resemblances between the first two deaths and the events associated with the first two trumpet blasts in the *Apocalypse*.

> "Did you not hear the seven trumpets?"
>
> "Why the seven trumpets?"
>
> "Did you not hear how the other boy died, the illuminator? The first angel sounded the first trumpet, and hail and fire fell mingled with blood. And the second angel sounded the second trumpet, and the third part of the sea became blood. . . . Did the second boy not die in the sea of blood? Watch out for the third trumpet! The third part of the creatures in the sea will die."
> (159)

Alinardo's theory is supported when, acting on the old man's hint about the water imagery associated with the third trumpet, William finds the body of a dead monk in the monastery bath. The apocalyptic *motif* seems confirmed when another body is found, its head broken by an armillary sphere that represents the stars associated with the fourth trumpet; and when yet another monk dies raving of the scorpions associated with the fifth trumpet.

William's recognition of the apocalyptic principle underlying the deaths eventually leads him to conclude that the murderer is Jorge of Burgos, the character most closely associated with the *Apocalypse*. As a young man Jorge had been sent to Silos to collect the editions of the *Apocalypse* that William and Adso discover in the library. Moreover, Jorge is preoccupied with apocalyptic themes and frequently alludes to them, most notably in a sermon he preaches in the abbey church. William assumes, because of his own Occamite interpretive bias, that Jorge's relationship to the apocalyptic pattern of the deaths must be individual and causal. He finds, however, that Jorge has not deliberately ordered the deaths in an apocalyptic mode. The degree to which Jorge is responsible for some of the deaths is itself problematic; his only deliberate use of apocalyptic imagery occurs after—and because—he has heard about William's belief in the apocalyptic ordering of the events at the abbey.

Refusing to consider the possibility of a principle of order that transcends the individual, William concludes that because Jorge's role in the apocalyptic pattern is not as William had conceived of it, the pattern itself does not exist. This belief is especially ironic because, even as William expresses his sense of failure to Jorge, the apocalyptic motif continues. In consuming the poisoned copy of Aristotle's treatise on comedy, Jorge pervertedly compares himself with the narrator of the *Apocalypse*:

> "Now listen to what the voice says: Seal what the seven thunders have said and do not write it, take and devour it, it will make bitter your belly but to your lips it will be sweet as honey." (480–81)

At the same time, unrecognized by William or Jorge, the imagery surrounding the sixth trumpet of the *Apocalypse* is being carried out. William has previously observed that the sixth trumpet is associated with horses, and, as he and Jorge speak, the abbot whose missing horse provided William's first opportunity for abduction dies of suffocation. The apocalyptic horse imagery described by Adso, concerning "horses with lions' heads from whose mouths come smoke and fire and brimstone" (418), is further represented when, during the destruction of the abbey, blazing horses with manes of fire spread the conflagration. The fiery destruction of the library clearly parallels the events following the seventh trumpet blast, and other details support this correlation. For example, the twenty-four elders in the verse above the library mirror—that is, the carved words themselves—fall on their faces, as the elders do after the seventh blast in the biblical text.

As these events suggest, William is not mistaken about the existence of an apocalyptic pattern in the story that unfolds in the abbey, nor is he mistaken in associating Jorge with apocalyptic themes. His error lies in his interpretation of this association, since his philosophical-theological attitudes prevent him from exploring the implications of the fact that Jorge's individual, deliberate actions were not the source of most of the novel's apocalyptic manifestations. In his *Postscript to "The Name of the Rose,"* Eco observes that his novel is

> a mystery in which very little is discovered and the detective is defeated. . . .
> After all, the fundamental question of philosophy (like that of psychoanalysis) is the same as the question of the detective novel: who is guilty? To know this (to think you know this), you have to conjecture that all the events have a logic, the logic that the guilty party has imposed on them.[9]

By this definition, William is indeed defeated; but this does not preclude an alternate view of his defeat as having occurred at a different moment, and for different reasons, than he himself believes.

William has determined a priori that whatever logic prevails in the events at the abbey must be the product of a single human mind. He correctly identifies the mind that is most congruent with the events but assumes that the identification is valid only if that mind conceived the events. The congruence is, in itself, meaningless to him because acknowledging that it has meaning would involve acknowledging the possibility of a transcendent logic of events in which Jorge's deliberate acts are no more or less significant and no more or less necessary than events that are apparently coincidental, such as Berengar's decision to place Venantius' body in a jar of pigs' blood, Berengar's choice of the monastery bath as a secluded place to read a forbidden book, and Malachi's use of the armillary sphere as a weapon.

The possibility that the events at the abbey are subject to a form of universal, rather than individual, ordering need not conflict with William's abductive method per se. Sebeok and Umiker-Sebeok point out that successful abduction is based on validated correlations between external reality and the invention of the thinker, which suggests that the mind, which has evolved as part of the world, is predisposed to think correctly about the world. In arguing this point, Sebeok and Umiker-Sebeok quote Peirce's observation "that there can 'be no reasonable doubt that man's mind, having been developed under the influence of the laws of nature, for that reason naturally thinks somewhat after nature's pattern'."[10] Thus, William's belief to the contrary, his basic abductive methodology supports rather than precludes the possibility of an extraindividual ordering of the events at the abbey. His method itself is based on the notion of an indefinable congruence between the human mind and nature, and this could explain not only the detective's successful reinvention of a real-life pattern of events but the unknowing cooperation of other individuals and circumstances in developing the pattern itself. William's refusal to consider this possibility is based not on his functional methodology or its conceptual basis but on a philosophical-theological bias that makes it impossible for him to consider the role of universals in a strictly rational manner. The nature of this bias is clearly defined in a conversation with Adso in which William claims:

> "To be sure, anyone who tests the curative property of herbs knows that individual herbs of the same species have equal effects of the same nature on the patient, and therefore the investigator formulates the proposition that every herb of a given type helps the feverish, or that every lens of such a type magnifies the eye's vision to the same degree. The science Bacon spoke of rests unquestionably on these propositions. You understand, Adso, I must believe that my proposition works, because I learned it by experience; but to believe it I must assume there are universal laws. Yet I cannot speak of them, because the very concept that universal laws and an established order exist would imply that God is their prisoner, whereas God is something absolutely free, so that if He wanted, with a single act of His will He could make the world different." (207)

Because he is preoccupied with the question of God's ability to change natural laws once they are established, William unwittingly circumscribes the free will of God by assuming that it can operate only in a nominalistic moral framework based on the deliberate acts and intents of individuals. He implicitly rejects the notion of a collective, universal pattern resembling Carl Jung's theory of synchronicity, which posits "the simultaneous occurrence of meaningful equivalences in heterogeneous, causally unrelated processes" within which the acts of individuals fall into place in a macropattern that the individuals themselves do not conceive, consent to, or even recognize.[11] As a result, William misses some of the implications of his own concluding analysis of his performance as a detective:

> "I arrived at Jorge through an apocalyptic pattern that seemed to underlie all the crimes, and yet it was accidental. I arrived at Jorge seeking one criminal for all the crimes and we discovered that each crime was committed by a different person, or by no one. I arrived at Jorge pursuing the plan of a perverse and rational mind, and there was no plan, or, rather, Jorge himself was overcome by his own initial design and there began a sequence of causes, and concauses, and of causes contradicting one another, which proceeded on their own, creating relations that did not stem from any plan. Where is all my wisdom, then? I behaved stubbornly, pursuing a semblance of order, when I should have known well that there is no order in the universe." (492)

It is at this point in the novel and not, as William believes, in his earlier confrontation with Jorge that he makes his final error. He accuses himself of having twisted the facts to fit his preconceived theories at the very moment when that is what he is doing. He concludes "that there is no order in the universe," when all that has actually been proved is that the order did not, in this case, come packaged the way he expected it to.

At the beginning of the novel William differs from Zadig because he has the courage to commit himself wholly to his Peircean methodology. At this early stage he is not, like Zadig, "unable to accept his fate as a Sherlock Holmes, [and] frightened by meta-abduction."[12] This early abductive daring is exemplified when William bases his inference about the monks' view of the abbot's horse on his belief that monks rely on authority rather than the evidence of their own senses. By the end of the novel William has become arbitrary and conceptually inflexible. He accepts defeat because he can claim success only by admitting that the apocalyptic pattern that points to Jorge is based on some form of universal and depends on a concatenation of actions by unwitting participants. This possibility threatens the primacy of the individual that is subjacent to his philosophy; he rejects it on doctrinal rather than strictly rational grounds. Therefore, William's conviction of failure is doubly ironic. A monk himself, William reverts to what he has identified as a universal monkish type by failing to pursue the evidence of his senses when that evidence points to universals whose possible existence conflicts with the doctrine that there are no universals.

In summarizing and evaluating the novel's events and his own performance, William tries to take a position between a dawning realization of postmodernist complexity and a more stereotyped medieval hierarchical mode of thought. Nevertheless, he is, in the final analysis, unable to deal with the possibility of unlimited connections. He never ceases to conceive of the world in a mannerist mode even while recognizing the possible existence of relationships beyond his grasp. His last words in the novel are thus understandable, significant, and poignant: " 'There is too much confusion here. . . . Non in commotione, non in commotione Dominus' " (493).

Notes

1. Umberto Eco, *The Name of the Rose*, trans. William Weaver (San Diego: Harcourt Brace Jovanovich, 1983), 15. Subsequent citations appear in parentheses in the text.

2. Eco, "Horns, Hooves, Insteps: Some Hypotheses on Three Types of Abduc-

tion," in *The Sign of Three*, ed. U. Eco and Thomas A. Sebeok (Bloomington: Indiana University Press, 1983), 206.

3. Eco, "Horns," 208.

4. Eco, "Horns," 209.

5. Eco, "Horns," 216.

6. Arthur Conan Doyle, *The Complete Sherlock Holmes* (London: Secker and Warburg, 1981), 497.

7. Compare Holmes's approach to deciphering coded messages in "The Dancing Men."

8. This is not to suggest that the mirror's relationship to the riddle is its only function in the novel. For example, Eco's *Semiotics and the Philosophy of Language* (Bloomington: Indiana University Press, 1984) includes observations that relate to other aspects of the mirror's significance, such as a definition of distorted mirrors as "[prostheses] with hallucinatory functions" (217) that stimulate a process "which shifts the boundaries between catoptrics and semiosis" (218). See also, Walter E. Stephens' discussion of Eco's adaptation of Borges' mirror imagery, "Ec(h)o in Fabula," *Diacritics* 13 (Summer 1983): 51–64.

9. Umberto Eco, *Postscript to "The Name of the Rose,"* trans. William Weaver (San Diego: Harcourt Brace Jovanovich, 1984), 54.

10. Thomas A. Sebeok and Jean Umiker-Sebeok, " 'You Know My Method': A Juxtaposition of Charles S. Peirce and Sherlock Holmes," in *The Sign of Three*, ed. Umberto Eco and Thomas A. Sebeok (Bloomington: Indiana University Press, 1984), 17.

11. Jung, "Synchronicity: An Acausal Connecting Principle," in *The Structure and Dynamics of the Psyche*, trans. R. F. C. Hull (New York: Bollingen Foundation, 1968), 531.

12. Eco, "Horns," 215.

6 The Detective Novel and the Defense of Humanism

Pierre L. Horn

The Name of the Rose uses for its main plot a series of seven shocking deaths set in what ought to be the ideal ivory tower. The novel, however, is not only a crime story devoted to the methodical and gradual discovery of the exact circumstances of mysterious events through rational means (though much of our enjoyment comes from its *whodunit* qualities) but a defense of enlightened humanism as well. Brother William of Baskerville—thanks to his training in philosophy, Christian dialectics, science, religious disputations, and empirical inquiry—is well suited to perform the mission of detective assigned him by the abbot. [1]

Even before he enters the monastery compound, "William demonstrates his great acumen" when he solves before an awe-struck audience the problem of Brunellus, the abbot's runaway horse (23–24) in a manner reminiscent of Voltaire's Zadig. [2] In both cases, their feats of observation and reasoning are accomplished more from the study of natural signs, which are visible and thus comprehensible to all, than through magic or intuition. [3]

In addition to several other fictional detectives, the Franciscan monk is clearly modeled on Sherlock Holmes. His Baskerville birthplace recalls the terrifying Conan Doyle tale and, like Holmes, he is tall and thin. He has sharp eyes made all the more penetrating by the use of magnifying eyeglasses[4] and, again like Holmes, during melancholy moods he partakes of narcotic herbs, probably hashish, a practice he learned from Arab scholars. His method of deduction "is founded upon the observation of trifles,"[5] while his disciple, assistant, and chronicler is named Adso (*Adson* in Abbé Vallet's book [1]), a near homophone for *Watson*. Finally, in deliberately choosing a Briton, Umberto Eco has established his investigator in the English Franciscan tradition of healthy skepticism, scientific methodology, and experiential verification of hypotheses as fostered and exemplified by Robert Grosseteste and Roger Bacon, and endowed him with a "special sensitivity in interpreting evidence" and in understanding people, largely derived from a knowledge of Occamian semiotic theories. [6]

To accomplish his task, William interrogates all pertinent witnesses who, of course, tell him what they know from their personal point of view. From their testimony he must decide what is true and what is false, although lies, half-truths, and obfuscations are useful tools, for they too reveal the psychology and motives of the speaker. Here, William's clerical training helps him get to the heart of the matter by focusing on apparently inconsequential words and phrases, as in his first interview with the abbot: "Speaking of a possible murder, you said, 'And if that were all.' What did you mean?" (34); or in his comment on the mysterious parchment's quality: " 'Strange': the very word Severinus used?" (443). At other times, the amateur detective is purposely misled, for instance, "because the murderer probably does not want attention to be concentrated on the library" (106). Yet he himself is not without guile when he reverts to deception with the cellarer, loudly announcing that Venantius' desk contains papers essential to his work, or when he insinuates that the abbot himself could be the murderer.

Clues inevitably play an important part in the conduct of William's investigation, whether they originate in the world (for example, water puddles) or are man-made (foot tracks in the snow). As signs, they serve to indicate various bits of evidence which are now to be read and interpreted. It is the power of observation—coupled with patience and persistence, on the one hand, and especially the ability to fit together into a significant picture these pieces of a jigsaw puzzle, on the other—that constitute the detective's skill and mastery. Since one must discriminate between good and bad clues, great care has to be taken to avoid pursuing red herrings—although this increases the human fallibility of the seeker and, tangentially, the suspense of the story—and such ratiocination, based on both deductions and inductions, requires intelligence (*inter* [between] and *legere* [to choose]): "Adso, . . . learn to use your head and think" (266). This application of one's gray cells to a problem is well known to readers of Hercule Poirot, but for William it represents more than a mental process that would consist of relying on reason. In fact, he admonishes his novice-charge:

> solving a mystery is not the same as deducing from first principles. Nor does it amount simply to collecting a number of particular data from which to infer a general law. It means, rather, facing one or two or three particular data apparently with nothing in common, and trying to imagine whether they could represent so many instances of a general law you don't yet know, and which perhaps has never been pronounced. (304)

By recognizing the value of signs and making cogent (but often tortuous) inferences, it is possible to arrive at the solution of the crimes so long as one does not "multiply explanations and causes unless it is strictly necessary" (91).

This paraphrase of Occam's apothegm, known as "Occam's razor," suggests how much discourse for its own sake is a vain intellectual exercise, made all the more absurd when Bernard Gui comes on the scene.[7] Historically famous for having written about the crimes of the Waldensian heretics, Gui acts in the novel as a pendant to William and his investigative methods. Unlike the cerebral Englishman, he enjoys sophistic, verbal parrying with his mainly illiterate victims, whom he badgers to such a degree that they do not know where to turn or how to respond. "This tells us that you were not only a heretic, but also a coward and a traitor," he accuses Remigio the cellarer, adding, upon the latter's oath,

> Here is another proof of your guile! . . . And so every oath will be further proof of your guilt! . . . You must do nothing. At this point, only I know what must be done. (380–81)

In further contrast to William, Bernard Gui, who alternately employs fear and torture to extract confessions and denunciations, is an implacable inquisitor overcome with a lust for power, "interested, not in discovering the guilty, but in burning the accused" (394). From his long professional experience (in November 1327 he is seventy), he is well versed in the psychology of punishment, which includes hypercritical indulgence, icy irony, merciless severity. Although William had once been an inquisitor, he had resigned his position because he did not want to burn a wretch on the basis of a misspoken word but, above all, because he had come to doubt man's inherent sinfulness and depravity. This explains how he can appreciate and forgive Adso's night of lust with the beautiful peasant girl in the same manner that he appreciates and forgives her unbecoming conduct, reasoning that, after all, the girl must have been compelled by hunger and an overriding need for "something for her and her family to eat" (253).

William's compassion for a young woman who prostitutes herself in exchange for "a pack of scraps" is, as a matter of fact, generalized to the entire female sex. Here again, William goes counter to the medieval position, which condemns women as incarnations of the devil; rather, he proves through convincing arguments that God could not have chosen "to introduce such a foul being into creation without also endowing it with some virtues" (252). This indulgence toward youthful experiences and a refreshing feminism are not the only examples of William's tolerance. He also understands Salvatore's and Remigio's heresies and sinful years of wandering as the result of misguided frustrations and well-intentioned desires for a more just world free from want and privilege. It is no wonder that William should once more readily accept the socialistic hopes of the Fraticelli and their followers, since he, too, is on the side of clerical poverty in the debate between the papal envoys and their imperial counterparts. Such a generous and humane outlook, plus an interest in and curiosity about all areas of science and philosophy, rounds out the portrait of this enlightened, "reasonable" humanist of the Gothic Middle Ages and is itself the complete opposite of Bernard Gui and especially of Brother Jorge of Burgos.[8]

Before turning to a discussion of the Spanish monk, let us examine the environment in which the crimes take place. Notwithstanding W. H. Auden's assertion that a murder in a monastery is either an impossibility or a contradiction,[9] Eco, perhaps rising to the challenge, sets the action in a fortified abbey and, in particular, inside its forbidding and foreboding Aedificium. Perched high atop a steep mountain, the monastery presents to the outside a world far removed from the worries and troubles of everyday life, a remoteness made all the more evident by the regularity of the liturgical schedule, punctuated as it is by the bell and the routine of daily tasks.

The Aedificium, designed according to a system of numerical symbols, houses the library and reading and work rooms. Since the abbot prizes books above all else ("Monasterium sine libris . . . est sicut civitas sine opibus" [36]), every monk who works there, whether commentator, copyist, illuminator, or translator, is well aware of his mission as guardian and protector of the many treasures within the confines of the abbey.

Clearly the jewel of the monastery for its rich collection of rare and magnificent manuscripts, this depository holds more books than any other Christian library. Nevertheless, despite the erudite and scholarly ambience, no text circulates freely because so many of them are of a profane, even subversive, nature. In fact, only the head librarian decides whether a brother will be allowed to consult a particular work, and only the head librarian has access to the shelves:

> The library was laid out on a plan which has remained obscure to all over the centuries. . . . Only the librarian has . . . the right to move through the labyrinth of the books, he alone knows where to find them and where to replace them. . . . (37)

In addition, the catalog's analphabetical call-numbering system is purposely complicated to discourage curious readers from finding a book's location.[10]

The architecture of the building itself further defends the inviolability of the stacks. Built as a mannerist labyrinth, "with many blind alleys," it includes many characteristics of a net as well.[11] Umberto Eco, summarizing Pierre Rosenstiehl, writes that "a labyrinth of this kind is a *myopic algorythm*; at every node of it no one can have the global vision of all its possibilities but only the local vision of the closest ones: every local description of the net is a *hypothesis*, subject to falsification about its further course."[12] Thus it behooves William (who has decided to transgress the abbot's proscriptions) to penetrate the maze so as to discover why the library is the focal point for all the deaths.

The library, which is, of course, always closed and locked at night, is protected by an additional series of ingenious devices. To enter, William and Adso must look for the mechanism that swings the altar open to a secret passage (by pressing the eyesockets of the fourth skull on the right) and descend through the old ossarium (a frightening experience at any time but all the more terrifying at night "in the play of shadows the lamp created as we walked on" [161]). There are as well blind rooms, distorting mirrors, noxious fumes, eerie sounds, invisible presences—all to deter the weak-hearted.

After their first venture has proved largely fruitless, William fabricates a compass and, as Rocco Capozzi pointed out, like Dumas' Dantès and Faria,[13] he matches his mind with those of the architects and builders, then draws a detailed floor plan (reproduced on page 321) to help them explore the library. No longer at the mercy of the "maximum of confusion achieved with the maximum of order" (217), nor of all the cunning impediments, William next realizes by sudden insight the method by which the books are distributed among the various rooms.

On his second visit, he understands the principle guiding their shelving: "the books are arranged according to the country of their origin, or the place where their authors were born, or . . . should have been born" (314). Entry to the *finis Africae*, the end of Africa, however, still eludes him, although he has been able first to bring out Venantius' code message written in invisible ink and made up of zodiacal signs and then decipher it, reading: "Secretum finis Africae manus supra idolum age primum et septimum de quatuor" (209). The Latin sentence still represents a seemingly unsolvable riddle, for the word *idolum* has several meanings and the phrase *primum et septimum de quatuor* seems nonsensical until William interprets them as referring to the first and seventh letters of *quatuor* found in the verse "carved over the mirror" (458). When *q* and *r* are depressed, the mirror swings open to a passageway that indeed leads to the forbidden center.

If the library is so cleverly defended, it is less to avoid damage through abuse than to prevent easy access to its collection. Once a symbol of the humanistic quest for knowledge and an instrument for disseminating the truth, the library now "lives to bury them" (396). By fostering secrecy, lies, and censorship, the library has betrayed in William's eyes its noble mission, becoming instead a "sink of iniquity."[14]

Such contempt for the intelligence and good sense of the monks shows both arrogance on the part of the ecclesiastical authorities—who, after all, know best what can be read and by whom—as well as their fear that readers will be overcome with doubts as to the truth and validity of Christian teachings and exegeses. Thus, while questions can lead to new interpretations at variance with those of the church fathers (for instance, about temporal power, sin, religious fervor, or Christ's poverty) and may often lead to heresies, ignorance remains an important tool, even when falsehoods mislead the susceptible. Because "the library is testimony to truth and to error" (129), and "Because learning does not consist only of knowing what we must or we can do, but also of knowing what we could do and perhaps should not do" (97), it seems obvious that the sole merit of books lies in their being read, regardless of the possibly inherent dangers found in their pages. Moreover, the very prohibition against certain works serves to awaken the desire to read them.

This, then, is the reason for all the deaths in the monastery: some monks wanted to consult and study these works and actually went to any length to fulfill their lust for knowledge, whereas others were willing to kill, the better to guard their secrets. As the old Adso reminds us in his Prologue, however, an omniscient God created the Word and is Himself the word—a concept allegorically presented in the bas-relief above the church's door where the Seated One holds a book, His companion holds out a book, and two monsters clutch a book (41). Who, then, he implies, can dare to fathom, let alone apprehend, God's purpose?

That the library, like so much else in the world, is thus "at once the celestial Jerusalem and an underground world on the border between terra incognita and Hades" (184) emphasizes again William's difficulty in reconciling his own contradictions concerning Christian doctrine in particular and in distinguishing true from false in general. However, in his confrontations with Brother Jorge of Burgos (who recalls Jorge Luis Borges), though respectful at first, he is explicit in his defense of intellectual freedom and in his ultimate, categorical rejection of the Spaniard's views and actions.

Besides his advanced age, Jorge is described chiefly in terms of his blindness—a physical, intellectual, moral, and metaphysical blindness that is contrasted with William's excellent eyesight, especially when aided by glasses. From the very first, this misanthrope stands against all lack of seriousness of heart and purpose as he speaks against laughter: " 'Verba vana aut risui apta non loqui' " (78). This peremptory statement leads to an interesting debate between Jorge and William, who, for his part, points out that witticisms render a sermon more vivid and act as sources of truth, which "can be revealed through surprising expressions, both shrewd and enigmatic" (82).

Yet the differences are not limited to a discussion of laughter and to whether or not Christ laughed, but to the more serious question of intellectual pursuit. To William's enlightened curiosity Jorge reveals a narrow-minded, even perverse form of obscurantism, which Teresa de Lauretis qualifies as "representative of the dark age's darkest dogmatism and religious zeal."[15] This is made evident when Jorge delivers to the monastic congregation and their guests a particularly intolerant sermon, in which he declares that only biblical and Christian writings hold the truth, that pagan texts are false and worthless and therefore must be suppressed, and that those monks who seek them sin against God and expose themselves to His just wrath.

The most pernicious of these works is Aristotle's volume two of the *Poetics*, which deals specifically with laughter. Long thought lost, a copy actually exists in the deepest recesses of the library. Jorge, viewing its contents as too subversive for the immature monks, has set himself up as the sole interpreter and absolute guarantor of Truth ("someone does not want the monks to decide for themselves where to go, what to do, and what to read" [126])—a position with which, incidentally, the priggish abbot also concurs.[16] That is why, to prevent the book from being read, the venerable Jorge has rigged an ingenious safeguard: the pages have been stuck together and their corners poisoned so as to kill anyone who, while consulting the manuscript, moistens his fingers to help him turn the pages.[17]

To underscore the ineluctability of divine punishment, Jorge follows the verses from Saint John's apocalyptic revelations, either when he rearranges murders done by others or commits them himself.[18] Far from considering himself a malignant madman bent on fratricide to protect the library, he asserts (to William, who has unmasked him): "I was only an instrument . . . I acted for His glory . . . I have been the hand of God" (471, 478). As expected, William does not agree with that immodest self-characterization calling him instead the Antichrist, the Devil (403, 477).

Jorge's grandiose mission as providential defender of God again reveals his pointless hubris, for an omnipotent and omniscient God can and must stand or fall on His own and thus needs no external, let alone human, defense. In fact, if, according to William, the function of philosophy is to question concepts, values, and conclusions ("sometimes it is right to doubt" [132]), to subject all books to inquiry, then intellectual questing is proper, even desirable. The reason Jorge is to be condemned with the opprobrium of his peers is that, in mistaking the appeal of the Devil, he has substituted himself for God, a God who in His infinite wisdom enjoys both unity and variety: "The hand of God creates; it does not conceal. . . . God created the monsters, too. . . . And He wants everything to be spoken of" (478).

Unlike other murderers in mystery fiction where "the crime symbolizes not only an infraction of the law but a disruption of the normal order of society," the Spaniard wants a universe immune to change and gladly kills to maintain his own warped conception of order and to salvage a world already on the verge of collapse.[19] Through his humorless fanaticism he discloses that "the most dangerous people in the world are those with an unshakable certainty that they are right. A man *that* certain of his cause . . . will justify any crimes."[20] Jorge offers an adulterated truth that is based on falsehood and delusion, whereas the Englishman, by his own example, illustrates that intellectual freedom leads to truth, and this truth in turn leads to greater spiritual freedom. Finally, despite the adversaries' mutual admiration, this Manichean struggle between Light and Darkness does not take place on the same moral or ethical plane: clearly, William is identified as the force of good, and Jorge as the force of evil.[21]

In a last, unrepenting act (such epithets as *horrible, distorted, malignant sweat, deathly white, bloodshot, ravening beast, disfigured, desperate, diabolical, disgusting* and *grotesque* appear in one paragraph), Jorge, the Minotaur at the heart of his labyrinth, eats the Aristotle manuscript, thereby poisoning himself—appropriately enough in Room Y (for *Yspania*)—and explodes for the first time not into liberating but into insane laughter. Under these circumstances, it is quite natural, maybe even right, that the library and the entire abbey—as projections of uncontrollable evil "consecrated to the pride of the word, to the illusion of wisdom" (60)—burn down in a general conflagration, although it bodes ill for humanity, which explains William's tears: "Now . . . the Antichrist is truly at hand, because no learning will hinder him any more" (491).

William has uncovered the mystery of the various deaths—by accident, as it were ("There was no plot . . . and I discovered it by mistake" [491]). But because he had looked for pieces of evidence to suit his preconceived pattern and had misunderstood their relationship, when he should have known that the surface order of the monastery hid the same chaos as in the outside world, Eco finds him "beaten in the end."[22] Through this process Adso has learned the difficulty of judging and the relativity of truth and has developed a love of books as well as undergone several initiation trials (oneiric, physical, mental) by which he has acquired a new way of being and thinking. At the end of his long life, the disciple opposes to his former master's longing for regeneration through inspired rationality and still hopeful words ("non in commotione Dominus" [493]) a more brooding existential conclusion: "Gott ist ein lauter Nichts, ihn rührt kein Nun noch Hier" (501).

Of course, nothing remains of the monastery, nor of Aristotle's study of laughter, nor of the dyadic seekers of truth, except this many times transcribed and retranscribed manuscript, with its eloquent attack on intolerant obscurantism and censorship and its shining apology of humanistic knowledge.[23] Nevertheless, on this ship of fools (to cite Adso), we are all implicated, ultimately, against the angels: "Any true detection should prove that we are the guilty party."[24] In the face of falsehood, darkness, mortality, chaos, and evil, only the "rosa pristina" remains in its original, nominal purity (502).

Notes

1. In fact, William exemplifies Raymond Chandler's lyrical characterization of the modern detective. See his "The Simple Art of Murder," in *The Art of the Mystery Story*, ed. Howard Haycraft (New York: Grosset & Dunlap, 1946), 237.

2. Umberto Eco, *The Name of the Rose*, trans. William Weaver (San Diego: Harcourt Brace Jovanovich, 1983), 21. Subsequent citations are in parentheses in the text. Edgar Allan Poe had already written that the analyst "derives pleasure from even the most trivial occupations bringing his talent into play . . . exhibiting in his solutions of each [mystery] a degree of *acumen* which appears to the ordinary apprehension praeternatural." "The Murders in the Rue Morgue," in *Poetry and Tales* (New York: The Library of America, 1984), 397.

Voltaire, *Zadig, ou La Destinée*, in *Romans et Contes* (Paris: "Bibliothèque de la Pléiade," Gallimard, 1954), 10–12.

3. "Often the hero's virtue is humanized, and his powers, rather than being supernatural, are the extreme realization of natural endowments such as astuteness . . . or even the logical faculties and the pure spirit of observation found in Sherlock Holmes." Umberto Eco, *The Role of the Reader* (Bloomington: Indiana University Press, 1979), 107.

4. In his essay-review, Verlyn Flieger calls William's glasses "device and metaphor" since they allow the wearer to observe more acutely up close and in the distance, "The Name, the Thing, the Mystery," *Georgia Review* 38 (Spring 1984): 180. It is no wonder, then, that before their parting, William offers Adso a spare set.

5. Arthur Conan Doyle, "The Boscombe Valley Mystery," in *The Complete Sherlock Holmes* (Garden City, N.Y.: Doubleday, 1953) I, 214. Furthermore, Eco's *The Sign of Three* (1983), which includes essays on Dupin's and Holmes's methods, owes its title to another Conan Doyle work, "The Sign of Four."

6. "There are two modes of acquiring knowledge," Roger Bacon declared, "namely, by reasoning and experience [although] reasoning does not suffice, but experience does," *The Opus majus*, trans. Robert B. Burke (Philadelphia: University of Pennsylvania Press, 1928) II, 583. Umberto Eco, *Postscript to "The Name of the Rose,"* trans. William Weaver (San Diego: Harcourt Brace Jovanovich, 1984), 26.

7. "Entities [of explanation] must not be multiplied beyond necessity."

8. Eco wrote to Stefano Rosso that William "in my novel is not rational but reasonable. This is why he believes in no single truth." "A Correspondence with Umberto Eco," trans. Carolyn Springer, *Boundary* 2, no. 12 (Fall 1983): 4. Corliss Lamont defines *humanism* as "a philosophy of joyous service for the greater good of all humanity in this natural world and advocating to the methods of reason, science, and democracy," *The Philosophy of Humanism*, 6th ed. (New York: Ungar, 1982), 12.

9. Auden, "The Guilty Vicarage," in *The Dyer's Hand* (New York: Random House, 1962), 150–51.

10. Eco, in a fascinating section on codes and grammars (*Semiotics and the Philosophy of Language* [Bloomington: Indiana University Press, 1984], 175–77), discusses this very concept of library shelving and gives as an easy example the expression "1.2.5.33" to "mean the thirty- third book on the fifth shelf of the second wall of the first room" (176).

11. Eco, *Postscript to "The Name of the Rose,"* 57.

12. Eco, *Semiotics and the Philosophy of Language*, 82.

13. Capozzi, "Scriptor et 'Lector in fabula' ne *Il nome della rosa* di Umberto Eco," *Quaderni d'italianistica* 3 (1982): 221. An avid reader of French serial novelists (Sue, Féval), Eco told *Le Monde* interviewers that he considers Alexandre Dumas a "pure" narrator (February 22, 1985): 16.

14. Earlier, quoting his compatriot Roger Bacon, William tells a still dubious disciple that "the aim of learning was also to prolong human life" (74).

15. Teresa de Lauretis, "Gaudy Rose: Eco and Narcissism," *SubStance* 14:2 (1985): 18.

16. Historically, as Eco reminds us, "the rules for good interpretation were provided by the gatekeepers of the orthodoxy, and the gatekeepers of the orthodoxy were the winners (in terms of political and cultural power) of the struggle to impose their own interpretation." *Semiotics and the Philosophy of Language*, 151.

17. See Dorothy L. Sayers, Introduction to *The Omnibus of Crime*, ed. Dorothy L. Sayers (Garden City, N.Y.: Garden City Publishing Co., 1929), 42, where she lists many "short cuts to the grave," among which is "licking poisoned stamps." In view of so many devices in popular novels (invisible ink, ciphers, secret passages, poisoned page corners), we should remember Eco's statement: "Two clichés make us laugh, but a hundred clichés move us. . . ." "*Casablanca:* Cult Movies and Intertextual Collage," *SubStance* 14:2 (1985): 11.

18. Thomas Narcejac explains that using enigmatic verses to announce future deaths, as in nursery rhymes, songs, or here in Revelation, "est une manière élégante

d'introduire quelque chose de fantastique dans une histoire policière d'une logique rigoureuse." *Une Machine à écrire: le roman policier* (Paris: Denoël/Gonthier, 1975), 164.

19. John G. Cawelti, *Adventure, Mystery, and Romance* (Chicago: University of Chicago Press, 1976), 83. Frank Kermode writes that "the detective is . . . concerned, not with the preservation of an old order, but with the institution of a new." "Novel and Narrative," in *The Poetics of Murder*, ed. Glenn W. Most and William W. Stowe (San Diego: Harcourt Brace Jovanovich, 1983), 187. This remark describes very well William's pre-Renaissance liberalism.

20. Robert Scholes, *Fabulation and Metafiction* (Urbana: University of Illinois Press, 1979), 204.

21. Discussing a similar archetypal opposition in Ian Fleming's novels, Eco asks, "The difference between good and evil, is it really something neat, recognizable?," "The Narrative Structure in Fleming," in *The Bond Affair*, ed. Oreste Del Buono and Umberto Eco, trans. R. A. Downie (London: Macdonald, 1966), 36. No such ambiguity exists here, however.

22. Stefano Rosso, "A Correspondence with Umberto Eco," 7.

23. Maryse Jeuland-Meynaud compares William and Adso with Anatole France's skeptical master-servant duo, Jérôme Coignard and Jacques Tournebroche. See her "Une Rose pour talisman," *Revue des études italiennes* 27 (1981): 255–56.

24. Eco, *Postscript to "The Name of the Rose,"* 81.

7 Holmes Goes to Carnival: Embarrassing the Signifier in Eco's Anti-Detective Novel

H. Aram Veeser

Critics have generally thought that detective fiction guarantees the triumph of clarity over ambiguity, and I would agree. This essay focuses on the ideological effects stemming from this essential movement toward clarity. Ideology may be understood as the imaginary forms in which people live out their relationships to the real conditions that govern their lives. Far from simply following the grooves that other, conventional detective stories have worn so deep, Eco's *The Name of the Rose* enters a dialogue with those works in order to contest the rigid patterning that characterizes the genre and to resurrect a medieval countertradition: the laughing satire that informs works by Lucian, Rabelais, and others.

Franco Moretti's *Signs Taken for Wonders* offers a convenient beginning.[1] Moretti argues that the detective constructs a chain of causality, gradually ruling out competing possibilities. The presence of this logical demonstration defines the genre. According to Moretti, such a novel performs the classical task of popular artifacts by hiding the labor that produces it and making it salable. Thus, Moretti simply extends Marx's theory of commodity fetishism to this particular cultural commodity—the consumable detective novel.

The commodity fetishism characteristic of capitalism and crime-stopping shapes Moretti's favorite example, the Holmes–Watson relationship. Watson does all the narrative work, only to have Holmes dismiss its importance, insisting that Watson can see only the inessential, irrelevant details. "You see," Holmes mutters, "but you do not observe." Yet, in the single instance when Holmes attempts to write his own version, he founders. "I am compelled to admit that, having taken my pen in hand, I do begin to realize that the matter must be presented in such a way as may interest the reader."[2] Never again does Holmes make such a confession. Watson's narrative labors soon return, in the great detective's opinion, to the category of the obtuse, obfuscatory, and laughably unimportant. "You have degraded what should have been a course of lectures into a series of tales," Holmes concludes ("The

Adventure of the Copper Beeches"). [3] Holmes's dismissive comments conceal from our gaze the forces that create the artifact and whatever value as a commodity it may have, that is, Watson's workaday writing. Moretti's analysis identifies other features in detective writing that form allegories of capitalist development. He reads the various criminals, for example, either as upstarts attempting to redistribute the social wealth too quickly or as aristocrats repairing their eroded fortunes and thereby criminally retarding the middle class and, what is the same thing for bourgeois ideology, dragging back civilization itself.

Eco's *Rose* has been sold and read as one of the conventional, fetishized products that Moretti describes. The dust jacket proclaims, for example, that the buyer of the hardcover edition will get an exciting and readable example of a recognizable genre:

> The year is 1327. Franciscans in a wealthy Italian abbey are suspected of heresy, and Brother William of Baskerville arrives to investigate. His delicate mission is suddenly overshadowed by seven bizarre deaths that take place in seven days and nights of apocalyptic terror. The body of one monk is found in a cask of pigs' blood, another is floating in a bathhouse, still another is crushed at the foot of a cliff.
>
> Brother William turns detective, and a uniquely deft one at that. His tools are the logic of Aristotle, the theology of Aquinas, the empirical insights of Roger Bacon—all sharpened to a glistening edge by his wry humor and ferocious curiosity. He collects evidence, deciphers secret symbols and coded manuscripts, and digs into the eerie labyrinth of the abbey, where "the most interesting things happen at night."

All signals announce a conventional detective novel. "William arrives to investigate" crimes that degenerate into murder. "Bizarre deaths" seize our attention. With tabloid accuracy the jacket blurb places and describes the bodies, one "crushed," another "floating," "a cask of pigs' blood" claiming a third. When William "turns detective," the reader stands assured that the medieval backlighting—the year, the abbey, the "logic" and "theology"— will not impede the main, all-too-familiar business of "collecting and deciphering the evidence." Confident that Brother William belongs to the fraternity of Holmes and Matt Helm, the reader can relax and enjoy "interesting things" without deep thoughts or experimental prose.

Unwary readers must experience some shock, then, as they pick their way through Eco's tongue-in-cheek preface about "finding" the novel at hand only to find that the mocking parodic complexities of tone redouble as they proceed to the story itself. Nevertheless, critics generally have grouped Eco's *Rose* with unself-conscious works in the suspense and detective genres. "The novel is a *mystery,* the most rationalist of all literary genres," stresses Franco Ferrucci, and the hero William, "like Sherlock Holmes," draws his method "from the philosophical school of Roger Bacon and William of Occam, the founders of cognitive empiricism, a philosophy based on the exact examination of real evidence revealed by the senses."[4]

These naive appraisals have come forth even in the face of Eco's reputation as a semiotician. The *Times Literary Supplement* adds that William epitomizes "the investigator—modern man pitting his cool intelligence against a medieval puzzle."[5] Italian reviewers join the chorus, finding William "Sherlock Holmes-like . . . a disillusioned inquisitor" who "embodies a spirit of scientific inquiry . . . modern man surrounded by religious fanatics."[6]

All these reviewers beg the central question: Can a book about another book—and not a conventionally valuable, gem-studded, Malteste Falcon-like object but, rather, a fabled literary critical text by Aristotle expounding the subversive genre of comedy—and the author of such a book really be asking us to read his work naively? Are we to ignore the parodic, stylized playing with the language of the characters and with our own conventional expectations, and simply read for plot and action? Suspense writers from Raymond Chandler on are quick to claim exemption from the popular genre that seduces readers to forget where they are and to believe that reason, logic, and unproblematic truth will win the day.[7] On the contrary, Eco's *Rose* concludes by literally burning to the ground the entire edifice of monastic logic within which the action takes place. Laughter, not logic, takes the palm, and just as the laughing tradition of Lucian and sacred parody immolate the imposing Aedificium and all its dead volumes, from those embers arise a new corpus of laughing texts, to which Eco's *Rose* belongs.

Eco has himself theorized about detective fiction, which, he says, usually bifurcates into "fundamental moves" and "incidental moves."[8] Eco's *Rose* might be taken as an exemplary case of "incidental moves" assuming greater importance than "fundamental" ones. Such a strategy was perhaps to be expected from an author steeped in semiotic theory and known for his deconstructions—literary-critical maneuvers that transmogrify the marginal into the essential and deny fixed oppositions between incidental and fundamental aspects of texts. Thus, the digressive forays into medieval thought concerning dreams, herbs, optics, and unicorns tend to reduce the fundamental crime and its discovery to little more than the scaffolding on which these richer historical materials can be lodged.

It was, of course, no accident that Eco employed the detective genre, with its stringent binarism, for his novel. But the sorting of the nonessential from the fundamental, the detective carving sensible narratives from chaotic details that a mindless scribe provides—this image has fetching appeal not just for structuralists who love formal ordering for its own sake but also for all who value their sanity. Eco invokes the genre of order, however, only to confound its familiar opposites. Thirty years earlier, Raymond Chandler distinguished similarly between two stories:

> One is known only to the criminal and to the author himself. . . . It is usually simple, consisting chiefly of the commission of a murder and the criminal's attempts to cover up after it. The other story is the story which is told. It is capable of great elaboration and should, when finished, be complete in itself.[9]

Chandler, like Eco, understands that in the postmodern reader's experience the "other story" matters more than the "fundamental" plot. "The things readers remembered," he remarks lyrically, "were not that a man got killed, but that in the moment of death he was trying to pick a paper clip off the polished surface of a desk, and it kept slipping away from him."[10]

The pinning of truth to the mat, which distinguishes the suspense-detective novel from other genres, has attracted pointed critical commentary. Structuralists find detection an exaggerated version of the closure that all fiction imposes on real events and that makes literature so attractive to minds boggled by life's formless dispersion. Freudians liken the moment of discovery to sexual climax, and even anti-Freudian Roland Barthes defines such "textes de desir" as performing a "single-minded discharge" and suspense as the fear that the promise of discharge will not be fulfilled. Pederson-King considers the detective's finest hour (when the drawing room door is closed and the crime is reconstructed before the assembled suspects) an allegory of return to "a more satisfying, less painful primal scene."[11] Although Geoffrey Hartman is better known for his defense of the undecidability of meanings in literature, he values detection because it reduces the undecidable. Detective novels offer, he says, to recover the repressed and to impale meaning once and for all: "To solve a crime in detective stories means to give it an exact location, to pinpoint not merely the murderer and his motives but also the very place, the room, the ingenious or brutal circumstances."[12] More determinedly political critics even contend that the detective's fight to repress chaos corresponds allegorically to other repressive mechanisms that regulate society at large.

Detective fiction thus belongs to the "discourse of the law," which serves to confine the new "disciplinary society" excavated by Michel Foucault.[13] Archly reactionary, "the thriller hero always *refounds* the state," emphasizes Jerry Palmer.[14] Moretti himself argues that the criminal always "has created a situation of semantic ambiguity"—clues always point to several suspects at once; and therefore the "detective must dispel entropy, cultural equi- probability . . . [and] reinstate the univocal ties between signifiers and signifieds."[15]

These radical critiques merely invert, in one sense, Marjorie Nicholson's affirmative comments made years earlier. She valued the conservatism and scholarship that detective fiction seemed to celebrate and, like her colleague at Columbia University, "Amanda Cross" (actually English professor Carolyn Heilbrun), felt that both scholars and sleuths have faith "in a universe governed by order [and] founded on eternal and immutable laws."[16] Mystery novels appeal to intellectuals, Nicholson said, offering an escape not from life but from literature. Crime stories give refuge from troublesome textuality and Joycean experiments. Critics of every stripe seem able to agree, then, that detective fiction polices not just the criminal underworld but also literary society, making our world safe for bourgeois democracy and philistine language and conducting a drive toward fixed identities for people, single meanings for words, and perfect closure for readers.

Yet incidental moves may assume such length and centrality that they overwhelm in importance the "fundamental moves." This is precisely what happens in Eco's *Rose*. A Greek friend and colleague tells me, for example, that the novel owes its popularity in his country to the long passages criticizing the Roman Catholic church, detailing its corrupt practices and tyrannical Inquisition. (These mildly scandalous canards also assured Eco a wide readership at the seminary and college attached to the Vatican, reports another colleague.) Although church politics have functional importance and frame what Chandler and Eco call the second, or "incidental," plot, Eco's piercing critique of Catholicism winds through the novel without ever really touching the "fundamental" plot of multiple murder, theft, and disclosure. Eco has acknowledged that even mainstream detective thrillers place value on "incidentals." Writing of the "aimless glance" that Ian Fleming casts on card tables, cigarette packets, fancy toiletries, and other trivial details, Eco attributes to it much of James Bond's popularity. Such passages afford knowledge of a high society that readers will never see, as well as provide suspense. Eco indulges his own "relish for the inessential" continually and promiscuously, stringing together page upon page of loving detail about medieval herb medicine, kitchen utensils, truffle hunting, gemology, and, most of all, architecture. Such passages offer more than a peep at inaccessible glamor; they provide a vision of forgotten history.

Perhaps the longest chapter of anticlerical satire describes the *Coena Cypriani,* an authentic tract concerning the marriage of King Johel at Cana of

Galilee, to which all kinds of persons from the Old and New testaments come. The entire biblical pantheon and roster of Catholic saints appear as gluttons, drunkards, and sexual perverts. The *Cyprian Feasts* attracted Mikhail Bakhtin's interest, and in his genealogy of laughing texts he writes that in such "parodia sacra," "it was permitted to turn the direct sacred word into a parodic-travestying mask. . . . Cyprian Feasts could enjoy enormous popularity even in strict church circles."[17] Eco's chapters involving the *Coena* prove far from merely incidental; they install the central theme of anarchic laughter and make Eco's *Rose* an antirationalist and therefore, in Moretti's sense, an antidetective text.

The *Coena* interlopes first as the narrator Adso recounts his dream (one modeled on this blasphemous banquet) then again as Jorge, the criminal, and William, the detective, discuss the custom of reciting the *Coena* at ecclesiastical tables. Even a glance at their debate shows that Eco's *Rose* belongs to Bakhtin's tradition of laughter, and not to Doyle's genre of logic. William's remarks virtually paraphrase Bakhtin's when the latter contends that in sacred parody,

> two "languages" (both intra-lingual) come together and to a certain extent are crossed with each other: the language being parodied (for example, the language of the heroic poem) and the language that parodies (low prosaic language, familiar conversational language, the language of the realistic genres, "normal" language, "healthy" literary language as the author of the parody conceived it). This second parodying language, against whose background the parody is constructed and perceived, does not—if it is a strict parody—enter as such into the parody itself, but is invisibly present in it.[18]

William defends the *Cyprian Feasts* as a pedagogical device, but Bakhtin's comments might also be considered as defining the relationship between Eco's *Rose* and the official language of detection. Like the *festa stultorum* amid solemn medieval pieties, Eco's *Name of the Rose* plops down among works that adhere to rigid strictures of the sort laid out in formulas such as S. S. Van Dine's "Twenty Rules for Writing Detective Stories."[19] The literary world has not seen laws so inflexible, I would argue, since the Puritans closed the theaters and Boileu codified neoclassical writing. Eco's novel joins Pynchon's *The Crying of Lot 49* and Robbe-Grillet's *The Erasers* in contesting this restrictive tendency and reasserting the tradition of laughter.

The pleasures of performing, of the circus and the sideshow, motivate William of Baskerville, whereas these pleasures leave the traditional detective unmoved. True, William greets the first murder in the fashion of Holmes, saying "I perceive you have been in Afganistan" to the gaping Watson. Thus William, on arriving at the abbey, induces universal "amazement," it is said, by deducing the location, size, and name of the abbot's horse for which all the monks are searching. Yet, as William privately admits to Adso, he owes his spectacular "deduction" to guesswork as much as to logic. "I didn't know which hypothesis was right," William confesses. "I won, but I might also have lost. . . . but they"—his spectators, the monks in the search party— "didn't know that a few seconds before winning I wasn't sure I wouldn't lose."[20] This markedly un-Holmesian admission points to a major difference between the two detectives. Whereas Holmes delights privately in the calculus of detection, saying "it is upon the logic rather than upon the crime that you should dwell," William merely uses logic—and luck—to dazzle others.[21] He wishes chiefly to create a sensation and, gloats William, he succeeds: "The others believed me wise because I won" the deductive gamble (305).

William has no illusions that reasoning can be pure, apolitical, or value-free, and this awareness sets him apart from the Holmes family of detectives. Instead of analyzing purely empirical evidence, William deduces his conclusions from texts, not nature. Identifying the horse's name, Brunellus, William deploys his knowledge of literary conventions: "even the great Buridan, who is about to become rector in Paris, when he wants to use a horse in one of his logical examples, always calls it Brunellus" (24). William later abandons all pretense of logic: "the first rule in deciphering a message is to guess what it means," he tells Adso (166). Later still, he expressly rejects logical method by saying to Adso that he has too much faith in syllogisms. Our narrator finally gets the message, but it disturbs him: "At that moment, I confess, I despaired of my master and caught myself thinking, 'Good thing the inquisitor has come.' I was on the side of that thirst for truth that inspired Bernard Gui" (306). Though in other ways a sensitive observer, Adso, like other adolescents, craves certainty and admires the dictatorial Bernard. As William explains, the papal inquisitor Adso admires "is interested, not in discovering the guilty, but in burning the accused," (394). A literalist of the law who violates the spirit by observing the letter, Bernard represents a pragmatist version of Holmes. His thorough skepticism allows that whatever people say is true, even under the compulsion of fire and tongs, is true indeed. The inquisitor, however, represents as well a principle that guides all the novel's villains: adherence to printed texts so inflexible that it proves Saint Paul's maxim. "The letter killeth," indeed.

Therefore it is up to William and the spirit of laughter to counter Bernard's and others' deadly allegiance to the letter, the official language, and the discourse of the law. The hero considers books as texts, as infinitely interconnected to other texts, as spurs to the speculative imagination—but never, like the villains, as deadly, clear-cut imperatives. Adso, a simpler soul in the tradition of most comic narrators, finds William's position alarming and at times scandalous. "Therefore you don't have a single answer to your questions?" asks the youthful scribe. "Adso, if I did I would teach theology in Paris," replies his mentor (306). William's mocking rejoinder brings to mind Rabelais' laughter, so often discharged against the Parisian schoolmen. When the grim villain of the piece, Jorge of Burgos, argues against his fellow monks that Christ never laughed, William denies Jorge's premise.

> "I wonder," William said, "why you are so opposed to the idea that Jesus may have laughed. I believe laughter is a good medicine, like baths, to treat humors and the other afflictions of the body . . . Laughter is proper to man, it is a sign of his rationality." (130–31)

Thus, for William—unlike Holmes, Jorge, and Bernard the inquisitor—laughter, and not reason, distinguishes man among the lower creatures. For Bernard, Jorge, and conventional detectives, all stern puritans of the imagination, laughter, along with the digressive pleasures of the text, presents unbearable threats to order.

Just as Eco reverses the importance of incidentals in relation to fundamentals, he revises the ordering, normative function of the detective: It is the villain who acts out the joyless work ethic. The villain's efforts to conceal Aristotle's secretly recovered treatise on laughter by smearing the book with poison bring on the deaths that cause William to turn detective. His diatribes against laughter fill out the antipapal dimension that entertained his Greek and ecclesiastical colleagues. While this unofficial debate over the issue, "Did Jesus laugh?" serves to cast in relief the official debate on the question, "Was Christ poor?", the unofficial question acquires as the novel proceeds greater intrinsic interest and actual importance. The official debate so farcically played out between the papal and imperial legations that clash in the abbey ostensibly touches events of world-historical significance. The Fransiscans and the far more radical sects of Minorites and Spirituals allied with them proclaim as doctrine the poverty of Christ, a tenet the well-heeled Benedictines and Dominicans believe veils an openly partisan attack on the Pope and his loyal retainers. Arranged as a formal disputation, the debate, however, crumbles into name-calling, face-slapping, hair-pulling brawls; and as serious matters turn laughable, Eco's favorite pattern reemerges. The incidental concern with laughter absorbs the fundamental concern with poverty, just as the normative, regulating role accorded to purportedly the wisest men is revealed as belonging to abject fools. Jorge, the villain, perceives the link that may join the two issues, marginal laughter and fundamental politics, but he works to keep the issues separate and their hierarchy undisturbed. For him, laughter belongs in the doghouse.

The criminal Jorge deplores the *Cyprian Feasts*, for example, and uses that text to define his hatred of laughter. His comments recall those of an actual scholar, F. J. E. Raby, whose sententious remarks appear in Holquist's edition of Bakhtin. Raby contends that the *Coena Cypriani*, "while puerile in itself, . . . might serve the purpose of instruction, if it did not rather move those who heard it recited to unseemly laughter."[22] Similarly, replying to William's argument that laughter is a sign of man's rationality, Jorge counters that "speech is also a sign of human rationality, and with speech a man can blaspheme against God" (131). Jorge goes even further than Professor Raby in his mistrust of the *Coena* among schoolboys:

> "Ah, yes," the old man said mockingly, but without smiling, "any image is good for inspiring virtue, provided the masterpiece of creation, turned with his head down, becomes the subject of laughter." (79)

Eco clearly takes pains to make Jorge diametrically oppose William, particularly about the salutary virtues of laughter.

This criminal alone should persuade us that Eco's *Rose* scarcely endorses the rationalism enshrined by ordinary detective fiction. As for Moretti's politicized thesis that villains in such fiction make language ambiguous by having it point all over the place, Jorge does just the reverse. "Our Lord did not have to employ such foolish things to point out the straight and narrow path to us," he fulminates. "But vulgarities, nonsense, and jests we condemn to perpetual imprisonment, in every place, and we do not allow the disciple to open his mouth for speech of this sort" (95). Usually detectives maintain that language and clues can have only one true meaning—witness Holmes's annoyance that Watson's literary embellishments have "degraded lectures into tales" or Chandler's comment on "the authentic power of a kind of writing"—hard-boiled detective stories—"that, even at its most mannered and artificial, made most of the fiction of the time taste like a cup of lukewarm consomme at a spinsterish tearoom."[23] Here, in Eco's book, it is the criminal and never the detective who insists that words have univocal meanings and narrow purposes easily discerned.

Despite his best intentions, Jorge creates ambiguities. This doubling of meanings occurs in his smallest gestures—as when he "emitted a grunt that could express either satisfaction or forgiveness" (134)—and clings to his most impressive feature, his blindness, an affliction that seems to place him in the noble regiment of blind seers, including Homer, Tiresius, and Milton, but which, in fact, has merely expressive relation to his more serious lack of inner vision. Blindness serves to sharpen not his imagination but only his hearing, an inferior sense on any medieval or Platonic scale and one that equips him for nocturnal crimes. Jorge's "Revelation" sermon, heralding the earthly apocalypse, prefigures the much smaller fire that consumes the abbey, a reductio ad absurdum that reduces Jorge's collosal prophecy to parody, his prophetic insight to demented paranoia. Eco's criminal, like his detective, serves to make *The Name of the Rose* an antidetective text. Jorge, and not the detective, dogs clear signs, trying (in Moretti's phrase) to "disambiguate language." And in the end he fails.

Eco has published an article bearing the title "Towards a New Middle Ages," which asserts something unexpected: the Middle Ages and late capitalism have fostered the same cultural effects.[24] The article helps to explain the setting Eco chose for the *Rose*. He was not, as he lightly suggests elsewhere, merely exploiting his scholarly beginnings as a medievalist. Whereas Eco's remark offers no help in understanding why he made his medieval narrative a detective novel, the article explains how the author came to enter the ongoing dialogue between mystery and other genres.[25] Eco's piece also suggests how Eco plans to enter the contestatory debate among writers and readers of the detective genre itself.

Eco's chief point is that rational debate over minor parochial issues, an apparently sterile exercise popular in both medieval and postmodern intellectual life, actually engages the deepest concerns available for discussion. Thus the *quaestio disputata,* or medieval forensic occasion (Eco's *Rose* provides a fine example with its debate about the poverty of Christ), "gave the outsider the impression of a monotonous and Byzantine game, while in it not only the great problems of man's fate were being debated, but also questions concerning property, the distribution of wealth, relations with the ruler, and the nature of terrestrial bodies in motion."[26] This recalls the claims Lukacs advances for written essays. What in that form appears secondary, superficial, latecoming, and parasitic actually probes the richest veins. Eco makes the same claim for the disregarded, derivative, drily academic debates over semiotic points that he and others have conducted in recent decades. "Nothing is closer to the medieval intellectual game," he argues, "than structuralist logic."[27] Formalism in all its expressions—logic, physics, contemporary mathematics, no less than Northrop Frye- or Russian formalist-style literary structuralism—embodies a panicky effort to impose even an arbitrary structure of thought on a "world whose official image has been lost or rejected."[28] In a society, whether medieval or postmodern, that class and intellectual rivalries have robbed of stable moorings, the monotonous games played by academicians of both periods accomplish far more than the meaningless and often absurd intellectual acrobatics they appear to indulge in. Eco takes the Marxist view that classes fight out their real conflicts in delusive forms, such as religious issues. During the medieval and postmodern eras, these "proposals for conflict" (the poverty of Christ, for example) remain in the hands of intellectuals, not of marching armies. Eco's discussion therefore takes a traditional left turn, finding that eventually all such proposals address the "reality of economic domination."

Eco's article helpfully illuminates the several topics I have considered and begins to pull them together. The play of "incidental" against "fundamental moves," for example, takes on expressly political implications. The debated questions of Christ's poverty and laughter gain an acute political edge as well. The carnivalesque in popular culture and fiction redefines itself as political intention and effect. The foregrounding of the narrator's ongoing work in the *Rose* also takes on a reddish tinge, as an act of defetishizing the consumable object and revealing the labor involved in its production.

In explaining how he made the intuitive leap necessary to deduce the sort of text Jorge has tried to conceal, William explicitly joins the social and textual bodies together. "I was struck," he says, "by the fact that here, too, there are references to the simple folk and to peasants as bearers of a truth different from that of the wise" (285). Laughter belongs to a political sector—simple folk and peasants—as their intellectual property or, perhaps better, as this group's particular "proposal for conflict" against the domineering, monologic, and, in this case, unsmiling official culture. The plot bears out these revolutionary notions. The riveting subplot involving Severinus, Salvatore, and their subversive political ties comes to its climax when Severinus breaks down and confesses his past. The sources of his fatal political apostasy, however, turn out to be anything but serious. "I believed in Dolcino's teaching," he admits, but he's not quite sure why.

> For Salvatore it was comprehensible: his parents were serfs, he came from a childhood of hardship and illness. . . . Dolcino represented rebellion, the destruction of the lords. For me it was different: I came from a city family. I wasn't running away from hunger. It was—I don't know how to say it—a feast of fools, a magnificent carnival. (271–72)

Elsewhere he confirms the carnivalesque spirit that motivated his rebellion:

> But I never really understood our learned disputes about the poverty of Christ
> and ownership and rights. . . . I told you, it was a great carnival, and in
> carnival time everything is done backward. (273)

The form of Severinus's utterance underlines its sense: he cannot find the
rational vehicle, the words, to express the emotion he felt ("I don't know how
to say it") and finds others' attempts to do so plainly ineffective ("I never
really understood our learned disputes"). Although the voice of Severinus
and, by extension, all his revolutionary cohorts is therefore so marginal as to
be actually inaudible, absent from monologic official histories, Eco gives
these excluded figures voice. Their groping utterance finally has more
compelling interest than the official pomposities against which these subversive speakers play.

In *The Name of the Rose,* emphasis always falls on the marginal, the liminal,
the nonessential things and people. The bizarre medievalia concerning gems,
pharmacology, martyrs, optics, and the occult migrate to the category of
"fundamental moves," as when William must teach the glazier optics in order
to replace his stolen spectacles and thereby read the essential coded clue.
Similarly, plenty of Derridean "undecidables" prove to have pivotal, not
marginal, standing. "The line between poison and medicine is very fine; the
Greeks used the word 'pharmacon' for both" (108). The Derridean word
invoked by the abby herbalist provides just one instance among many in
which literal meaning branches in different directions. The former rebel
Salvatore "is apparently a monk," for example, "though his torn and dirty
habit made him look like a vagabond. . . . Whether the gaze was innocent or
malign I could not tell" (45-46). Moreover, "his speech was somehow like his
face, put together with pieces from other people's faces, or like some precious
reliquaries I have seen" (47). The kitchen-helper's face thus molds a living
carnival masque. His appetite has a carnivalesque aspect, for he gorges
himself as though he has never eaten before and introduces Adso to such
holiday fare as fried cheese with sugar. Most of all, however, he perfectly
embodies the multivoicedness that Bakhtin finds the hallmark of the novel as
literary form. Salvatore serves as a fleshly macaronic, a congeries of different
idioms:

> Cave basilischium! The rex of serpenti, tant pleno of poison that it all shines
> dehors! Che dicam, il veleno, even the stink comes dehors and kills you!
> Poisons you . . . And it has black spots on his back, and a head like a coq,
> and half goes erect over the terra, and half on the terra like the other serpents.
> And it kills the bellula . . .

The bellula?
Oc! Parvissimum animal, just a bit plus longue than the rat. . . . (308)

As Bakhtin observes of other macaronic parodies, the vernacular portion "sharply ridicules the sacred Latin word" and "is a crude earthly rejoinder to the other-worldy pomposity."[30] Within this single figure, Salvatore, Eco propels incompatible class voices into open-ended, contestatory play.

Language forms the most essential of the novel's marginalities. And Adso, as our narrator, necessarily confronts the duplicity and carnival-quality of all speech and writing. Just as the foregrounding of Adso's narrative work tarnishes the mystique of printed books, the play of endlessly branching language never obscures the labor that conceives, prints, and conserves the material book-as-object. In *The Name of the Rose,* Eco fulfills the left-accented concerns of his article cited above by insisting that language takes on material form and has political consequences. Very much concerned with the constructing, binding, copying, illustrating, storing, and retrieving of books, the *Rose* opens with Eco's prefatory reverie about the physical pleasure he felt in handling "those large notebooks from the Papeterie Joseph Gibert in which it is so pleasant to write if you use a felt-tip pen" (1). The book's central action, taking place in a medieval scriptorium, provides occasion to discuss types of paper and parchment, writing implements and accessories, illuminating inks and illicit monkish marginalia, the rule of silence, fingers cramped with overlong labor—in short, all the aspects of physically inscribing the text. The housing and placement of books in the library is the subject of an equally exhaustive account. These and other passages, in their naturalistic density, counterweight the butterflylike playfulness and skittish ambiguity attributed to language as it is spoken.

Although he longs for certainties, Adso, as narrator, has to come to grips with a language that seems always to be slipping anchor. Even his words evade his intentions:

> But if love of the flame and of the abyss are the metaphor for the love of God, can they be the metaphor for love of death and love of sin? Yes, as the lion and the serpent stand both for Christ and the Devil. The fact is that correct interpretation can be established only on the authority of the fathers, and in the case that torments me, I have no *auctoritas* to which my obedient mind can refer, and I burn in doubt (and again the image of fire appears to define the void of the truth and the fullness of the error that annihilate me!). (248)

Adso's soliloquy tends to consume itself, as Stanley Fish might say, and the proliferating meanings of his words drive them and him toward the abyss, or rather the fire, as is right in a work which mass conflagration brings to an end.

To conclude, the "incidental" overwhelms the "fundamental" and produces a carnivalesque text, just as the normative, policing role falls to the villain, not the detective. *The Name of the Rose* exchanges the joys of closure and finally fixed guilt for the pleasures of open form and endless play. Rather than offer his upscale readers an escape from literature and politics, Eco engaged his chosen genre with another, older escape literature, the laughing antitexts of Lucian and Rabelais. Far from a severe logician hostile to "tales," as is Holmes, Eco's detective William of Baskerville frankly encourages his "Watson," Adso, to record this tale in all its naturalistic profusion. "In any case, Adso, write it all down: let at least some trace remain of what is happening today" (346). By novelizing detective fiction, the *Rose* not only incorporates the "incidental" language spoken so oddly by marginal types— the cellarer and his heteroglossic side man, whose name *Salvatore* means both savior and healthy, thus joining spirit and body. The novel actually features these officially excluded persons and the subversive carnival they themselves lack words to describe. As "incidental" languages, genres, and classes overtake the monologic officialdom—the "Latin Middle Ages"—detective work acquires a different setting. The solution to all "fundamental" mysteries seems not to reside in the detective's cerebral parts but in the victims', criminals', and onlookers' lower bodily functions. Restoring the medieval meaning of *fundament*—that is, "excrement"—the "fundamental moves" of this novel conclude only when the villain *eats* the mysterious text he has so zealously guarded. That book, Aristotle's treatise on laughter, another text that attempts to render the margins of discourse, therefore achieves its purpose. Somber officialdom literally dies of laughter. As the library burns, Eco's innumerable, now somewhat less somber readers can only smile and, like the Creator Himself, say that it was good.

Notes

1. Moretti, *Signs Taken for Wonders* (London: Verso and New Left Books, 1983).

2. "The Adventure of the Blanched Soldier," in Moretti, *Signs*, 258n.

3. Arthur Conan Doyle, "The Adventure of the Copper Breeches," in *The Sherlock Holmes Illustrated Omnibus* (New York: Shocken Books, 1976), 156.

4. Franco Ferrucci, "Murder in the Monastery," *New York Times Book Review* (5 June 1983): 1, 20–21.

5. Masolino D'Amico, "Medieval Mirth," *Times Literary Supplement* 4058 (9 January 1981): 29.

6. Michael Dirda, "The Letter Killeth and the Spirit Giveth Life," *Book World—The Washington Post* (19 June 1983): 5, 14. See also, Gian-Paolo Biasin, "Il nome della rosa," *World Literature Today* 55 (Summer 1981): 449–50.

7. Chandler, *The Notebooks of Raymond Chandler,* ed. Frank McShane (London: Weidenfeld and Nicholson, 1976), 42.

8. Umberto Eco, "The Narrative Structure in Ian Fleming," *The Bond Affair,* ed. O. del Buono and U. Eco (London: Macdonald, 1966), 53–56, quoted in Dennis Porter, *The Pursuit of Crime* (New Haven: Yale University Press, 1981), 28.

9. Chandler, *Notebooks,* 42.

10. Chandler, *Notebooks,* 51.

11. Geraldine Pederson-Krag, "Detective Stories and the Primal Scene," *Psychoanalytical Quarterly* 18 (1949): 212; quoted in Porter, *Pursuit of Crime,* 239.

12. Hartman, "Literature High and Low: The Case of the Mystery Story," *The Fate of Reading* (London and Chicago: University of Chicago Press, 1975), 204.

13. According to Porter, *Pursuit of Crime,* 120.

14. Palmer, *Thrillers: Genesis and Structure of a Popular Genre* (London: E. Arnold, 1978), 203.

15. Moretti, *Signs,* 146.

16. Nicholson, "The Professor and the Detective," in *The Art of the Mystery Story,* ed. Howard Haycraft (New York: Simon & Schuster, 1946), 110-27.

17. Bakhtin, *The Dialogic Imagination,* trans. Michael Holquist (Austin: University of Texas Press, 1981), 73.

18. Bakhtin, *Dialogic,* 75.

19. Van Dine, "Twenty Rules for Writing Detective Stories," in *The Art of the Mystery Story,* (New York: Simon & Schuster, 1946), 189-93.

20. Umberto Eco, *The Name of the Rose,* trans. William Weaver (San Diego: Harcourt Brace Jovanovich, 1983), 305. Subsequent citations appear in parentheses in the text.

21. Doyle, *Sherlock Holmes,* 156.

22. Raby, *A History of Secular Latin Poetry in the Middle Ages,* 2 vols. (Oxford: Oxford University Press, 1934), I, 220; in Bakhtin, *Dialogic,* 70n.

23. Chandler, *Trouble Is My Business* (1934; reprint New York: Ballantine, 1973), vii.

24. Eco, "Towards a New Middle Ages," in Marshall Blonsky, ed., *On Signs* (Baltimore: Johns Hopkins University Press, 1985), 448-504.

25. Gian-Paolo Biasin observes that the *Rose* may be read as "a gothic novel, a thriller, a novel of ideas, even [as] an allegory." Review of *Il nome della rosa,* 450.

26. Blonsky, *On Signs,* 500.

27. Blonsky, *On Signs,* 500.

28. Blonsky, *On Signs,* 500.

29. Blonsky, *On Signs,* 500.

30. Bakhtin, *Dialogic,* 78.

SEMIOTICS

8   Sign and De-Sign:
Medieval and Modern Semiotics
in Umberto Eco's *The Name of the Rose*

Helen T. Bennett

"In the beginning was the Word and the Word was with God, and the Word was God." This is the opening of both the Gospel According to John and the manuscript of the medieval monk Adso in Umberto Eco's novel *The Name of the Rose*. The "beginning" referred to may constitute the last time language and meaning were unequivocally united. Since antiquity, Western thinkers have consistently been concerned with the relationship between signs and words, on one hand, and the external reality they represent, on the other. One striking parallel in attitudes toward sign and meaning involves medieval nominalism, as represented by the fourteenth-century philosopher William of Ockham, and twentieth-century semiotics, a field in which Umberto Eco is a major figure. The intellectual parallel enhances the suitability of Eco's medieval setting in *The Name of the Rose*. Eco exploits the similarities in semiotic concerns and differences in degree of questioning between the medieval and modern periods in creating the novel's characters, plot, and overall meaning.

William of Ockham sought to distinguish questions of ontology from questions of terminology. Modern semiotics focuses on the processes of sign production and perception. To formulate their theories, both Ockham and Eco explore, one, how humans perceive and, two, how language affects and records (accurately or inaccurately) the process of perception.

William of Ockham offered a radical change from his predecessors in defining what is knowable and how it comes to be known. Before Ockham, reality was thought to consist of universal natures or essences, which were the expression in the world of God's ideas. These essences came to be known through direct cognition by the intellect. The intellect could not have direct cognition of individuals. The senses perceived individuals; the intellect perceived universals, that is, reality.[1] Ockham argued that, on the contrary, only individuals are real and that universals have no independent existence, that they are only concepts created to grasp the similarity among individuals.[2] He also contended that real knowledge comes only through direct cognition of individuals, and direct cognition does not involve inference. Ockham called this knowledge based on direct cognition "intuitive knowledge" and said it has to precede all other knowledge.[3] Therefore, all valid, rational conclusions about the world must be based on direct cognition of individuals in the world. Everything except the individual being is, in some sense, a construct or a sign. The word is a conventional or artificial sign imposed on the concept, which is the natural sign in the soul.[4]

Modern semioticians believe that there is no perception (knowledge) without inference. Charles Sanders Peirce, the father of modern semiotics, formulated the concept of the *interpretant,* the idea created in the mind through contact with an object in the world. This interpretant, which allows the interpreter to understand what is viewed, seems equivalent to Ockham's "concept" or "natural sign." For Peirce, the interpretant exists in all cognition.[5] John Deely distinguishes mere sensation (a lower order of awareness) from perception by the production of a construct in the mind that permits understanding to take place. These constructs involve inference.[6] Eco says that a semiotics should analyze the "complex cognitive process" behind what looks like "intuition"; he subscribes to Piaget's belief that perception itself is the interpretation of disconnected sensory data and involves creating a cognitive hypothesis based on previous experience.[7] As an example, Eco equates the observation "This is a cat" in the presence of a real cat with the same observation in the presence of an iconic representation of a cat.

Although the contemporary semiotician sees inferential processes as even more pervasive in cognition than did Ockham, both confirm the complex cultural and conventional relationship between a sign and what it signifies. To Ockham, a sign, something which through its presence makes something else known, cannot give direct or actual knowledge of something else. It can only call up knowledge already in the mind through past experience: "A sign is only representative of what is known habitually."[8] Ockham's example is that a person seeing a statue of Hercules will see it only as signifying Hercules if the person already knows who Hercules is.[9] Eco sees the sign as functioning under culturally precoded conditions. He says that signs are not things but correlations, between expression and content, so that we should actually speak of *sign-functions* instead of signs. A sign-function occurs when a certain expression is correlated to a given content, and these correlations are culturally created. Eco goes so far as to call the content of an expression not an object but a cultural unit. One of his examples is "dog." The referent is not a particular dog perceivable by the senses but all existing dogs.[10] We can understand a sign only if we know the proper code of correlations between expression and content.

The artificial and conventional nature of sign-meaning correlations is most intrinsic to the semiotic system called language. Thus, while both Eco and Ockham devote the bulk of their theories to classifying terms according to modes of signification, how terms acquire and communicate meaning and how they function in propositions, both share common concerns about the instability or unreliabilty of language. Ockham makes clear that knowing the meaning of a term does not guarantee that the knowledge is true.[11] One function of what Ockham calls the "connotative term" is to signify something unreal, for example, "chymera."[12] Similarly, Eco speaks of a sign-function operating in every lie to signify something not in the external world, and of a given code enabling us to understand propositions that are false, as well as those that are true.[13] Ockham and Eco both deal with univocal and equivocal terms. For Ockham, concepts as natural signs in the soul are univocal; but words, which are artificial signs, can be univocal or equivocal, depending on whether they stand for one or more mental concepts.[14] With numerous qualifications, Ockham posits the possibility of a univocal term, whereas Eco virtually eliminates the univocal term as he indicates in his very definition of a sign-function that the correlation between expression and content is transitory and provisional, that a term can exist in different and changing semantic fields.[15] Therefore, Eco's distrust of language exceeds Ockham's.

To formulate their theories of words and signification, both Ockham and Eco take on the same tradition of Western thought: Aristotle's *Categories* and the interpretation of Aristotle by the third-century Phoenician, Porphyry.[16] But again, Eco questions the tradition more fundamentally than does Ockham. Porphyry adopted Aristotle's categories of kinds to set up a hierarchical structure for defining terms, using a limited number of general terms from which to build all definitions. For Porphyry, this most general level represents the nature, or essence, present in all individuals. For example, "man" represents the humanity in all individuals. Ockham objects to the independent existence given nature or essence, arguing that even the most general terms denote real individuals. For Ockham, in "Socrates is a man," "man" stands for the individual "Socrates," as it could stand for many individuals.[17] Ockham, however, believes in the principle of a Porphyrian tree. He believes that one can work back to a level of generalization where categories involve a minimum of presuppositions and can classify all categorematic terms (terms, such as nouns, that stand for something) without any overlapping. Eco does not believe this. In *A Theory of Semiotics,* he shows that, if a term cannot be interpreted, its meaning cannot be understood; once it is interpreted, it becomes explainable only by another sign. Therefore, categories will overlap, and we have a process of infinite recursivity, unlimited semiosis, in the form of a labyrinth rather than a tree.[18]

In all areas of the preceding comparison, we see that William of Ockham did not take his questioning quite as far as the twentieth-century semiotician, but he certainly demonstrated enough philosophical similarities to make him a congenial prototype for Eco's fictional hero, William of Baskerville, in *The Name of the Rose*. William of Baskerville is a medieval reader of signs caught in a modern semiotic dilemma, and this dilemma involves his roles as both theologian and detective.

Theologically, Ockham followed his predecessor, Duns Scotus, in attributing to God two kinds of power—ordained, which is his law for the world, and absolute, whereby his omnipotence is limited only by logical self-contradiction. Because of God's absolute power, and because all but God himself is contingent upon God's will and therefore subject to change at any moment, no knowledge beyond immediate, individual experience can be certain. Ockham used the concept of absolute power to put theology out of reach of reason.[19] In the novel, William of Baskerville repeatedly refuses to define theological truth and right.[20] Since, according to Ockham, theological questions do not lend themselves to proof but must be left to faith, William of Baskerville has resigned his post as inquisitor, being unable to conclude rationally that the devil acted in certain crimes on which he had to pass judgment (29–31).

Although a theologian is dealing with what William of Ockham would deem rationally unknowable, detective work seems to fall within the realm of Ockham's knowable. Referring to the traditional view of creation as a great book, William of Baskerville distinguishes between the obscurity with which it speaks of "ultimate" (spiritual) things and the clarity of its message in earthly matters (23–24). Detective work employs rational inference based on direct earthly experience. Peirce calls the inferential process *abduction* and defines it as the logical process of forming an explanatory hypothesis based on facts or on a single fact that is puzzling.[21] The observer tries to explain the fact so that it is no longer puzzling. Peirce distinguishes between the general, unconscious method by which everyone acquires the truth and the self-conscious, theoretically developed method of discovering truth used by scientists and detectives.[22] Detectives must pay close attention to individual details because they do not know which ones will ultimately be important signs. Thus are they constantly testing semiotic values for various expressions and objects and forming hypotheses to account for the facts as found.

The collection of essays in *The Sign of Three: Dupin, Holmes, Peirce* is based on just this identity between Peircean abduction and the methods used by Sherlock Holmes and C. Auguste Dupin. William of Baskerville is a name that could certainly be added to this list. From the moment we meet him, he is performing abductions, and he consistently affirms his belief in the abductive process as leading to valid conclusions. Even before William and Adso reach the monastery, and without being told anything about the situation, William directs members of the monastic community to the place where they can find the lost horse Brunellus. Upon Adso's request, William traces his abductions. We see him use signs from the various semiotic categories Eco defines in his theoretical works: nonverbal imprints (hoof-prints) and clues (a broken branch), and clues from texts (the source for the name *Brunellus*). Over and over again in the novel, we see William reading signs correctly: he deciphers codes in manuscripts and in the arrangement of the library, he deciphers clues to crimes, he figures out that victims were not murdered where their bodies were found.

As William of Baskerville repeatedly goes through the abductive process and explains his thinking, he sounds as much like a theoretical semiotician as a detective. He actually defines *abduction*, in contrast to induction and deduction and, like Peirce, singles it out as the only logical process generat-ing new ideas.[23] He tells Adso,

> solving a mystery is not the same as deducing from first principles. Nor does it amount simply to collecting a number of particular data from which to infer a general law. It means, rather, facing one or two or three particular data apparently with nothing in common, and trying to imagine whether they could represent so many instances of a general law you don't yet know, and which perhaps has never been pronounced. (304).

He goes on to describe how unexpectedly a result may indicate a better line of reasoning but how testing hypotheses continues and uncertainty remains until a final solution is perceived (305).[24]

William uses modern semiotic categories and fourteenth-century Ockhamist concepts to define and classify the various signs he uses in his abductions. Eco's "imprint" (signifying a past agent) and Ockham's "connot-ative term" (signifying something unreal) are two examples. William com-pares the prints left in the snow by one of the murder victims to the print of a unicorn, an unreal object.[25] A print of something indicates that the some-thing must exist, either in the world or in our minds. A print can be a print of an idea. "The idea is sign of things," William says, "and the image is sign of the idea, sign of a sign. But from the image I reconstruct, if not the body, the idea that others had of it." When Adso asks if this is enough, William answers, "No, because true learning must not be content with ideas, which are, in fact, signs, but must discover things in their individual truth" (as Ockham would say). But, says William, that is not always possible "without the help of other signs." Adso, formulating the definition of unlimited semiosis, asks, "Then I can always and only speak of something that speaks to me of something else, and so on. But the final something, the true one—does that never exist?" William answers, "Perhaps it does: it is the individual unicorn. And don't worry: one of these days you will encounter it, however black and ugly it may be" (317), referring to historical accounts of the rhinoceros being identified as the unicorn. This final response of William's is disturbing in a number of ways: it is self-contradictory, stating both doubt ("Perhaps") and certainty ("you will"); and it reflects that the individual truth, if it exists, may be ugly and threatening or only true in wholly unexpected ways.

The truth William finds at the end is indeed negative. It represents the logical conclusion of Ockhamist thought that no knowledge except the direct cognition of individuals is certain. The final truth William of Baskerville perceives also demonstrates how nihilistic Ockham's belief is; ultimately it applies to William's roles both as theologian and as detective. William discovers that, because there was no pattern to the crimes, all of his abductions were worthless. Abduction can only lead to discovery of a pattern; when there is no pattern, when the reality is irrational, that reality cannot be discerned by reason. Any "clues" must be nonrational, unrelated to patterns. In this case, the key clue to penetrating the mystery of the library is provided by Adso's dream, and William discovers the murderer's method by accident. Despondently, William says to Adso: "I have never doubted the truth of signs, Adso; they are the only things man has with which to orient himself in the world. What I did not understand was the relation among signs."[26] He asks what happens when signs do not derive from any plan: "Where is all my wisdom, then? I behaved stubbornly, pursuing a semblance of order, when I should have known well that there is no order in the universe." When William attributes this lack of order to God's absolute power, Adso asks whether affirming God's absolute omnipotence and freedom of choice is tantamount to demonstrating that God does not exist since both situations constitute chaos. William responds with a question: "How could a learned man go on communicating his learning if he answered yes to your question?" Adso now asks for clarification of the question: "Do you mean . . . that there would be no possible and communicable learning any more if the very criterion of truth were lacking, or do you mean you could no longer communicate what you know because others would not allow you to?" (493)

This last question is left unanswered verbally as at that moment the burning monastery crumbles, even as the logical and theological structures are crumbling in William's and Adso's minds. Describing all levels of action, William says, "There is too much confusion here."

Just as in his last appearance William of Baskerville despairs of abduction leading to meaning, so Adso, writing years later, is full of semiotic doubts about language and meaning. He tells of having returned to the site of the monastery after some time, only to find all the structures in ruins and of having collected scraps of parchment, "amputated stumps of books" (500), from which he tries to grasp but fails to decipher some meaning. He ends with uncertainty about his own manuscript having any meaning.

With all these doubts about meaning, where should we go to resolve our own questions about the meaning of the novel? Are there any more clues to bring to bear in our abductive process? Because Eco speaks of the aesthetic text as creating correlations through figurative language, and because the medieval mind had a panmetaphorical attitude toward the world,[27] it seems appropriate to seek as signs of theme the central images and metaphors of the novel. Two that have the most bearing on the parallels between medieval and modern semiotic thinking are the labyrinth and the rose.[28]

While the labyrinth is a powerful image in both medieval and modern thought, medieval thinkers see it more as threatening and are more uncomfortable with the idea of being in one. In medieval churches, labyrinths represent, among other concepts, human desires leading one away from God. Labyrinths in medieval literature signify loss of meaning, or the confusion of truth and falsehood. In contrast, Eco is quite comfortable with the idea of an endless labyrinth from which it is impossible to exit.[29] He uses it in his theoretical works as the symbol for (1) unlimited semiosis, in that signs are explainable only by other signs, and each sign ultimately leads to all others; (2) for texts, whose "maze-like structures" combine various codes and signs; and (3) for reading aesthetic texts, whose "labyrinthine garden . . . permits one to take many different routes."[30]

If we view the labyrinth as representing the abductive process, then William of Baskerville's problem is that he is a medieval man in a modern labyrinth.[31] The idea of a labyrinth is threatening unless getting to the heart of the monastery's labyrinthine library means decoding the mystery of the murders. In successive tries, William gets thoroughly lost, finds his way to the walled-up room, and finally penetrates the room. By the time he gets into the finis Africae, however, he knows that no solution awaits him there. What he finds instead is a murderer who admits to having no plan. The modern labyrinth has no heart or center; the center of the novel's library is indeed an empty space, around which the sections of the structure are built. Neither does the modern labyrinth have an end, a place where one can grasp a pattern. Thus, William is disappointed because, despite all his doubts and philosophical questionings, he has medieval expectations of some truth and finality, of signs leading to a meaningful, understandable pattern ("relation among signs").

The labyrinth points to the difference between medieval and modern philosophies. The rose highlights the similarity—though not an identity. In his *Postscript to "The Name of the Rose,"* Eco explains his title by referring to the lines that close Adso's manuscript: "stat rosa pristina nomine, nomina nuda tenemus" (the rose of former days remains in the name, the bare name is all we have). The medieval source is *De contemptu mundi* by Bernard of Morlay, a twelfth-century Benedictine. Eco also refers to Abelard's *Nulla rosa est,* "to demonstrate how language can speak of both the nonexistent and the destroyed."[32] Therefore, to the medieval mind, the rose could represent the transience of things and the gap between language and reality. But again, the twentieth-century mind takes the transience and uncertainty a step further. For Eco, in *A Theory of Semiotics,* the rose signifies the transience of language itself. He speaks of many codes being "weak and transient, thus lasting *l'espace d'en matin,* like a rose. But a rose is no less a rose . . . because it is so short-lived; in the same way a code is a code . . . as long as the correspondence exists and society accepts it."[33] Thus, just as Eco is comfortable in an endless, self-contained labyrinth, so he is at home with a sign system that cannot be expected to last. In the course of his manuscript, Adso makes considerable progress—from trusting the Word as God to seeing that the word divorced from a fleeting reality is all that endures. Adso's despair at the uncertainties of language separate him from Eco, the modern semiotician, who accepts the semiotic limbo.

In drawing his characters, plot, and overall meaning, Eco uses the significant intellectual parallels between the fourteenth and twentieth centuries. The questions raised link the two eras; the belief in answers separates the medieval mind from the modern. It is finally Eco's fictional, contemporary editor who articulates the modern position. He decides to publish Adso's manuscript "as if it were authentic," "with no concern for timeliness," "for sheer narrative pleasure" (5), pleasure we surely derive, whatever the novel means, and for however long it has that meaning.

Notes

1. Gordon Leff, *The Dissolution of the Medieval Outlook* (New York: New York University Press, 1976), 38.

2. William Ockham, *Ockham's Theory of Terms: Part 1 of the Summa Theologicae*, trans. Michael J. Loux (Notre Dame: University of Notre Dame Press, 1974), 3; and William Ockham, *Philosophical Writings*, trans. Philotheus Boehner (New York: Bobbs-Merrill Company, 1964), 30, 38.

3. *Philosophical Writings*, 21–28.

4. *Ockham's Theory of Terms*, 50; *Philosophical Writings*, 52.

5. Peirce, *Principles of Philosophy*, I, 339, *Elements of Logic*, II, 227–42, in *Collected Papers* (Cambridge: Harvard University Press, 1931–32); and John F. Boler, *Charles Peirce and Scholastic Realism* (Seattle: University of Washington Press, 1963), 11, n28, and 49, n47.

6. Deely, *Introducing Semiotic: Its History and Doctrine* (Bloomington: Indiana University Press, 1982), 101.

7. Eco, *Semiotics and the Philosophy of Language* (Bloomington: Indiana University Press, 1984), 9; and *A Theory of Semiotics* (Bloomington: Indiana University Press, 1976), 165.

8. William Ockham, cited in Gordon Leff, *William of Ockham: The Metamorphosis of Scholastic Discourse* (Manchester: Manchester University Press, 1975; reprinted Totowa, N.J.: Rowman and Littlefield, 1977), 127.

9. Ockham, cited in Leff, *William of Ockham*, p. 127.

10. Eco, *Theory of Semiotics*, 61–66.

11. Gordon Leff, *Medieval Thought: St. Augustine to Ockham* (Chicago: Quadrangle Books, 1958), 282.

12. Leff, *William of Ockham*, 140.

13. Eco, *Theory of Semiotics*, 58, 64; and Umberto Eco, *The Role of the Reader: Explorations into the Semiotics of Texts* (Bloomington: Indiana University Press, 1979), 179.

14. Ockham, *Philosophical Writings*, 63–64.

15. Eco, *Theory of Semiotics*, 49, 64; and *Role of the Reader*, 87–88.

16. Eco, *Semiotics*, 46. For a summary of Porphyry's place in the history of semiotics, see Deely, *Introducing Semiotic*, 15–17, 26–27.

17. *Ockham's Theory of Terms*, 90–100.

18. Model Q, in *A Theory of Semiotics*, 68–71. The idea of "infinite regression" appears in Peirce in connection with his concept of interpretants: "[t]he meaning of a representation can be nothing but a representation. . . . So there is an infinite regression here. Finally, the interpretant is nothing but another representation to which the truth is handed along; and as representation, it has its interpretant again. Lo, another infinite series" (*Principles of Philosophy*, 339). The agreement here between Eco and Peirce can be overstated. Philosophically, Peirce is a realist, agreeing more with Duns Scotus than with Ockham on the reality of generals or universals: where

Ockham sees generals only as words or mental constructs, Scotus posits metaphysical common natures ("formalities"), and Peirce posits laws. See Boler for a complete discussion of Peirce's realism; and Eco, *Role of the Reader,* 191–92 for attempts to reconcile the seeming contradiction between unlimited semiosis and Scotist realism.

Eco's labyrinth is not a unique modern semiotic metaphor; Deely repeatedly speaks of a *"semiotic web,* . . . a structure of experience built up through sign relations" (101–102) and refers to "the semiotic web of natural language" as opposed to an artificially organized and controlled sign system (76).

19. Julius R. Weinberg, *A Short History of Medieval Philosophy* (Princeton: Princeton University Press, 1964), 240.

20. Umberto Eco, *The Name of the Rose,* trans. William Weaver (San Diego: Harcourt Brace Jovanovich, 1983), 203, 205, for example. Subsequent citations appear in parentheses in the text.

21. Peirce, *Elements of Logic,* 96, 623–24; Eco, *Semiotics,* 8; and Umberto Eco and Thomas Sebeok, eds., *The Sign of Three: Dupin, Holmes, Peirce* (Bloomington: Indiana University Press, 1983), 16.

22. Peirce, *Elements of Logic,* 755; and *Sign of Three,* 40, 143, 190.

23. Peirce, *Elements of Logic,* 96; and Boler, 85–88.

24. According to Boler, Peirce objects to the nominalist position which holds that "the only actualities are past events," and only these past events are uniform: "a law is simply a particularly striking uniformity." Peirce sees more than uniformity involved; the crucial inferential leap is the *connection,* the *relation* among events or signs. Once the connection is discovered, one can predict future events. And a future actuality is a current *real* possibility. Prediction is the essential aspect of Peirce's concept of general law (Boler, *Charles Peirce,* 111–12).

25. Eco also uses the unicorn to explain a sign-function in *The Role of the Reader,* 179.

26. Of course, it is the "relation" among signs that is crucial to understanding, that, in fact, defines understanding. But there must *be* a relation, a pattern, if there is to be a Peircean "law," if there is to be meaning. Here, the lack of *relation* is what defeats William.

27. Eco, *Semiotics and the Philosophy of Language,* 103.

28. For a discussion of the monastery as deconstructive symbol, see my forthcoming article "Deconstructing the Monastery in Umberto Eco's *The Name of the Rose,* " in *The Medieval Monastery,* University of Minnesota Press.

29. W. H. Matthews, *Mazes and Labyrinths: Their History and Development* (New York: Dover Publications, 1970), 67–68; Piero Boitani, "Chaucer's Labyrinth: Fourteenth-Century Literature and Language," *Chaucer Review* 17 (1983): 209. Eco outlines three types of labyrinths, the last being the rhizome, in which each point ultimately is connected to every other: *Postscript to "The Name of the Rose,"* trans. William Weaver (San Diego: Harcourt Brace Jovanovich, 1983), 57–58; and *Semiotics and the Philosophy of Language,* 81–82.

30. The references are to Eco's *A Theory of Semiotics*, 68–71; *The Role of the Reader*, 9; and *A Theory of Semiotics*, 256, 275, respectively.

31. Eco would disagree since he says that William knows the world is rhizomaic (*Postscript*, 58).

32. *Postscript*, 1.

33. Eco, *A Theory of Semiotics*, 160.

9 Traversing the Labyrinth: The Structures of Discovery in Eco's *The Name of the Rose*

Jocelyn Mann

In Umberto Eco's *The Name of the Rose,* a murder mystery set in a medieval monastery, the learned Franciscan, Brother William of Baskerville, discovers that his misguided interpretation of the significance of a series of clues has led him to erroneously link several deaths that have taken place in the abbey. [1] He comes to realize that there is ultimately no "right way" through and out of any labyrinth of clues, or signs. Although the signs themselves can be useful and valid, the idea that it is possible to create an enduring thread of meaning by linking them together and following them to a permanent truth is an illusion. "I have never doubted the truth of signs," says William to Adso, his young novice assistant; "they are the only things man has with which to orient himself in the world. What I did not understand was the relation among signs" (492).

The pursuit of signs in the quest for truth—the structure of every detective novel—is most metaphorically embodied in *The Name of the Rose* by the monastery's library. A huge labyrinthine construction with secret passageways, cryptic indices, and rooms within rooms of ancient books and scrolls holding diverse cultures and philosophies, it is guarded by zealous monks and is open only to a select few. Through the twists and turns of a plot that is yet another maze, William and Adso end up trying to utilize the library's winding structure and coded contents to lead them to the murderer.

In this novel, a parallel search to the hunt for the murderer goes on at the same time. Casually introduced in the first few pages as the purported subject of the frame story, in this optional search (the whodunit can be enjoyed without undertaking it), the reader is the detective, and the discovery he or she seeks is no less than the text itself. In an attempt to learn the nature and authority of its creator and its ultimate truth and reality, if any, the reader must penetrate the labyrinth of the novel's structure, find a way through and by its twists and turns of signs, genres, translated codes, parodies, and intertexual culture clashes, to an awareness of the shape of the novel's universe.

There is, then, both a fictional and a metafictional quest occurring simultaneously in Eco's novel. On the fictional level it is the story of a Franciscan cleric and his companion using clues to solve the mystery of a series of deaths that take place in an isolated abbey in medieval Italy, a country torn by internal power struggles and threatened by apocalyptic movements heralding the collapse of the church-centered culture of the Middle Ages and the rise of a new, less rigidly structured society.[2] On the metafictional level, it is the story of a text whose readers must search for ways to enter and exit; a deceptive structure, which shifts its shape as the readers help to build and explore it. This story—or chains of signs about other chains of signs—is about the ways in which cultures encode signs and signs become books and books become cultures. The search has its own apocalyptic movement; it, too, is a story about the crumbling of rigid structures and their more plastic reconstitution. Ultimately, the search can be viewed as a semiotic, cultural exploration of fiction and how its interrelationship with its reader generates the structure of its own particular universe.

The labyrinth as the expression of a semiotic-cultural exploration is discussed by Eco in his *Semiotics and the Philosophy of Language*.[3] In the chapter, "Dictionary vs. Encyclopedia," Eco, referring to Porphyry's *Isogage,* describes the medieval dictionary type of knowing, or "competence," that branches out like a tree, defining by genera and species, substances and their differentiae. He then opposes this dictionary competence to the encyclopedic type of competence initiated by the encyclopedists of the Enlightenment, Diderot and d'Alembert, and developed by C. Deleuze and F. Guattari into the more radical concept of the vegetable-like network known as the "rhizome."[4] Translating both dictionary and encyclopedic competences into a metaphor of the labyrinth, Eco proceeds to describe the three types of labyrinth: classical, Mannerist, and rhizomic, the last two representing, respectively, the opposed competences.

The classical labyrinth, as exemplified by Theseus entering the labyrinth of Crete, is linear and predetermined; that is, one enters, must reach the center, and from there, the exit. The Minotaur is there merely "to make the whole thing a little more exciting . . . and . . . one *cannot* get lost; the labyrinth itself is an Ariadne thread."[5]

The Mannerist maze corresponds to the dictionary competence. It contains many paths, and some are dead ends. "If one unwinds a maze, one gets a particular kind of tree in which certain choices are privileged in respect to others. . . . Only one among them leads to the way out."[6] An Ariadne's thread *is* needed for this Porphyrian-tree type of labyrinth, and the monster that lurks in its corridors is the trial-and-error process itself.

The encyclopedic labyrinth, which evolves into the more radical rhizomic labyrinth, has no single way out, no one correct interpretation. It models itself, rather, on a view of human culture as a network capable of limitless, ever-changing interpretations.

In the fictional quest, William is at first confident that he can solve his case by way of the Mannerist maze through a combination of hypothesis and trial-and-error, with the entire procedure resembling the deciphering of a coded message. He tells Adso,

> "Perhaps this is the right track. But it could also be just a series of coincidences. A rule of correspondence has to be found. . . . "
> "Found where?"
> "In our heads. Invent it. And then see whether it is the right one. But with one test and another. . . . —remember this—there is no secret writing that cannot be deciphered. . . . (166)

William is aware, too, that there are many possibilities involved in forming more complex hypotheses. Dramatizing the theories set forth in "Horns, Hooves, and Insteps," his essay on Sherlock Holmes and Charles Peirce, the American semiotician upon whose theories much of his semiotic philosophy is based, Eco has William tell Adso how he arrived at the identity and location of the missing horse, Brunellus.[7] The brilliant, English-trained Franciscan monk describes to his young Watson-surrogate the process of forming a hypothesis—or, to use Peirce's term, an "abduction"—and the way in which this process opens up various avenues to the truth. This shocks Adso, who is used to addressing the problem of truth with a medieval sensibility, looking for first causes and reflections of God's thought:

> I understood at that moment my master's method of reasoning, and it seemed to me quite alien to that of the philosopher, who reasons by first principles, so that his intellect almost assumes the ways of the divine intellect. I understood that, when he didn't have an answer, William proposed many to himself, very different one from another.
> "But then," I ventured to remark, "you are still far from the solution. . . ."
> "I am very close to one," William said, "but I don't know which."
> . . . . .
> "And you . . . never commit errors?"
> "Often," he answered. "But instead of conceiving only one, I imagine many, so I become the slave of none." (305–306)

The structure of thought of medieval society did not allow for this model of conjecture, which resembles the encyclopedic labyrinth of interpretive competence more than it does the defining rigidity of the Porphyrian tree. William's thought, however, is still rigid in the way it "considers a typology of signs as if they were entities, whereas in fact they are relations," as Eco says in a rare but important criticism of Peirce's theory.[8] As already noted, William laments, at the end of the events that culminate in the destruction of the library labyrinth, that he had seen the truth of signs but not their relation. He had seen what each clue stood for but not their function of *standing for.*[9] As we shall see, it is precisely the deconstructive nature of relation, as opposed to entity, that underlies the fiery end of the Aedificium, with all that appeared to be held so securely within its walls.

Just as William originally puts his faith in his virtuoso ability to decipher codes, so the discerning reader of the novel in which he figures is confident that he or she is in a familiar structure that, however winding or deceptive, inevitably will provide the way out. The unmistakable signs of the genre of the detective novel have been set forth: the name, William of Baskerville, echoing that most famous Sherlock Holmes vehicle, "The Hound of the Baskervilles"; and the methods of the super-sleuth himself suggested in the Brunellus episode. The metafictional whodunit—the problems of validity, origin, and meaning, of the reliability of narrators and the truth of translations—should be solved by keen perception and rational vigor. Both William and the reader initially see their respective universes of abbey and book, and the larger cultural universe implicit in the two, as modeled on the Mannerist labyrinth, needing only an Ariadne's thread of possible correspondences and a willingness to undergo the trial-and-error process to provide a "true" exit.

The labyrinth as a "mode of conjecture" is related by Eco to his novel in *Postscript to "The Name of the Rose,"* an illuminating commentary on the writing and reception of the book: "The labyrinth of my library is still a Mannerist labyrinth, but the world in which William realizes [by the end of the novel] he is living already has a rhizome structure: that is, it can be structured but is never structured definitively."[10] Thus we may assume from his comment that this aspect of its composition—to be structured but never structured definitively—carries for Eco the greatest importance of the rhizomic labyrinth to the novel. To understand its significance and the role it plays in the universe of the novel and the universe of human culture, a longer look at the characteristics of the rhizome is necessary.

The rhizomatic structure, as suggested by Deleuze and Guattari, is a "tangle of bulbs and tubers appearing like 'rats squirming one on top of the other.' "[11] A partial list of its characteristics is given by Eco in *Semiotics and the Philosophy of Language*, which further reveals the nature of its radical departure from previous modes of conjecture, such as its network composition: "Every point of the rhizome can and must be connected with every other point . . ."; and its negation of one correct interpretation: "No one can provide a global description of the whole rhizome; not only because the rhizome is multi-dimensionally complicated, but also because its structure changes through the time."[12] From a combination of this quite radical view and the somewhat more modified plan of the eighteenth-century encyclopedists, who in seeking to transform the Porphyrian tree into a map, "made in fact the rhizome thinkable," Eco concludes that

> the universe of semiosis, that is, the universe of human culture, must be conceived as structured like a labyrinth of the third type: (a) It is structured according to a *network of interpretants*. (b) It is virtually *infinite* because it takes into account multiple interpretations realized by different cultures: a given expression can be interpreted as many times, and in as many ways, as it has been actually interpreted in a given cultural framework. [13]

Since the universe of semiosis or human culture is "virtually infinite" because it holds all past, present, and possible future cultural interpretations, it can be investigated only through the application of one or more of the codes it contains. As the noted Soviet semiotician Juri Lotman observes in "Problems in the Typology of Culture":

> The entire hierarchy of codes that constitute this or that type of culture can be deciphered either with the help of an identical structure of codes, or with the help of a structure of another type of codes that intersects only partially with the one used by the text's creators or else is completely extraneous to it. [14]

Although he speaks of deciphering, Lotman, as well as Eco, rejects the idea of any culture-deciphering tool that is not—however helpful—ultimately as vulnerable to change and interpretation as culture itself. Furthermore, as Lotman goes on to say, a change in the cultural context in which it is read can alter the semantics of even a word-for-word reproduction of a text. "The modern reader of a medieval religious text obviously deciphers its semantics by having recourse to codes different from those used by the text's creator. Furthermore, he even changes the type of text: in its creator's system it belonged among sacred texts."[15]

Eco illustrates Lotman's concepts in both fictional and metafictional aspects of his novel by first constructing a carefully accurate medieval world so that his fiction can represent itself, for most of its pages, as a medieval chronicle of events. "Writing a novel," he says, "is a cosmological matter, like the story told by Genesis. . . . What I mean is, to tell a story, you must first construct a world."[16] And Eco creates a world that abounds in signs. As Lotman observes, "The medieval type [of culture] is distinguished by its high semioticity. It not only tends to impart the character of a cultural sign to everything that has meaning in natural language, [it] proceeds from the assumption that everything is significant."[17]

On the fictional level, William is forced to pick his way judiciously through a maze of signs. He must find his way through this labyrinthine medieval construct by putting into operation the deciphering skills noted by Lotman. As an Englishman from another order, exposed to different educational and philosophical influences, William can bring to the Benedictine monastery in Italy the different cultural angle of vision provided by his familiarity with the logic of Bacon and Occam and the philosophy of Aristotle. As the novel progresses, William investigates each of the suspects and victims from the vantage point of his partially intersecting cultural code. He explores what they read, wear, and do; how they express themselves; and, above all, what they put above all: the hierarchy of their desires. Jorge's extreme abhorrence of laughter, for example, becomes an important clue because William is able to utilize his "exotic" point of view to discern a norm—a cultural code—about attitudes toward laughter and comedy, hence the extremity of Jorge's departure from this norm. All the signs revealed in the winding corridors of the narrative are culturally coded in the recalled history, anecdotes, sermons, descriptions, and dialogue that William examines through the ground-to-order spectacles of his own cultural code. Even with his superior background in interpreting signs, however, he is led astray by his interpretation of the clues which meretriciously link the murderer to the apocalyptic revelation of Saint John of Patmos, so that it appears the murders are a fulfillment of the Seven Seals of Revelation and an enactment of its iconography. Icons of icons—a rhizomatic tangle of superimposed codes—and for awhile William loses his spectacles and his way.

When we turn to the modern reader's corresponding metafictional quest, we must reexamine Eco's created world. As a medieval chronicle, that world must at least appear to be constructed in the design—the conjectural mode—of the Mannerist labyrinth. Even as a modern novel, a historical murder mystery must have a linear unfolding. That is, it must follow certain historical events chronologically and try to solve the mystery; it must seek a way out of the labyrinth. A modern semiotician who sees the world as rhizomatic in structure, however, will, at the same time, look for a way to create a rhizome labyrinth. In *The Name of the Rose*, its reader's metafictional exploration is a rhizome labyrinth—a mode of conjecture consisting of a semiotic scanning of a novel that can be understood and enjoyed without it but with which the reader who undertakes it, the writer who devises it, and the work itself are enlarged, redefined, and enriched. This is the ironic game of the postmodern novel, as Eco tells us in *Postscript:*

> . . . it is possible not to understand the game and yet to take it seriously. . . . the collages of Max Ernst, who pasted together bits of nineteenth-century engravings were postmodern: they can be read as fantastic stories, as the telling of dreams, without any awareness that they amount to a discussion of the nature of engraving, and perhaps even of collage.[18]

The "collage" of which Eco speaks, the putting together of bits and pieces of other, earlier works on the same subject, illustrates, among other things, the postmodern handling of "the echoes of intertextuality," the fact that "books always speak of other books, and every story tells a story that has already been told."[19] The setting of Adso's chronicle within three other narrative frames and the creation of a twentieth-century narrator attempting to find the "real" manuscript through various times and places sets the tone of postmodern irony. At the same time, the reader's alternate metafictional quest is initiated. In the process of showing at the outset the inevitability of intertextuality, the network quality of the rhizome—every point of the rhizome can and must be connected to every other point—is introduced. In reciting his problems with the translation of Adso's manuscript, the narrator-translator is also educating the reader on the equivalence of the universe of semiotics and the universe of culture, with its rhizomatic, Einsteinian considerations of constant change, overlapping influences, and lack of absolutes:

> First of all, what style should I employ? The temptation to follow Italian models of the period had to be rejected as totally unjustified: not only does Adso write in Latin, but it is also clear from the whole development of the text that his culture (or the culture of the abbey, which clearly influences him) dates back even further; it is manifestly a summation, over several centuries, of learning and stylistic quirks that can be linked with the late-medieval Latin tradition. (4)

In this way, even before William begins to interpret signs in the context of a culture, the reader has been eased into the starting gate of the corresponding textual semiotic quest. The question of the "truth" of Adso's manuscript has been broached and questioned. Layer after layer of context-culture must be traversed before and after the faulty filter of an old German monk writing in Latin, trying to remember a traumatic week in his youth.

There are, for example, the comments on the manuscript that are found in Buenos Aires by the present-day narrator among the shelves of a "little antiquarian bookseller" in a Castilian version of an Italian translation of a work, *On the Use of Mirrors in the Game of Chess* (3). This reference to Jorge Luis Borges' famous story in *Labyrinths,* "Tlon, Uqbar, Orbis Tertius," is an illustration of Eco's statement on Ernst's collage and postmodern irony. To those familiar with its contents, Borges' story adds much to Eco's semiotic commentary (some may consider the story a key to the commentary); but uunfamiliarity with Borges does not cancel the reader's understanding and enjoyment of *The Name of the Rose.*[20] Nor, for that matter, does this unfamiliarity impede the reader's semiotic pursuit. Indeed, as the narrator proceeds to divulge that the Castilian version of the work was written by a presumably Slavic writer, Milo Temesvar, in Georgia and that it contained "copius quotations" from Adso's manuscript written by the Jesuit scholar— Father Athanasius Kircher "(but which work?)" (3)—the reader, in the midst of being delightfully entertained by the ridiculous ramifications of the search, has been made to realize, or at least to sense, the ubiquitous and inevitable presence of intertextuality. The subversion of the very decoding process that Eco, for much of the novel, appears to be extolling in the persona of William has begun. The modern reader, peering through his irony-coded twentieth-century spectacles, has started his own inquest into the nature of this collage of clues.

A change of viewpoint is involved in irony which demands our taking another look at a norm or code that is being so treated.[21] Scholes refers to irony as the one figure that "must always take us out of the text and into codes, contexts, and situations."[22] He cites as an example a "brief reworking" of Balzac's *Eugenie Grandet* by Donald Bartheleme, called "Eugenie Grandet," which combines portions of the original with "newly constructed absurdities" in a "collage of discourses presented without reference to an interpretive center."[23] One of the ways in which Eco achieves an ironic collage of discourses is with Adso's narrative, which allows the modern reader to observe the medieval codes operating in the language of a narrator who believes himself to be accurately recording the history of a series of events. When Adso speaks of an apocalyptic movement, he uses apocalyptic language; when he describes animals, he uses the language of *The Bestiary.* When he makes love, Eco tells us in the *Postscript,* Adso uses a combination of religious texts to describe it: the Song of Songs, Saint Bernard and Jean de Fecamp, or Saint Hildegard of Bingen.[24] He records events without understanding them, and Eco admits that it was his aim to "make everything understood through the words of one who understands nothing."[25] In this way, the texts that influence Adso's life turn what he believes to be a chronicle of events into a more literary exercise than he realizes. Hayden White has suggested that historical narratives "are not only models of past events and processes, but also metaphorical statements which suggest a relation of similitude between such events and processes and the story types that we conventionally use to endow the events of our lives with culturally sanctioned meanings."[26] With this in mind, the reader can construct an icon of the structure of those literary traditions in the culture that sanction the meanings in his discourse.[27]

If we combine Eco's comments on Adso's "transparency" as a character with White's ideas of the cultural iconicity of historical discourse, we can look at Adso's narrative semiotically as an intertext. His text refers—consciously and unconsciously—to other texts harbored within it that give the text its meaning. Add to this the fact that the reader knows from the frame narrative that in its passage from one translator to the next, it has absorbed various cultures and interpretations and becomes a model of intertextuality while, at the same time, becoming a collage of discourses illustrating the postmodern ironic sensibility.

The Name of the Rose invites the interpretive exploration of its reader because, set in its tangled series of interrelated frames and presented through the different culture codes of its unstereotyped and three-dimensional protagonists, it fulfills the conditions of an "open" novel, Eco's term in *The Role of the Reader* for a work that allows for maximum interpretive and generative participation of its reader.[28] In the "closed" work (Eco gives Ian Fleming's James Bond novels as one example), "The reader finds himself immersed in a game of which he knows the pieces and the rules—and perhaps the outcome—and draws pleasure simply from following the minimal variations by which the victor realizes his objective."[29] In the myth of Superman, another Eco example of the closed work, "the stories help define their expressive structure as the circular, static conveyance of a pedagogic message which is substantially immobilistic."[30] That immobilistic, pedagogic structure is the world of Superman—and of the Aedificium in *The Name of the Rose*.

In contrast, Eco compares the open text to the universe of Einstein and Spinoza, since both have a multiple polarity and an absence of "an absolute conditioning center of reference."[31] This more ambiguous structure does not imply random interpretation, however; Eco feels that it does possess a "structural vitality" which prevails but does not preclude different interpretations. Quoting Edmund Wilson on James Joyce, "Joyce's world is always changing as it is perceived by different observers and by them at different times," Eco makes further comments on Joyce's *Finnegans Wake* that could be used as a description of the rhizome network mode of conjecture:

> The book is molded into a curve that bends back on itself, like the Einsteinian universe. . . . the work is *finite* in one sense, but in another sense it is *unlimited*. Each occurrence, each word stands in a series of possible relations with all the others in the text. According to the semantic choice which we make in the case of one unit so goes the way we interpret all the other units in the text. This does not mean that the book lacks specific sense. If Joyce does introduce some keys into the text, it is precisely because he wants the work to be read in a certain sense. But this particular "sense" has all the richness of the cosmos itself.[32]

In *The Name of the Rose,* the final debate between Brother William of Baskerville and Jorge of Burgos behind the looking glass in the Aedificium unites the fictional and the metafictional pursuits of detective and reader and carries the quest into the heart of the labyrinth. As William discovers the prize he covets above the solution of the murders—the lost second book of the *Poetics* of Aristotle—the brilliant Franciscan, who has correctly construed its major premises from his readings of other works by Aristotle, defends the philosophical validity of its purported subject—comedy—to Jorge, whose hatred of its contents has prompted him to keep it hidden from the world:

> Comedy does not tell of famous and powerful men. . . . It achieves the effect of the ridiculous by showing the defects and vices of ordinary men. Here Aristotle sees the tendency to laughter as a force for good . . . though it tells us things differently from the way they are, as if it were lying, it actually obliges us to examine them more closely. . . . (472)

Jorge, fearing the loss of theocentric control inherent in such a view, cries out against it:

> "But on the day when the Philosopher's word would justify the marginal jests of the debauched imagination, or when what has been marginal would leap to the center, every trace of the center would be lost. . . . But if one day somebody, brandishing the words of the Philosopher and therefore speaking as a philosopher, were to raise the weapon of laughter to the condition of subtle weapon, if the rhetoric of conviction were replaced by the rhetoric of mockery, if the topics of the patient construction of the images of redemption were to be replaced by the topics of the impatient dismantling and upsetting of every holy and venerable image—oh, that day even you, William, and all your knowledge, would be swept away!" (475–76)

Calling Jorge the devil because, like the devil, Jorge possesses "arrogance of the spirit, faith without smile, [and] truth that is never seized by doubt," William proceeds to defend comedy and condemn Jorge's stand in terms that ultimately condemn any closed world:

> The Devil is grim because he knows where he is going, and, in moving, he always returns whence he came. . . . like the Devil you live in darkness. . . . And now I say to you that, in the infinite whirl of possible things, God allows you also to imagine a world where the presumed interpreter of the truth is nothing but a clumsy raven, who repeats words learned long ago.
>
> . . . . .
>
> The hand of God creates; it does not conceal.
>
> . . . . .
>
> God created the monsters, too. And you. And he wants everything to be spoken of. (477–78)

William's defense of comedy encompasses Eco's defense of the freer, more reader-involved work. The final debate between William and Jorge is the same confrontation of two cultures, two ways of knowing, that we have seen in Eco's nonfiction works on semiotics. It is the difference between the "open" and the "closed" novel, the dictionary versus encyclopedic competence, that he has given the metaphor of the two labyrinths. The last gasps of Jorge as he consumes the philosophy he has impregnated with poison, rather than give to the world a new way of perceiving—a way of unlimited possibilities—are the last gasps of a culture to whom the truth was a closed, mysterious, rigid, tortuous accumulation of secret passages guarded by high priests of privileged knowledge. The reasons for the apocalyptic thrust of the novel become clear as we see in the ensuing fire that consumes labyrinth and monastery the end of one kind of world: "The Aedificium, which had seemed so solid and tetragonous, revealed in these circumstances its weakness, its cracks, the walls corroded from within" (488). On the metafictional level, the apocalypse that takes place is the destruction—or, rather, the deconstruction—of the rigidly defined, one-meaning, author-centered work. The reader's faith in the text's expected solution provided by its author-creator through the persona of the infallible detective has been shaken by the revelation of William's inability to foresee the "accidents," the network of relations, that compound and confound interpretation. William's answer to Adso's attempted reassurances on the subject of his mentor's success in solving the case brings the rhizomatic labyrinth concept to the structure of the text and its troubling-to-some implications of a centerless universe of unlimited interpretability: "It's hard to accept the idea that there cannot be an order in the universe," he tells the young novice, "because it would offend the free will of God and His omnipotence" (492–93).

Adso's marvelously reactionary response is not unlike the dismay voiced by many in the world of literary criticism to the more radical ideas of deconstruction, as voiced by Jacques Derrida, Paul de Man, and others:

> "But how can a necessary being exist totally polluted with the possible? What difference is there, then, between God and primigenial chaos? Isn't affirming God's absolute omnipotence and His absolute freedom with regard to His own choices tantamount to demonstrating that God does not exist?" (493).

William replies characteristically with another question: "How could a learned man go on communicating his learning if he answered yes to your question?" (493). One may be reminded here of Eco's comments, quoted above, on the structural vitality or authority of a text that prevails regardless of the endless possibilities of interpretation. Or one may be reminded of something that seems to apply more closely to William's words. Neither would be wrong. This is, after all, an open novel. Adso, though, always pressing for a definitive answer, now asks William to distinguish between two possible interpretations of William's reply. When William refuses to respond because of the noise and confusion after the fire, the point is made that neither Adso nor the reader is going to receive reassuring, prefabricated answers to the larger "global" questions. The old, closed structure—the Mannerist maze—has burned down, and the confusion and openness of the rhizome-structured world in which William and Adso find themselves have been worked into the very fabric of the novel, providing a good example of the postmodern novel and semiotic irony.

In the final section of the novel, Adso, about to "enter this broad desert" of death (501), ends his recollection of the events at the abbey, and the reader discovers that this account is literally as well as literarily a *re-collection*. Years after the fire, Adso returns to the scene and collects the few fragments remaining of the books of the old library and reassembles these relics into a "lesser library," which he uses as an oracle or icon for his narrative. He tells the reader that his manuscript is "only a cento, a figured hymn, an immense acrostic that says and repeats nothing but what those fragments have suggested to me" (501). This suggests that the narrative of those seven days is not an indisputable account of specific events but rather a fragmented memory conceived of and perceived through a network of changing cultural codes— the "immense acrostic" or "collage of discourses" that each of us, as well as Adso, carries within us. As Scholes points out in his discussion of semiotics and intertextuality, "parallel to the unlimited semiosis of signs we have the infinite regress of texts as well."[33] Adso and the reader are now in a strange new world, an unfamiliar mode of conjecture, where linear boundaries have been destroyed, and not only old authorities divested of their singular power (although Adso steadfastly refuses to see this) but both narrator and reader robbed of their ancient right to locate the center of the labyrinth. Eco illustrates spatially the missing center of the rhizome world when Adso revisits the destroyed monastery, climbs a circular staircase to the ruins of the old library, and realizes that it is now only a "sort of gallery next to the outside walls, looking down into the void at every point" (500).

The deconstruction of structure as an entity, a dismantling that consists primarily of doing away with a definitive center, is posited by Jacques Derrida in his landmark essay, "Structure, Sign, and Play in the Discourse of the Human Sciences."[34] Derrida claims that the attempt to conceive of structure as an entity is a desire that can never be fulfilled, since an entity must have a center, a "transcendental signified." What we call a center is only a name given to that which does not exist:

> The whole history of the concept of structure . . . must be thought of as a series of substitutions of center for center, as a linked chain of determinations of the center. Successively, and in a negative fashion, the center receives different forms or names.[35]

This absence of the center as an entity or presence does not preclude the concept of center as a function, "a sort of non-locus in which an infinite number of sign-substitutions come into play. . . . the absence of a transcendental signified extends the domain and interplay of significance *ad infinitum.*"[36] Derrida's concept of the loss of the center as an entity but not as a function is much the same as that proposed by Eco (cited above as one of Eco's rare criticisms of Peirce). In this passage, Eco goes on to say that "signs stand for something else, but the problem of their meaning does not concern the 'they' or the 'something,' but the function of *standing for.*"[37] Both Derrida and Eco see the need to recognize the lack of a centered structure in order to allow the free play of interpretation or unlimited semiosis.

To demonstrate that the conception of a permanent, centered structure is no longer valid, Eco first builds a structure and then destroys it. In *The Name of the Rose* he creates a medieval society with a powerful authoritarian center and shows that that center kept its authority by virtue of its narrowly defined premises and its hierarchical structure descending from a rigidly conceived Divine Order. On the semiotic level, both the culture of the medieval world, with its logic of first causes and dictionary competence, and that of William's nascent modernity, with its investment in the rational intellect, are shown to be dependent on the idea of a center—an ultimate Truth—an idea of entity that imposes false limits on epistemological possibility.

Thus the very structures that lead to the discoveries in *The Name of the Rose* must, for the reason they were created, be destroyed. They were neither permanent nor centered, or rather, their centers were shown to be imagined and nothing but the names they were called and the action they evoked. Library-labyrinth or detection procedure (both William's and the reader's), they were not entities; they were functions, some of them useful but not truths in themselves. "The order that our mind imagines is like a net," says William to Adso, trying to communicate what he has learned from his quest, "or like a ladder, built to attain something. But afterward you must throw the ladder away, because you discover that, even if it was useful, it was meaningless. . . . The only truths that are useful are instruments to be thrown away" (492).

Jorge is the exemplar of the person who can't let go of his truth. Looking back at Jorge's obsessive hatred of Aristotle's book on comedy, William comments on the blind monk's reasons:

> "Jorge feared the second book of Aristotle because it perhaps really did teach how to distort the face of every truth, so that we would not become slaves of our ghosts. Perhaps the mission of those who love mankind is to make people laugh at the truth, *to make truth laugh,* because the only truth lies in learning to free ourselves from insane passion for the truth." (491)

At the end of the novel, Eco, as well as William (and for the same reasons) throws away the order that his mind has imagined, dismantling the elaborate labyrinth he has created and revealing its lack of a "transcendental signified" or unchanging center. Eco has jettisoned the traditional role of author as absolute and controlling god of his book-universe to create a text which, to use his own definition of a novel, is "a machine for generating interpretations."[38] By dramatizing the culture-created, constantly changing, multi-interpretational aspect of his fictional world with its rhizome-labyrinth complexity, he negates the Mannerist maze as an outmoded model of conjecture for the reader's world as well. There can be no isolated single story, single murderer, single definitive truth in this whodunit, because it demonstrates the network interrelationship of all its signs as it unbuilds itself. Nevertheless, like its evocative title, *The Name of the Rose* carries a kind of immortality; not in the fixed and everlasting divinity of an absolute Truth but in its revelation of the endless dance of interpretation in Eco's semiotic world of infinite possibility.

Notes

1. Umberto Eco, *The Name of the Rose,* trans. William Weaver (San Diego: Harcourt Brace Jovanovich, 1983). Subsequent citations to this edition appear in parentheses in the text.

2. For information on apocalyptic movements of this time in Italy, see Lois Zamora, "Umberto Eco's Revelation: The Name of the Rose," *Humanities in the South: Newsletter of the Southern Humanities Conference,* no. 61 (Spring 1985): 3–5.

3. Eco, *Semiotics* (Bloomington: Indiana University Press, 1984).

4. Eco, *Semiotics,* 81.

5. Eco, *Semiotics,* 80.

6. Eco, *Semiotics,* 81.

7. Eco, "Horns, Hooves, Insteps: Some Hypotheses on Three Types of Abduction," in *The Sign of Three: Dupin, Holmes, Peirce,* ed. Umberto Eco and Thomas A. Sebeok (Bloomington: Indiana University Press, 1983), 198–220.

8. Eco, "Looking for a Logic of Culture," in *The Tell-Tale Sign: A Survey of Semiotics,* ed. Thomas A. Sebeok (Lisse, The Netherlands: Peter de Ridder Press, 1975), 13.

9. Eco, "Looking for a Logic," 13.

10. Eco, *Postscript to "The Name of the Rose,"* trans. William Weaver (San Diego: Harcourt Brace Jovanovich, 1984), 58.

11. G. Deleuze and F. Guattari, *Rhizome* (Paris: Minuit, 1976), cited by Umberto Eco, *Semiotics and the Philosophy of Language,* 81.

12. Eco, *Semiotics,* 81–82.

13. Eco, *Semiotics,* 83. Eco's definition of culture in "Looking for a Logic of Culture" anticipates the changing network of the rhizomatic mode of conjecture: "Culture structures (the way in which a given society organizes the world which it perceives, analyses and transforms) are semiotic structures and therefore systems of units each of which can stand for another," 15.

14. Lotman, "Problems in the Typology of Culture," in *Soviet Semiotics,* ed. and trans. Daniel P. Lucid (Baltimore: Johns Hopkins University Press, 1977), 215–16.

15. Ibid.

16. Eco, *Postscript,* 23.

17. Lotman, "Problems," 216–17.

18. Eco, *Postscript,* 68.

19. Eco, *Postscript,* 20.

20. Borges, "Tlon, Uqbar, Orbis Tertius," in *Labyrinths: Selected Stories and Other Writings,* ed. and trans. Donald Yates and James E. Irby (New York: New Directions Books, 1964). The story, by the famous blind Argentine, starts with a search for an encyclopedia of which a copy is found in Buenos Aires. It builds to a description of the imaginary planet of Tlon, which is "surely a labyrinth, but it is a labyrinth devised by men, a labyrinth destined to be deciphered by men." About Jorge of Burgos, Eco says, "I wanted a blind man who guarded a library, . . . and library plus blind man can only equal Borges, also because debts must be paid," in *Postscript,* 28.

21. See Robert Scholes, "A Semiotic Approach to Irony in Drama and Fiction," in *Semiotics and Interpretation* (New Haven: Yale University Press, 1982), 76–77.

22. Scholes, 84–85.

23. Scholes, 85.

24. Eco, *Postscript,* 45.

25. Eco, *Postscript,* 34.

26. White, *Tropics of Discourse: Essays in Cultural Criticism* (Baltimore: Johns Hopkins University Press, 1978), 88.

27. White, 88.

28. Eco, *The Role of the Reader* (Bloomington: Indiana University Press, 1979), passim.

29. Eco, *Role,* 160.

30. Eco, *Role,* 122.

31. Eco, *Role,* 61.

32. Eco, *Role,* 54–55.

33. Scholes, 145.

34. Derrida, "Structure, Sign and Play in the Discourse of the Human Sciences," in *The Structuralist Controversy: The Languages of Criticism and the Sciences of Man,* ed. Richard Macksey and Eugenio Donato, a republication of the 1966 symposium at Johns Hopkins University (Baltimore: Johns Hopkins University Press, 1972).

35. Derrida, "Structure," 249.

36. Derrida, "Structure," 249.

37. Eco, "Logic of Culture," 13.

38. Eco, *Postscript,* 2.

10 Answering Idle Questions: Open and Closed Readers in *The Name of the Rose*

Deborah Parker

In the *Postscript to "The Name of the Rose,"* Umberto Eco writes of his refusal "to answer idle questions on the order of 'Is your novel an open work or not?' "[1] Coming from the theorist of *Opera aperta,* this insistence that such a question is "idle" might surprise the reader. Eco's explanation of his refusal is curt—"How should I know? That is your business, not mine"—but effective as a reminder of how the categories of open and closed function. To designate a novel "open" or "closed" in an absolute sense implies that these categories are attributes of the work alone, not indicators of a method of reading or of a reader's attitude toward a text. Such a decision is precisely "our business," as it was Eco's when he discussed *Finnegans Wake* as an exemplary open work in *Opera aperta.* But this makes the original question more vexatious than "idle"; such a question would simply indicate a mistaken—and, consequently, bothersome—application of Eco's own theory. A better explanation of this idleness might be found by examining the context of Eco's remark. It comes as an introduction to "of all idle questions the most idle" one raised by those who "suggest that writing about the past is a way of eluding the present."[2] To this acme of idleness Eco devotes the rest of the chapter, rephrasing the question ("What does writing a historical novel mean?"), identifying three ways of "narrating the past," and finally setting down the general aims of the historical novel.

Similarly, the question of open or closed can be productively recast. As it stands, in its binary either-or form, one could only answer that *The Name of the Rose* is resolutely closed, a novel which, as Maria Corti writes, "is so lucidly constructed and closed as to respect in a way exceptional today the Aristotelian unities of time, place and action."[3] But if, as Teresa De Lauretis proposes, one understands the concept of the open or closed work not only as an "aesthetic given but as an epistemological fact," the question of how open and closed ideologies function in the novel is a pressing one.[4] The question is idle only if posed as an either-or: *The Name of the Rose* is both closed and open, and the tension between the two positions is central to an interpretation of the novel. Eco, quoting Pousseur, has succinctly declared the open work one that "produces in the interpreter acts of conscious freedom, putting him at the center of a net of inexhaustible relations among which he inserts his own form."[5] Derived from Eco's study of Joyce, Calder, Stockhausen, Pousseur, and other contemporary and near-contemporary artists, this concept is opposed to the traditional closed work, which allows the reader or viewer far less choice in interpretation. The categories are ideal—no work can be completely open or closed—but they function well in making distinctions between kinds of art. Adopting the proper attitude toward an open work has political and social ramifications: the open work denies conventional views of the world, replacing them with a sense of its discontinuity, disorder, and dissonance. Eco sees the alienation attendant on this realization as beneficial, since, from this feeling of crisis, one may derive a new way of seeing, feeling, understanding, and accepting a universe in which traditional relationships have been shattered.

In *The Name of the Rose* the categories of open and closed work on two levels—that of form and that of content—in a way that might be described as paradoxical. Formally, as Maria Corti states, it is determinedly closed. Eco carefully provides the reader with explanations and structures, even if these violate the expectations of detective fiction Eco has so diligently planted in the reader. Although William does not proceed in the inexorable, hyperlogical way of Sherlock Holmes (the novel is, in fact, a record of William's errors and limitations as investigator), by the end of the novel, we are, nonetheless, just as clearly informed of the chain of events. Like its labyrinthine library, *The Name of the Rose* has a clear formal structure, one that virtually forbids us to project one of our own. Whereas Eco seems to forbid us an open attitude by giving us a resolutely closed work, his protagonist William clearly embodies this attitude. William is a remarkably open interpreter of the world and a lucid exponent of the utility of this stance. His conversations with Adso—a suitably closed foil for William's ideas—assume the form of a debate for the reader. Adso's confusion at William's method is somewhat like that of a traditional reader confronted with *Finnegans Wake*. While Adso struggles with doubt, "seeking an auctoritas to which my obedient mind can refer,"[6] William stresses the *use,* not the final truth of signs, and delivers Wittgensteinian quips about the insufficiency and eventual disposability of sign systems.

The Brunellus episode provides our first look at William in action. From a set of tracks in the show, a bit of horsehair on a tree, and a knowledge of what monks read, William deduces that the abbot's horse, Brunellus, has escaped. The success of this calculated risk, which stupefies the search party as well as

Adso, serves as a powerful introduction into the abbey for William, announcing both his arrival and his acumen. His reputation is confirmed. The incident has a great effect on Adso as well, who presents it in his narrative as an example of how William thinks: "This was my master's way. He not only knew how to read the great books of nature, but also knew the way monks read the books of Scripture, and how they thought through them" (20). Adso has the highest praise for William's deductive powers; he remarks on "the power of the truth" and on the "splendid revelation" which is the fruit of this process. Adso's admiration is misplaced, however. William's very Holmesian deductive process does not constitute his "way." Adso's elevation of the incident to paradigmatic status is the first in a series of unreliable analyses on Adso's part, and we must be careful to read through his accurate but naive account of William's thought. Adso is a closed reader, and this colors his narrative (and, ultimately, our reaction to it). He longs for an ordered universe and seizes on William's deductive insights as evidence of such a universe. Despite Adso's determined presentation of William's stance as closed, William's own words imply an open ideology. He begins explaining the Brunellus incident to Adso by reminding him of what he had said earlier: "during our whole journey I have been teaching you to recognize the evidence through which the world speaks to us like a great book" (18). He then invokes Alanus de Insulis as an authority for this perspective. After the explanation, Adso picks up William's metaphor—"he not only knew how to read the great book of nature"—but with a substantial difference: Adso's omission of the word *like* tends to reify the image. William's formulation of this metaphor emphasizes its provisional nature. It is a way of proceeding, a methodology, not the statement of some deep truth. His authority, Alanus, also keeps this distinction: *"omnis mundi creatura/quasi liber et pictura"* (emphasis mine). Adso, however, because of his closed ideology, tends to collapse metaphor into reality.

The difference here is slight, but William's later references to the Brunellus episode show the degree to which his ideas are misrepresented by Adso and the zeal with which he attempts to correct his follower. Adso is an unreliable narrator, but the narration itself is reliable. After a long explanation of heresy (Third Day, Nones), William discusses his inability to know whether the universe is ordered or not. Adso, understandably upset by this blunt exposition of an open attitude, tries to comfort him:

> "Yours is a difficult life," I said.
> "But I found Brunellus," William cried, recalling the horse episode of two days before.
> "Then there is an order in the world!" I cried, triumphant.

"Then there is a bit of order in this poor head of mine," William answered. (244)

Adso misinterprets the Brunellus episode, and William corrects him by reasserting the provisional nature of his epistemological metaphor. An experiential consistency—that his model seems to explain certain facts—is not truth, and William is unwilling to make the leap from metaphor to reality so boldly taken by Adso. The Brunellus episode means one thing to William and quite another to Adso.

The gap between these two interpretations widens as the novel progresses. In a discussion of hypotheses (Fourth day, Vespers), Adso reports another frank account of William's open attitude:

> I line up so many disjointed elements and I venture some hypotheses. I have to venture many, and many of them are so absurd that I would be ashamed to tell them to you. You see, in the case of the horse Brunellus, when I saw the clues I guessed many complementary and contradictory hypotheses.
> . . . Then I understood that the Brunellus hypothesis was the only right one, and I tried to prove it true, addressing the monks as I did. I won, but I might also have lost. The others believed me wise because I won, but they didn't know the many instances in which I have been foolish because I lost. . . . (367)

William's description of the Brunellus episode is not an ineluctable process of deduction; logic is less important than proposing many possibilities. This frustrates Adso, who demands a "single answer." William continues his commentary on the Brunellus episode: "I imagine many [hypotheses] so I become the slave of none" (367). If an explanation seems to explain the facts, William is pleased; but he never confuses his models with reality.

Just as William is consistent in his ideology, Adso is in his. After the configuration, Adso tries to hearten William by reminding him of his efficacy in other situations—"But it was true that the tracks in the snow led to Brunellus" (599). Again he insists on the episode as a bulwark against the chaos he fears; but William patiently explains: "I behaved stubbornly, pursuing a semblance of order, when I should have known well that there is no order in the universe" (599). Adso reports the conversation faithfully, but his epilogue shows how little he comprehends it.

Despite Adso's enthusiasm for it, the Brunellus episode is not the best example of William's thinking. Its position in the story, its familiarity as a harbinger of a certain kind of story (Holmesian detective adventure), and Adso's unreliability give it a misleading prominence. A better paradigm is

William's discussion of heresy (Third Day, Nones), in which his open perspective is apparent.

What William says in his explanation of heresy is far less important than the way he says it. He attempts to clarify the situation by way of an analogy: "You see, it's as if, over the last two centuries, and even earlier, this world of ours had been struck by a storm of intolerance, hope, and despair, all together" (232). He abruptly shifts his approach, asking Adso to "imagine a river." William pursues this analogy for a time, but upon hearing Adso's confused explanation of it, he drops his metaphor entirely: "Forget this story of the river" (237). This kind of exchange, in which William consciously and deliberately uses metaphor, is fundamental to his open perspective. He constructs and projects an explanation; he does not claim to reveal the truth. His analogizing implies that there are several hypotheses, each of which may be useful in clarifying a situation and none of which possess indisputable truth.

William's second explanatory technique is related to his analogizing but is more subtle. In his discussion of marginality and the sign of leprosy, he again attempts to describe society in terms of useful metaphors. Unlike the discarded river metaphor, however, these have a relational, rather than an essential, cast. They focus on the position of heretics in relation to other parts of society, not on what the heretics believe. What counts is where you are in relation to groups in power, not what you are. "Scratch the heresy and you will find the leper" (239)—essences, or heretical beliefs, are not at stake in this game; position and relation, signified by leprosy here, are the motive forces. This relational cast of mind is further explored by William:

> "How can I discover the universal bond that orders all things if I cannot lift a finger without creating an infinity of new entities? For with such a movement all the relations of position between my finger and all other objects change. The relations are the ways in which my mind perceives the connections between single entities, but what is the guarantee that this is universal and stable?" (243)

At issue here are the primary assumptions of William's open perspective. His metaphoric explanations are useful but unsatisfying: "the most we can do is look more closely" (242). William's open methodology is based upon a construction or projection of order on the world by metaphor and hypothesis. By definition, it cannot guarantee universality or stability. Throughout the novel, William will return to the issues raised in this section, but he does not shift his basic position. His final words to Adso as the abbey burns are essentially a restatement of what he has enacted here:

> What I did not understand was the relation among signs. . . . I behaved
> stubbornly, pursuing a semblance of order, when I should have known well
> that there is no order in the universe. . . . The order that our mind imagines
> is like a net, or like a ladder, built to attain something. But afterward, you
> must throw the ladder away, because you discover that, even if it was useful,
> it was meaningless. (599–600)

The emphasis on relation rather than essence and the implicit assertion of the
metaphoric or constructed basis of order are familiar. William again indulges
his passion for multiple analogies in explanation—first order as a "net"
(which is the image Eco himself uses in *Opera aperta* to describe his perspective), then as a "ladder."[7] The necessity of throwing away the ladder, or
discarding the metaphor, is bluntly asserted here under the humorous aegis of
the German "mystic" Wittgenstein. The only real difference between this
final, pithy statement of William's open perspective and earlier conversations
with Adso is one of knowing and knowing deeply and well. At the end of the
investigation William returns to the fundamental assumptions of his methodological stance, not, in some ephiphanic way to know that place for the
first time, but to "look more closely."[8]

The other characters in *The Name of the Rose* function as closed foils to
William, allowing us to see clearly his open perspective. Like Tolstoy's
unhappy families, all the closed characters are closed in different ways. Adso
ardently seeks the truth, which he equates with authority. He is incapable of
living with the doubts so liberally sown by William. His inability to
understand William benefits the reader; without his questions, we would
have many fewer or no explanations from William. Adso is a structural device
to ease the delivery of William's ideas.[9] Despite Adso's faithful transmission
of what William says, he himself is unchanged. Adso, writing decades after
the events at the abbey, awaits a death which he imagines will offer a return to
"dumb silence," to a prelinguistic state in which "all differences will be
forgotten" and which would provide him with the certainty he so fervently
desires. The dominant image of Adso's "Last Page" is his retrieval of scraps
from the library, whose origins he dutifully traces: "I studied them with
love," he writes, "as if destiny had left me this bequest, as if having identified
the destroyed copy were a clear sign from heaven that said to me: Tolle et lege"
(609). Adso never relinquishes his faith in design, in authority, in closure.
His reconstruction of a much smaller library from the fragments gathered at
the site of the greater one reveals the extent to which Adso, even in his old
age, continues to seek signs of order and design in the universe.

Bernard Gui, the inquisitor, displays a more knowing and manipulative
closure. To Adso, frustrated by what he perceives as William's inability to

distinguish between Spirituals, saints, and heretics (which he attributes to William's having lost the assistance of God), Gui's arrival represents the possibility of a swift reestablishment of the discriminating power necessary for order: "I despaired of my master and caught myself thinking, 'I was on the side of that truth that inspired Bernard Gui', " (368). Reading through Adso's perceptions, however, provides a strikingly different picture of Gui. His search for truth is a pragmatic and expedient method of furthering the aims of the papal court at Avignon. Remigio, Salvatore, and the girl are doomed as heretics, but Gui must employ considerable inquisitorial skill to bring about the confession he desires. His conclusions are set; only the means of execution are in question.

Ubertino, like Gui, seems to offer Adso an alternative. For Adso, his ability to make distinctions is an immense relief from William's relentlessly shifting hypotheses. His closure is based on mystery and prophetic insight, and he advises William to give up his open perspective: "Mortify your intelligence, learn to weep over the wounds of the Lord, throw away your books" (68). Ubertino wants William to submit to authority, to one interpretation of everything. He seems to recall another William, one who had not been corrupted by Bacon and Occam, and he seeks to call this William back.

Throughout the novel, these characters serve to create a dialogue between open and closed; but it is Jorge, William's antithesis, whose presence provokes the sharpest exchanges. His first appearance in the book sparks a heated debate with William on the value of metaphor. But it is in his final confrontation with William that the arguments for an open perspective are most clearly stated. In the moments before Jorge's suicide and the fire, William's perspective triumphs hands down over that of Jorge, and it does so in an important way—by revealing that Jorge's closed system is based on choice, a blunt assertion of the will, an axiom, not on some received, incontrovertible bit of truth. Jorge has either repressed or is oblivious to the knowledge that at the center of his system lies an ideological stance, and it is the clash between these two systems that we witness in the finis Africae. Jorge justifies his actions by invoking not so much truth but necessity. He fears the discovery of the lost *Poetics* not because of what it is but because of what it can do:

> But on the day when the Philosopher's word would justify the marginal jests of the debauched imagination, or when what has been marginal would leap to the center, every trace of the center would be lost. (578)

The metaphors of marginality and centrality are those used by William in his earlier discussion of heresy. What this discussion—which, significantly, takes place in what has become the center of the mystery, the finis Africae—reveals is that the reliance of Jorge on authority ("When you are in doubt, you must turn to an authority, to the words of a father or of a doctor; then all reason for doubt ceases" [151].) is actually a decision on how the world shall be read. It makes up the rules of a vast interpretive game. William and Jorge are faced with the same problem—how to read the world—and each must project or construct a method. The difference lies in Jorge's insistence on one and only one hypothesis and in his tendency to act as if he had forgotten this primary act of projection. He has raised an epistemological metaphor to the order of truth. Put in Nietzsche's terms, Jorge has raised an illusion to the status of truth by forgetting that it is an illusion. [10]

This exchange goes far beyond a simple critique of Jorge. What is apparent in the finis Africae is not a revelation of truth but a decision regarding what system one will use in understanding the world. Eco, as he has done in his critical works, clearly distinguishes between methodological and ontological conceptions of structure: between William's open *use* of projections and constructions, and the claim of Lévi-Strauss' brand of structural anthropology to the discovery of existing, even transcendent, structures in reality. [11]

William stands alone in the novel as the exponent and defender of the open faith, vanquishing Jorge and even surviving Adso's incomprehension. This exponent of aperture, however, is in sharp contrast to the "Aristotelian" closure of the book itself. We read of the virtues of William's attitude, but we do not experience them as we would reading *Finnegans Wake* or hearing Stockhausen. This discrepancy remains: Why has Eco chosen to deliver what seems a pitch for aperture in a resolutely closed form?

The answer is implied in Eco's discussion of the modern and postmodern novel in his *Postscript*. There he defines *postmodern* as "an ideal category—or better still, a Kunstwollen, a way of operating. We could say that every period has its own postmodernism, just as every period would have its own mannerism." [12] The postmodern novel recognizes that the past "must be revisited: but with irony, not innocently." *Opera aperta's* avant-garde sentiments, its manifesto-like quality in which it trumpeted "acts of free consciousness" with clear social and political ramifications, constitute a usable past for Eco, and *The Name of the Rose* is a record of one of these ironic postmodern visits. Teresa De Lauretis has commented on Eco's tendency to revise *Opera aperta* in each of its three editions: "There are therefore not one but three *Opere aperte* by Eco, the reader of himself." [13] *The Name of the Rose*, in its own way, is also a revision of *Opera aperta:* Eco has again visited his past to re-situate the gesture of eighteen years earlier.

A quick look at what happened to the avant-garde in Italy in these eighteen years is helpful here. Shortly after the publication of *Opera aperta,* a group of artists and critics, including Eco, formed Gruppo 63, whose fundamental purpose was "making art reflect in its form the social and economic conditions which it inhabited."[14] Their proceedings—and, consequently, their advant-garde agenda—received widespread media attention. The group praised "experimental works, novels that caused scandal and were rejected by the mass audience."[15] Literature was given a privileged position. In it, and not through direct political action, lay hope for society—a revolutionary cognition was anticipated. The second meeting of the group, in 1965, produced a shift in attitude. The old equation between popularity and worthlessness in literature was being challenged by the success of Gruppo 63 itself. The avant-garde had become an integral (or, at least, accepted) part of Italian society and was itself in danger of becoming a tradition. Eco called for a reexamination of the "dichotomy between . . . a work for popular consumption and a work for provocation," an analysis from "another point of view."[16] This dichotomy, though general, clearly includes the closed and the open work. The decline of Gruppo 63 came in 1968–69. The general strike and student unrest of 1968 offered new possibilities for social and political change. The rationale for Gruppo 63 slipped away, and the Gruppo itself was outflanked by student radicals and striking workers.[17] This new threat of irrelevance added to the existing threat of being coopted, of being perceived as having a safe niche in the society it wished to transform (many of its members had academic posts, its artists achieved a measure of fame, a large publishing house—Feltrinelli—produced its literature, and it had acquired a periodical, *Il Verri*). Its demise was reported and analyzed by its own members in the pages of the periodical it had founded, *Quindici.*

In the frame of *The Name of the Rose,* the transcription of the Abbé Vallet's volume refers to this bit of artistic history:

> there was a widespread conviction that one should write only out of a commitment to the present, in order to change the world. Now, after ten years or more, the man of letters (restored to his loftiest dignity) can happily write out of pure love of writing . . . for sheer narrative pleasure. (xviii)

The retreat from action hinted at here is an echo of that widespread retreat in 1968 by the radical thinkers of Gruppo 63; but it is an echo amplified by the determination of this flight into a literature "gloriously lacking in any relevance for our day, atemporally alien to our hopes and certainties" (xix). It is a step away from the tendentious component of the open work toward entertainment.

What the tension between open content and closed form may imply, then, is that the theorist of the open work has recognized two things: that the world is more resistant to the construction and projection involved in the open "acts of conscious freedom"; and that the old retrograde, closed form has a charm and an interest that readers and writers are unwilling to lose. *Opera aperta*, like other avant-garde works, called for destruction of the past. It is clear, though, that the past has claims on us. Our visits to it cannot be innocent of irony, of even an extremely sophisticated version of sentimentality; but we still find it worth our while. The closed work is, as William's discussions of aperture with Jorge imply, simply a construction or projection on reality become so familiar that its metaphoric status is forgotten, and as with other metaphors of cognition—William's Wittgensteinian ladder—it ought to be thrown away. Yet we like this ladder. In fact, it has a crucial function: closed and open do not cancel but instead complement each other.

Notes

1. Eco, *Postscript to "The Name of the Rose,"* trans. William Weaver (San Diego: Harcourt Brace Jovanovich, 1984), 73.

2. Eco, *Postscript,* 71.

3. Corti, "E' un'opera chiusa," *L'Espresso*" (10 October 1980). All translations of Corti and De Laureti's are my own.

4. De Lauretis, *Umberto Eco* (Florence: La-Nuova Italia [I] Castorol, 1981), 16.

5. Eco, *Opera aperta* (Milan: Bompiani, 1962), 36. Translation mine.

6. Umberto Eco, *The Name of the Rose,* trans. William Weaver (New York: Warner Books, 1984), 294. All subsequent quotations are from this edition.

7. Eco, *Opera aperta,* 9.

8. Teresa De Lauretis contends that William's understanding that the universe is open comes only at the end of his investigation; "What he discovers at the end is that the work is open, that there is not an order in the universe" *Umberto Eco,* 85. I find this contention hard to accept, since William himself says "I behaved stubbornly, pursuing a semblance of order, when I should have known well that there is no order in the universe." Throughout the narrative William implies that he understands the open perspective: "In order for there to be a mirror of the world, it is necessary that the world have a form" (136). But this misreading is interesting because it is indicative of the disjunction between the detective novel form and the very different type of investigation that William is involved in. One of Adso's functions is to place the generic grid of detective fiction on the events surrounding William. A reader sensitive to the generic markers that the story provides would expect an almost epiphanic moment at the end of the story.

9. Eco describes Adso's function in the *Postscript:* "Adso was very important to me. From the outset I wanted to tell the whole story (with its mysteries, its political

and theological events, its ambiguities) through the voice of someone who experiences the events, records them all with the photographic fidelity of an adolescent, but does not understand them (and will not understand them fully even as an old man, since he then chooses a flight into a divine nothingness, which was not what his master had taught him)—to make everything understood through the words of one who understands nothing" (34).

10. *The Philosophy of Nietzsche,* ed. Geoffrey Clive (New York: Mentor, 1962), 506.

11. Eco's "methodological" rather than "ontological" conception of structuralism and semiotics was developed primarily in response to the view prevalent in the late 1960s, promoted by Lévi–Strauss' essays on anthropology, that structural analysis served ultimately to reveal the perennial laws that govern the working of the human mind. Eco's disagreement with this position is documented in great detail in *La struttura assente* (Milano: Bompiani, 1968). See also a summary of Eco's position in David Robey, "Umberto Eco," *Writers & Society in Contemporary Italy,* ed. Michael Caesar and Peter Hainsworth (Leamington Spa, Warwickshire: Berg Publishers, 1984), 76.

12. Eco, *Postscript,* 66.

13. De Lauretis, 13.

14. Christopher Wagstaff, "The Neo-avant-garde," in Caesar and Hainsworth, 39, 59.

15. Eco, *Postscript,* 61.

16. Ibid., 63.

17. Wagstaff, "Neo-avant-garde," 37.

POSTSCRIPT

The Name of the Rose as Popular Culture

Roger Rollin

I was of that first generation which grew up after the war, who were able to think simultaneously about Disney and Shakespeare, or Beethoven and the Beatles.
—UMBERTO ECO[1]

The Problem of Popularity

Personal popularity is the golden fleece of the callow, sought by many an adolescent but found by few. Mature men and women, in the main, have given up on the quest, though few of us, doubtless, would object if somehow it came our way. In reality's cold light adults recognize that popularity is compounded of knowledge and love, and that most people will neither know them nor love them. And so, we wince at the pathos of Willy Loman, that indefatigable seeker of popularity, whose fate it is never to be well known or well liked.

Among adults it is chiefly entertainers and politicians who actively continue to seek popularity. Some of them may do so for the same psychological reasons that youths pursue personal popularity—to upgrade their identities and reinforce their egos. But surely for most entertainers and politicians, popularity is simply a career necessity: whether it is show biz or political biz, one has to be both known and loved. Popularity, then, becomes a professional more than a psychological desideratum.

Popularity inevitably involves quantification—the greatest number of votes for "Most Popular Senior Girl," the survey that yields the list of "The Ten Most Admired Men," or the movie exhibitors' poll that indicates which movie stars are the current top draws at the box office. As these examples suggest, popularity must be purchased but with various kinds of coin. In the publishing industry, it is mainly the coin of the realm. Warner Brothers, the American publishers of the paperback of *The Name of the Rose* (hereafter *Rose*) purchased the rights for $500,000, then to that sum added $100,000 for advertising—in major metropolitan newspapers, in *People* and *US* magazines, in forty U.S. college newspapers, in six urban transit systems, and in bookstore displays and giveways.[2]

However purchased, popularity is to some extent transferable. The wife of the President of the United States invariably makes the list of "The Ten Most Admired Women," regardless of what she is or does. Some tickets for the film version of *Rose* were purchased by those who read the novel or merely heard that the movie was based on a best-seller. Of course, many more movie tickets than books must be sold before the film version of *Rose* comes to be regarded as a "popular" film by the movie industry—that is, one that drew larger audiences than its current competition but also audiences comparable in size to those that patronized the more financially successful movies of the past decade or so.

Although popularity may simply be a matter of the bottom line for the producers of popular culture, students of popular culture as yet have been unable to agree about what the term *popular* means. The *OED* defines it as: "4. The fact or condition of being approved, beloved, or admired by the people, or by many people; favour or acceptance with the people." But "the people," who? And how many is "many"? One of Umberto Eco's heroes, Woody Allen, has said somewhere that just once he would like to make a movie that everyone wanted to see. Such a remark may well give pause to all those fans and scholars of the cinema who think of Allen as "popular," both as an actor and as a filmmaker. Since he seems to be able to finance the films he wishes to make (unlike a Robert Altman, for example), are we not to assume that his films are "popular," that is, that they are commercial successes? And yet, Allen's *Sleeper* was no *Star Wars* at the box office, nor was *Annie Hall* by any means an *E.T.* Regardless of the art and the craft with which they are made, few critics (even those who hail him as a genius) would claim that Allen's films are anything other than brilliant examples of "popular culture"—that is, commercial culture, culture meant to make a profit.

Agatha Christie mystery novels turn a handsome profit over time. Only occasionally best-sellers in the United States, they are prime examples of that publishing-industry phenomenon, the "steady seller." Some popular culture scholars argue, however, that detective fiction, though it exhibits the salient characteristics of popular culture (it is eminently accessible, more entertaining than illuminating, more "conventional" than "inventional," and so on), remains pretty much a coterie phenomenon, like modern jazz or dirt-track racing. Not even all "mass culture" is "popular." Witness the fate of most new U.S. television series that are introduced with such fanfare each fall. Yet the sheer numbers of those who watch a cop show that is dropped by its network after a few months far exceed the number who have even heard of Eco's novel, much less read it. *Rose*, however, is a famous "best-seller," while the TV series that was watched by merely ten million people each week is a flop. The medium, then, is the measure; when it comes to culture, popularity is less a matter of qualification than it is of an equation: P(opularity) = C(ornering) X% of the M(arket) in a given ME(dium) [where X represents more than the minimum number of consumers needed to ensure a reasonable return on the investment in the popular-culture artifact].

Tedious though such formulas may be, the alternative—defining popular culture qualitatively—is fraught with difficulties. Eco himself, in spite of his professed admiration for popular culture (see the epigraph to this essay), has exacerbated these difficulties. With allowances for an academican's put-on, he has revealed that he has a "secret formula" for writing best-sellers. Moreover, anybody, he has said, "can write a best-seller; if you cannot, it is because you have not read well."[3] On the other hand, he has also taken pains to stress the difference

> between the text that seeks to produce a new reader and the text that tries to fulfill the wishes of readers already to be found in the street. In the latter case we have the book written, constructed, according to an effective, mass production formula; the author carries out a kind of market analysis and adapts his work to its results.[4]

This latter kind of hack, Eco implies, he is not. He himself is, rather, the kind of writer who "plans something new," who "conceives [of] a different kind of reader," who is "a philosopher who senses the patterns of the *Zeitgeist*" (*Postscript*, 49). This, of course, is scarcely a profile for a best-selling author, nor from it can a plausible "secret formula" that could explain the popularity of *Rose* be extrapolated. Attempts to describe popular fiction *qualitatively* and formally—that is, in terms of convention and inventions or various combinations of the two—invariably run into the problem that many novels exhibiting such qualities never achieve popularity.

When it comes to defining the *popular* in "popular culture," then, quantification will invariably crunch qualification. Viewed formally, *Rose* does not appear to be the stuff of which best-sellers typically are made; yet *Rose* has the numbers. It makes no difference whether Eco's novel was, as the *New York Times* alleged, "one of the great unread sellers of recent years"; the book *was* bought, and bought in extremely impressive quantities. Undoubtedly, some bought it for intellectual chic; undoubtedly, others bought it but never opened it or read only a few pages. (Two bookstore managers, independently of each other, volunteered to me that a number of their customers had mentioned they had not finished the novel.) Nevertheless, if a novel considerably more accessible than *Rose* must invariably run into stiff competition from other potential best-sellers, it would be almost impossible for Eco's book to have made the list at all unless the enthusiasm of those who read *Rose* with pleasure outweighed the disgruntlement of those who found themselves unable to finish it.

Still, Eco's novel remains an improbable best-seller at best, and speculation about "man's fascination with puzzles" or his "pleasure in the imposition of order upon disorder and meaning upon mystery" or his "penchant for alternate worlds" remains just that—speculation. It does not appreciably advance our understanding of the phenomenon of book-selection; nor does it go far toward explaining how people psychologically "process" a novel; nor does it clarify the social dynamics of the interpersonal recommendation of books.

Fortunately, there are marked advantages to inquiring into the popularity of an artifact such as *Rose* over investigating the popularity of a person. Charisma does not readily submit itself to testing. Moreover, human beings, subject to space and time, continually deconstruct and reconstruct themselves. The arrangement of ink on the pages of Eco's novel is static, however much in flux may be those who mentally process that arrangement. Considerations such as these dictated that any attempt even to begin to solve the mystery of *Rose*'s popularity would have to focus on its *readers* more than on the text itself. Accordingly, I devised a modest experiment. Its modesty was a function of constraints of time, funding, and the experimenter's limited expertise in matters social scientific. I would have preferred to design something along the lines of Norman N. Holland's reader-response project, complete with the psychological testing of a group of the novel's readers, free-association interviews focusing on *Rose* in depth, and the correlation of subjects' psychological profiles with their responses to the text.[5] Such an experiment, in addition to being beyond the resources at hand, might be more likely (as Holland's account suggests) to uncover significant differences in readers' responses than significant likenesses—and my interest was chiefly in consensus, in the possible causes of a best-seller. Thus the only procedure that seemed feasible was that of a questionnaire distributed to a target sample and voluntarily completed by those who claimed to have read Eco's book.

A Modest Experiment Described

Although I could not employ the experimental methods developed by Holland, it seemed to me that reader-response theory still constituted the most reliable guide to developing an instrument that might yield robust findings that could contain clues to the mystery of *Rose*'s popularity. As the questionnaire began to take shape, however, it became clear that there were limits on the extent to which what was essentially a social scientific instrument might elicit essentially psychoanalytic data. For example, reader-response theory postulates that a reader of Eco's novel will unconsciously draw upon characteristic personal fantasies during the reading process.[6] How can one devise a question that might get at such sensitive matters without such a question being perceived as threatening? The experiment would have to rely on the kindness of strangers, and strangers generous enough to take the trouble to fill out a questionnaire must not feel threatened or burdened.

Accordingly, I made the questionnaire (see pages 162-63) brief and endeavored to bury potentially threatening questions among more innocuous ones (such as questions 5 and 10). Similarly, the entry into the questionnaire (questions 1–3, and exit, questions 12–14) were meant to disarm the respondent and at the same time yield demographic data that might shed some light on *Rose*'s popularity. (Those data did not, in fact, shed much light—but it is necessary to know that they did not.)

In retrospect, it appears probable that such efforts to make the questionnaire less threatening were not entirely successful. For example, 42% of the respondents either left blank Question 6 ("Which character . . . is most like you?") or denied that *any* of Eco's characters were like themselves. Some denials were so vehement as to raise the suspicion that the respondent doth protest too much: "Characters *all* overdrawn—each so dramatic, the fiction is difficult to relate to oneself and I don't want to locate myself in any novel." Males were the most vigorous deniers, although males and females avoided Question 6 almost equally (8/6). Question 6 was designed to probe the psychological phenomenon known as "projection"—the unconscious imposition of one's own personality traits on another. Question 11 ("Which character . . . would you most want to be like?"), on the other hand, sought to get at the opposite phenomenon, "introjection," the unconscious imposition of the traits of others on oneself.

Projection and introjection are fundamental to the complex psychological process of identification. That 37% of the respondents avoided Question 11 and 24% denied wanting to be like any of Eco's characters may well indicate that this question was consciously or unconsciously perceived as threatening, a possible revelation of one's inner life. Long ago, Sigmund Freud observed that people are reticent about their inner lives and tend to be ashamed of their fantasies.[7] Because of the importance of personal fantasy-recreation to readers' gratification, however, I sought to probe that aspect of respondents' mind-sets without alienating them. Accordingly, I asked them what I hoped was a

SURVEY OF READERS OF "THE NAME OF THE ROSE"

I am doing a study of Umberto Eco's novel, *The Name of the Rose*. If you have read this book, would you please take a few minutes to respond to the questionnaire below? (If you haven't read it, but know someone who has and who might be willing to complete the questionnaire, kindly pass it along to them.)

QUESTIONNAIRE

1. How did you obtain your copy of *The Name of the Rose*?
   Bought (24)   Borrowed (9)
2. In which version did you read *The Name of the Rose*?
   Hardbound (15)   Paperback (18)
3. What prompted you to obtain *The Name of the Rose*? (Check more than one if appropriate.)

   Mail advertisement (1)   TV review/feature___
   Newspaper advertisement ___   Radio review/feature (3)
   Magazine advertisement (2)   Magazine review/article (14)
   Someone's recommendation (17)   Newspaper review/article (5)
   Other ___ (skimming the book: 2)
4. Which elements of the novel would you say weighed most heavily in your decision to read it? (Please list in order of priority: 1, 2, 3, etc.)

   The medieval setting (123 pts.)   The "detective story" aspect (101 pts.)
   The religious context (68 pts.)   Umberto Eco's reputation (33 pts.)
   The character (and narrator),   The character, "Brother William
      "Adso of Melk" (15 pts.)   of Baskerville" (14 pts.)
   Other (please name or describe):

   _____

5. Did you finish the book?   Yes (30)   No (3)
6. Which character in the novel would you say is most like you? (Blank or "none": 14)

   (Adso: 9) (William: 9) In what respects?
   (Adso: youthfulness; innocence or naiveté; curiosity; involvement)
   (William: logic; objectivity; competence; success)
7. If there was anything you *disliked* about *The Name of the Rose*, briefly indicate what that was, using the back of this sheet if necessary:
   (Length: 5; religious history/theology: 4; Latinity: 3; plus 11 assorted complaints)
8. Have you ever dreamed (or day-dreamed) about (check as many as apply):
   Living in the Middle Ages (12)
   Solving a mystery (15)
   Devoting your life to some religious calling (17)

9. Please indicate what you *liked most* about *The Name of the Rose*, using the back of this sheet if necessary:
   (Historical verisimilitude: 16)
   (Eco's handling of plot, characterization, style, etc.: 11)
   (Mystery/puzzle aspect: 8)
10. If the contemplated movie version of *The Name of the Rose* is made, do you think you might like to see it?   Yes (17)   No (5)   Not sure (9)
    Your reasons?_____
11. Which character in the novel would you most want to be like?
    (William: 10; Adso: 3)   Your reasons? ("None": 8; "Don't know": 3;
                                                            left blank: 9)
12. Your age range: Under 18 __   18-25 (1)   26-35 (13)
    36-45 (12)   46-55 (3)   55-65 (2)   Over 65 (2)
13. Your sex: female (16)   male (17)
14. Your occupation_____
15. If a follow-up could contribute importantly to this study, would you be willing to undergo a 4-5 minute interview?   No __   Yes __
    by phone only __?   in person only __?

OPTIONAL: Name _____Phone_____

Thank you for your help.

less threatening question (no. 8) about their dreams and daydreams. But fully one-third denied (or avoided denying) ever having had a medieval, mystery, or ecclesiastical fantasy—a probable indication that this question, too, roused some unconscious defenses.

Approximately 250 copies of the finished questionnaire were sent out to the faculty, staff, and graduate students of Clemson University's College of Liberal Arts. Thirty copies each were left at our small town's bookstore, its magazine shop, and its used bookstore. By the time the completed forms had stopped trickling in (the process took more than a month), 33 usable questionnaires were in hand. As might be expected, the sampling technique used did not by any means yield a cross section of the American public. Of the respondents, slightly over half were members of the teaching profession; the rest were students, professionals, business or clerical people, and retirees. Fully 76% were in the 26–45 age bracket. Gender, at least, was happily divided, almost 50/50. (Gender, incidentally, seems to have played hardly a role in most responses, perhaps giving credence to the hypothesis that, aside from certain kinds of reading such as Barbara Cartland romantic tales and Zane Grey westerns, novel-reading is more of an androgynous than a strongly sex-typed activity.)

Given the academic bias of the sample, it is not surprising that two-thirds of the respondents indicated that they were prompted to obtain a copy of *Rose* because of reviews they had read or heard. Some of these were among the 50% that reported also being influenced by the recommendations of others—yet another confirmation of the importance of word-of-mouth advertising to the success of those popular-culture artifacts that feature direct costs to the consumer. What motivates readers to take such risks as spending their money and even recommending that others spend money (as well as their time) is, apparently, a cluster of factors.

A Calculated Popularity

With the limitations of the investigation's instrument and its skewed sample as disclaimers, this essay suggests that *Rose's* popularity is due to its poly-valent or overdetermined character, and further, that this overdeterminancy appears to be the result of the author's contrivance.

By *polyvalent* or *overdetermined* here is meant that Eco's book especially lends itself to being positively processed by a wide if distinctive range of readers. Whereas a Harlequin romantic novel might be said to be "underde-termined," written to a very strict formula for an audience defined in highly specific demographic terms; and whereas a Jackie Collins novel might be said to be "determined," written to a somewhat more relaxed formula that appeals to men as well as women susceptible to soft-core sex; *Rose* is a compound of formulas that transcends formula, offering something, if not for everyone, at least for a sizable group of readers who cherish a fantasy of innocence or a fantasy of experience, a would-be Adso of Melk or William of Baskerville.

By virtue of its vision of the medieval, its detective-story plot, its intellectual texture (a synthesis of philosophy, theology, and semiotics), and its accessible protagonists, *Rose* offers readers an array of materials for reinforc-ing and/or developing their individual identities. Furthermore, as became evident after I had read Eco's *Postscript to "The Name of the Rose"* (well after the last questionnaire had been returned), the novel's overdeterminancy has been deliberately brought about by Eco himself, a writer sufficiently desirous of selling his book as to defer to his Italian publisher with regard to its title.[8] If, that is, we can trust the teller of the tale; if *Postscript* is not, in fact, an elaborate put-on, yet another of Eco's fictions written as much in self-justification and self-defense as by way of an explanatory afterword, brought out to satisfy an insistently curious public.

For the purposes of this essay, I intend to take *Postscript* at face value and to cite it liberally in order to underscore the deliberation behind *Rose's* polyvalency.

> *Postscript:* The fact is that everyone has his own idea, usually corrupt, of the Middle Ages.[9]

Whether or not they shared Eco's obsession with the period, a major appeal of *Rose* for my respondents was their perception of it as a "historical novel." When asked to rate those elements of the book that weighed most heavily in their decision to read it (Question 4), the item, "medieval setting," received the highest score (123 points in a system that assigns six points to a first-priority rating, five to a second-priority rating, and so on). Moreover, given the opportunity to indicate what they liked best about the novel (Question 9), 49% replied, in effect, that its historical verisimilitude had appeal for them. If most of these readers did indeed have a "corrupt" idea of the Middle Ages, as Eco maintains, his own vision proved to be one they were readily able to install in the "defective" one's place.

> *Postscript:* . . . I said to myself that, since the Middle Ages were my day-to-day fantasy, I might as well write a novel actually set in that period.[10]

Although none of the respondents admitted to be thus preoccupied with the medieval, 36% of them acknowledged having dreamed or daydreamed about living in that era. Medieval fiction or medieval pseudofact, *Rose* participates in a popular literary tradition that goes back to such Renaissance chapbooks as *Palladin of England*, to such nineteenth-century romances as Scott's *Ivanhoe*, to modern best-sellers such as *The Silver Chalice*, and to all of those films, like *Excalibur*, set in a glamorized Middle Ages. Eco's audience, then, could be said to have been ready-made: medieval is "in" and in fact has been "in" almost since the Middle Ages themselves.

> *Postscript:* . . . to tell a story you must first of all construct a world.[11]

That Eco amply succeeded in doing so is certainly suggested by this modest experiment as well as by *Rose's* sales. A number of respondents indicated that they particularly enjoyed the medieval "ambience," "the mood of the abbey," the "careful description," "the way the time-place setting was handled," the capturing of "the flavor of the middle ages," "the fine evocation of [the] medieval atmosphere," the sense of entering into the medieval mind-set. The creative writer, says Freud, "creates a world of phantasy which he takes very seriously—that is, which he invests with large amounts of emotion—while separating it sharply from reality."[12] That world is re-created in the reading process, in part as a way of "correcting" the deficiencies readers perceive in their own reality, its lack of romance, for example, or its drab secularism. One respondent, a middle-aged physician, became so caught up in Eco's most complex "construction," the Library, that he "nearly wept when it burned." On the other hand, another reason why Eco's world works for some readers is, paradoxically, that it is perceived as a threatening fantasy.

> *Postscript:* And since I wanted [readers] to feel as pleasurable the one thing that frightens me—namely, the metaphysical shudder—I had only to choose [from among the model plots] the most metaphysical and philosophical: the detective novel.[13]

Put another way, the first appealing thing about a detective novel is that we know someone is going to get killed. We also know it won't be us. But we seldom know who, when, where, or, of course, whodunit. It was the detective-story aspect of *Rose* that respondents reported as being the second most important factor in their decision to read it (Question 4), and eight readers volunteered the information that its mystery or puzzle aspect was what they liked most about the book (Question 9)—"a rousing good mystery." The frisson of being a voyeur of death may be equalled only by that of spiritual sadism—forcing others to reveal their guilty secrets. The fictional detective enjoys both privileges, which may be why 46% of the respondents admitted that they themselves had fantasized about "solving a mystery" (Question 8)—even more than had daydreamed about living in the Middle Ages.

> *Postscript:* It is no accident that the book starts out as a mystery (and continues to deceive the ingenous reader until the end, so the ingenuous reader may not even realize that this is a mystery in which very little is discovered and the detective is defeated).[14]

The fact that almost twice as many respondents reported having fantasies about solving a mystery as indicated that what they most like about *Rose* was its detective-story quality can be explained by a certain disappointment in the novel's outcome, the sense of being somewhat cheated of the genre's conventional pleasures. However, in response to Question 7 (whether there was anything about *Rose* they did not like), there were no clear indications of such disappointment, and only one respondent faulted the novel as a detective story—and that perhaps a shade too wittily: "The detective quality was elementary." It is possible, then, that Eco himself underestimates the satisfaction readers gain from discovering that the murderer is a blind man and the motive is a legendary and priceless manuscript. It is also possible that, in accordance with the principle of overdetermination, a given reader's pleasure in *Rose's* medievalness, for example, might well serve to counterbalance any sense that Eco ends up deconstructing his own mystery.

Indeed, the latter possibility may find support in the fact that the more traditional murder mysteries of Ellis Peters, though popular enough to have become a seven-volume series, have never approached *Rose's* popularity—its 1,356,000 paperback copies in print up through 1985 in the United States and Canada alone, for example.[15] (Although the earlier novels in this medieval mystery series antedate the writing of *Rose*, in his various references to the sources and influences of his novel in *Postscript*, Eco does mention Peters.)

Peters' detective, Brother Cadfael, is a former Crusader turned Benedictine monk at a monastery in the vicinity of present-day Shropshire. The author's effort to construct a world—in this case, the world of twelfth-century Britain rather than fourteenth-century Italy—is not unsuccessful, but that world lacks the intense theocentricity that lends such verisimilitude to Eco's narrative. *Rose's* "religious context," in fact, ranked third among the factors respondents cited as weighing heavily in their decision to read the novel (Question 4). While four respondents said that *Rose's* religious and theological elements were what they disliked about it (Question 7), seven readers acknowledged having dreamed or daydreamed about devoting their lives to some religious calling (Question 8). Eco, a lapsed Catholic who "found Catholicism anthropologically and philosophically very enlightening,"[16] in *Postscript* has some things to say about the theology and philosophy that went into making *Rose* a novel of ideas (so satisfying to readers in their role as intellectuals, as a number of respondents implied); but he is silent about the psychology of faith. Nevertheless, the reader who at some level gains pleasure from reliving an ecclesiastical fantasy may well be able to find sufficient material for the construction of one in the exhaustive details of Eco's re-creation of the world of 1327.

Given the academic bias of this experiment's sample, it may not be surprising that the fourth most influential factor in respondents' decisions to obtain *Rose* was its author's reputation (Question 4). (By the spring of 1984 even the readers of *Vogue* had been provided with a brief but sophisticated introduction to Umberto Eco as a scholar and an author.) Regardless of the extent to which they were aware of Eco's academic reknown, his skill as a novelist did impress respondents. Asked what they most liked about *Rose*, one-third of them replied in effect that they thought the book was well written, volunteering positive, even enthusiastic responses to Eco's handling of plot, characterization, and/or style (Question 9). Some of those who said they would not likely go to see the movie version of *Rose* (Question 10) gave as their reason the inability of the film medium to "do justice" to a novel. "No movie," said one, could "capture the intellectual wonderment." Such reservations explain why 27% of the respondents simply were not sure they would make an effort to see the Jean-Jacques Annaud film. On the other hand, as an example of what might be called "the inter-media carryover effect," some of the more than half of the respondents who said they would likely see the movie version gave their admiration for the novel as their prime motivation (Question 10). There was also some consensus among respondents with regard to *Rose*'s two principals, William of Baskerville and Adso of Melk.

> *Postscript:* They identified with the innocence of the narrator, and felt
> exonerated even when they did not understand everything.[17]

In response to the "projection" question (Question 6), nine respondents said that Adso was most like themselves, and the same number, William. Qualities typically associated with Adso were those of youth—naiveté, curiosity, impressionability, and involvement. Eco, however, characterizes those who identify with Adso as "unsophisticated readers"—probably not an apt description of the sample in question. What Eco may not be taking into account here is the fantasy factor in identification: even older readers and sophisticated readers can take pleasure in identifying with an innocent, particularly one who happens to be the centered consciousness of the narrative.

> *Postscript:* [Through Adso] I gave [readers] back their fear and trembling in
> the face of sex, unknown languages, difficulties of thought, mysteries of
> political life. . . . These are things I understand now, *apres coup*; but perhaps I
> was then transferring to Adso many of my adolescent fears.[18]

Some respondents who claimed to identify with Adso described him as puzzled and occasionally fearful—"like I would be," according to one respondent. Even the anxiety a text can stimulate can, of course, be a factor contributing to the text's popularity, as the writers of Gothic novels and the makers of horror films (*Rose* has roots in both genres) have always known. Horror films, of course, are especially appealing to adolescents, and the Gothic novel perhaps appeals to the adolescent still lurking within the adult. What attracted one respondent to Eco's novel was "the dark mystery of its superstitious world." For another, "The mood of the abbey and the happenings is easily felt." In creating Adso, Eco (Freud might hypothesize) drew upon "a memory of an earlier experience," "from which there [proceeded] a wish which [found] its fulfillment" in the novel; "altering and disguising" the nature of his "egotistic daydream" he maximized its appeal to the reader,[19] the reader who perceives Adso as a hero-figure, who follows him "through his perilous adventures" enjoys "the true heroic feeling," expressed in the notion that "Nothing can happen to me!" even though circumscribed by physical, social, emotional, and intellectual dangers. The pleasure of vicarious danger, of risk-free mystery, of fear and trembling mastered, is available to the reader of *Rose* just as it is to the many fans of those ubiquitous adventure, espionage, intrigue, and private-eye novels that clog paperback racks. Amid the various reasons given for liking *Rose* (Question 9)—some of them sophisticated in the extreme—almost one-third of the respondents indicated that, for them, the novel had the traditional appeal of the thriller.

> *Postscript:* A text is meant to be an experience of transformation for its readers.[20]

Fear and trembling are also components of most initiation rituals. The events of the novel become, in effect, such rituals for Adso and thus for readers who closely identify with him. In spite of the fact that 27% of the respondents identified most closely with Adso, in response to Question 11 ("Which character . . . would you most want to be like?"), only three chose Adso. (Two of these had also named him as the character most like themselves, with the other seeing herself as more closely resembling William of Baskerville.) Ten respondents wished to be more like William. Of those ten, apparently only three were sufficiently satisfied with their self-images to indicate in response to Question 6 that they saw a good deal of William in themselves. Twice as many respondents *identified* with Adso while *aspiring* to become William—perhaps a case of the child within dreaming of transforming itself into the parent-figure. (Although reliable inferences cannot be drawn from such limited data, the fact that six self-identified "Adsos" expressed a desire to become "Williams" lends support to those reader-response critics who argue that ego-*development* as well as ego-*reinforcement* can be a function of the positive reading experience.)

> *Postscript:* [William of Baskerville's] emotions were all mental, or repressed.[21]

There was more consensus among respondents about William's character than reader-response theory might lead us to expect. The nine respondents who saw something of themselves in him (Question 6) typically referred to his mental discipline—his logic, his objectivity, his capacity to become dispassionate: "I'm very analytical," said one. Eco, as already noted, claims that his detective, in the end, is defeated, but there was little indication that these respondents saw it that way. Indeed, several mentioned that they admired him for his competence and success. *Contra* Eco, Baskerville does (circumstances and their aftermath aside) solve the mystery. Moreover, Eco may not have taken three other factors sufficiently into account: (1) the conventional pattern of the detective-story plot, which climaxes with the anastrophe and the epiphany of the sleuth-hero and which, because it is conventional, a source of expectations, readers are likely to impose on a novel's resolution; (2) the fundamental human desire to merge with successful others such as William; (3) the fundamental human desire to merge with parent figures. "It is characteristic of the young," opines Adso, "to become bound to an older and wiser man not only by the spell of his words and the sharpness of his mind, but also by the superficial form of his body, which proves very dear, like the figure of a father. . . ."[22] Although films having to do with male bonding seem to be especially popular, Eco's novel is less a book about brothers than about an archetypal father and son. Thus it remains true to another of its popular sources, Conan Doyle's accounts of the education of John Watson at the hands of Sherlock Holmes.

> *Postscript:* Poe said that the effect of a work is one thing and the knowledge of the process is another.

Reader-response theory holds that individuals come to *dis*like a text because they are unable to "defend" against it, to protect their egos from its perceived threats; because they find themselves unable to impose some literary category or meaningful interpretation on it; or because they have not been able to use the text to generate acceptable variations upon their identity themes.[24] Eco is aggressively defensive with regard to criticism of his technique. For example, his novel's title, he says, "rightly disoriented the reader" in accordance with his view that "A title must muddle the reader's ideas, not regiment them."[25] Only one of the respondents, however, complained about the title, though several indicated that they found the narrative to be heavy going at times, weighted down by what they felt was an excess of historical or philosophical or ecclesiastical baggage—"Baskerville running on about the categories of Aristotle and mechanical engineering." Eco himself acknowledges that the first hundred pages of the book in particular are "difficult" and "demanding" —deliberately so, he says, for they constitute a kind of "penance or initiation, and if someone does not like them, so much the worst for him."[26] But the author's attitude toward his readers is not, on the whole, as cavalier as this statement might suggest: he is, in fact mindful of the relationship between reading fiction, whether elite or popular, and of the Pleasure Principle.

> *Postscript:* While you write, you are thinking of a reader . . . I wanted the reader to enjoy himself, at least as much as I was enjoying myself. . . . The

ideal reader of *Finnegans Wake* must, finally, enjoy himself as much as the reader of Erle Stanley Gardner. Exactly as much, but in a different way.[27]

"Ideal readers" are, of course, as much an author's fictional creation as any of his dramatis personae. Perhaps more so, because the ur–reader of any text is its author; thus an ideal reader must be some clone of that original. For Eco, this is a sporting reader, one who "would play my game," but who would gracefully lose under the fictive pressure, becoming "the prey of the text."[28] Eco's desire to create his own fit audience, in effect, turns upside down reader-response theory, which holds that it is the readers who create a text—and in *their* own images. Eco characterizes the reading process as a "dialogue [between] the text and its readers,"[29] but reader-response theory holds that a text cannot act, it can only be acted upon. Although respondents gave the impression that they were willing to play Eco's game, their remarks suggest they were not so much the "prey of the text" as its predators. They indicated that they enjoyed the chase (though not always) and that there were some things about their "prey" that they did not wholly admire (its occasional "bravura," its length, its vocabulary and Latinity, its "Wagnerian" ending). Yet the majority found much about the book to admire, and 91% of them pursued their quarry to its conclusion.

> *Postscript:* There is no question that if a novel is amusing, it wins the approval of a public. Now, for a certain period, it was thought that this approval was a bad sign: if a novel was popular, this was because it said nothing new and gave the public only what the public was already expecting. . . . It can be said that the "popularity–lack of value" equation was supported by the polemical attitudes of some writers, including me.[30]

If he has not been forced to eat his book (as Jorge of Burgos was), Eco has eaten a few of his words. He has discovered the truth of what students of popular culture have been saying for some time, that it is possible "to find elements of revolution and contention in works that apparently lend themselves to facile consumption."[31]

That *The Name of the Rose* lent itself to "facile consumption" is not borne out by the results of the experiment described here. Nor does the data suggest that these readers found much that was "revolutionary" or "contentious"—ideologically, at least—in Eco's book. What does seem clear is that in its overdeterminacy, its unique synthesis of the historical novel—the detective story, the novel of ideas, the father-son initiation tale—made *Rose* a book with something for, if not everyone, at least for the many would-be Adsos and Williams among the frequentors of modern scriptoria.

Notes

1. Melik Kaylan, "Umberto Eco . . . Man of the World," *Vogue* 174 (April 1984): 329.

2. Edwin N. McDowell, "New Bloom on the 'Rose,' " *New York Times* (15 June 1984): C26.

3. Albino Castro Filho, "Italy's Unlikely Bestseller," *World Press Review* 31 (March 1984): 60.

4. Eco, *Postscript to "The Name of the Rose,"* trans. William Weaver (San Diego: Harcourt Brace Jovanovich, 1984), 48–49.

5. Norman N. Holland, *5 Readers Reading* (New Haven: Yale University Press, 1975), 41–46.

6. Ibid., 117ff.

7. Freud, "Creative Writers and Daydreaming," *The Standard Edition of the Complete Psychological Works of Sigmund Freud*, trans. James Starchey and others (London: Hogarth Press, 1959), IX, 145.

8. Eco, *Postscript*, 2.

9. Ibid., 77.

10. Ibid., 14.

11. Ibid., 23.

12. Freud, "Creative Writers," 144.

13. Eco, *Postscript*, 53.

14. Ibid., 54.

15. Daniel Goldin, publicity manager for Warner Books; correspondence with the author.

16. Kaylan, "Umberto Eco," 330.

17. Eco, *Postscript*, 34.

18. Ibid., 34.

19. Freud, "Creative Writers," 151, 153.

20. Eco, *Postscript*, 53.

21. Ibid., 35.

22. Umberto Eco, *The Name of the Rose*, trans. William Weaver (San Diego: Harcourt Brace Jovanovich, 1983), 15.

23. Eco, *Postscript*, 11.

24. Holland, *5 Readers Reading*, 113–29.

25. Eco, *Postscript*, 3.

26. Ibid., 41.

27. Ibid., 47, 59.

28. Ibid., 50, 55.

29. Ibid., 47.

30. Ibid., 60.

31. Ibid., 63–64.

Appendix:
A Preliminary Checklist
of English-Language Criticism

Jackson R. Bryer and Ruth M. Alvarez

This listing presents the major published commentary on Eco found in English-language periodicals. It makes no claims to completeness and is based primarily on a list graciously supplied by Mr. Eco himself and on the files of his American publishers, Indiana University Press and Harcourt Brace Jovanovich, to whom we are also grateful for their assistance. We have not listed any item we have not actually seen; but in several instances, we have listed as incomplete references items viewed as clippings. In the case of an incomplete item, we were not able to verify date and other information about it as given on the clipping.

Obviously, the great preponderance of commentary on Eco is in Italian, French, German, and a few other major languages. Because the vast majority of this material was unavailable for verification, we have restricted our listing to the more readily available English-language sources. In those instances where a review or essay deals with Eco among other writers, we have listed the page numbers for the full essay, then, in brackets, the pages dealing with Eco.

Mention should be made of *The Key to "The Name of the Rose"* by Adele J. Haft, Jane G. White, and Robert J. White (Huntington Park, NJ: Ampersand Associates, 1987), which summarizes Eco's ideas on semiotics and medieval thought and includes a chronology of the Middle Ages, an annotated guide to historical and literary references in the novel, notes on the text, and translations of all non-English passages.

I. Essays, Interviews, and Articles

Agena, Kathleen. "The Return of Enchantment." *New York Times Magazine* (November 27, 1983): 66, 68, 72, 74, 76, 79–80. *Brief mention of* The Name of the Rose.

Artigiani, Robert. "The 'Model Reader' and the Thermodynamic Model." *SubStance* 47 (1985): 64–73. *Applies Ilya Prigogine's model of change to Eco's "description of the transition of medieval into modern culture."* The Name of the Rose *is "a casebook examination of cultural transition described in Prigoginian terms, as relevant to the present as to the fourteenth century."*

Bachman, Gideon. "The Name of the Rose." *Sight & Sound* 55 (Spring 1986): 129–31. *Interview in which Eco discusses films in general as well as, specifically, the movie version of* The Name of the Rose.

Balducci, Gioacchino. "Umberto Eco in New York: An Interview." *Communication Quarterly* 24 (Spring 1976): 35–38. *Eco discusses his interest in semiotics and the semiotics of film.*

Bentley, Logan. "The Thorny Issue in Umberto Eco's *The Name of the Rose* Is Murder in the Monastery." *People* 20 (August 29, 1983): 40, 43. *Brief biographical piece which describes the success of the novel.*

Bruss, Elizabeth, and Marguerite Waller. "Interview With Umberto Eco." *Massachusetts Review* 19 (Summer 1978): 409–20. *Eco discusses semiotics, resistance to semiotics in the United States, structuralism, and Marxist theory of superstructure.*

Burgess, Anthony. "Taking the Best Sellers Seriously: Where Sex Meets Self-Improvement." *New York Times Book Review* (June 1, 1986): 3. *Cites* The Name of the Rose *as an atypical best-seller offering "titillation" and "instruction."*

Carluccio, Charles, M.D. "MD Talks With . . . Umberto Eco." *MD* 28 (March 1984): 36, 41, 44. *Eco discusses multiple readings of* The Name of the Rose, *film version, and semiotics.*

——————. "Person to Person—Umberto Eco." *Attenzione Magazine* 6 (April 1984): 64. *Shortened version of* MD *interview.*

Catania, Thomas M. "What Is the Mystery of 'The Name of the Rose'?" *New Catholic World* 228 (July/August 1985): 157–61. *Sees Eco as making the novel "a complex metaphor for his epistemological and aesthetic musings"; his "fundamental concern" is "the accessibility of truth to mind and art."*

Chase, Donald. "Cover Story—A Movie with Monks and Murder." *USA Today* (March 31, 1986): 1D, 2D. *Account of filming of* The Name of the Rose—*interviews with actors, director, and producer.*

Christian, George. "Author Notes—Eco Says Brother William Could Return; Dan Jenkins on Tour Travails; Bette Bao Lord's Eighth Year." Houston *Chronicle* (November 4, 1984): Zest section, 12, 17. *Account (p. 12) of talk in which Eco speaks of origins of* The Name of the Rose *and of a sequel.*

——————. "The Making of the Rose." Houston *Chronicle* (June 17, 1984): Zest section, 14, 19. *Interview in which Eco discusses the origins of his novel, which he sees as making a statement about "the everlasting problems of tolerance and violence."*

Churchill, John. "Wittgenstein's Ladder." *American Notes and Queries* 23 (September/ October 1984): 21–22. *Allusion in* The Name of the Rose *to Wittgenstein's Tractatus Logico-Philosophicus is "an instance of disclosed concealment."*

Conroy, Sarah Booth. "Book Biz Buzz—Toasting Umberto Eco & the Rise of the 'Rose.' " *Washington Post* (May 28, 1984): D1, D8. *Quotes Eco's observations on his novel at a party in his honor.*

De Lauretis, Teresa. "Gaudy Rose: Eco and Narcissism." *SubStance* 47 (1985): 13–29. *What the novel "finally affirms is the truth of discourse, the* name *of the rose, and thus the continuity of the very institution it seems to challenge: the name of the Father."*

De Mallac, Guy. "The Poetics of the Open Form—(Umberto Eco's notion of *Opera Aperta*)." *Books Abroad* 45 (Winter 1971): 31–36. *Calls* Opera Aperta *"in many ways the author's major achievement."*

Dionne, E. J., Jr. "Outside of Rome, A Medieval Whodunit Unfolds." New York *Times* (February 16, 1986): section 2, 21, 28. *Account of filming of* The Name of the Rose.

Dipple, Elizabeth. "An Interview with Umberto Eco." *Arts & Sciences* (Northwestern University) 9 (Fall 1986): 6–9, 12–13. *Eco comments on his changing reputation, his next novel, the relation of theory and fiction, wrong interpretations of* The Name of the Rose, *and the film version of the novel.*

Dunsmore, Peter. "Eco's Rose." *Encounter* 66 (March 1986): 77. *Letter to the editor, highly critical of Eco and his novel.*

"Extras." Boston *Globe*, (August 30, 1983): p. 60. *Brief note on high sales figure of paperback rights to* The Name of the Rose.

Filho, Alvino Castro. "Italy's Unlikely Best Seller." *World Press Review* 31 (March 1984): 60. *Interview in which Eco discusses* The Name of the Rose *and* The Sign of the Three.

Fleischer, Leonore. "Talk of the Trade." *Publisher's Weekly*, 224 (August 26, 1983): 381. *Comments on* The Name of the Rose *by Howard Kaminsky, president of Warner Books.*

Freedman, Adele. "Hit Novel Comes as a Surprise." Toronto *Globe and Mail* (June 21, 1983): 17. *Interview in which Eco comments on the genesis of* The Name of the Rose *and on James Joyce.*

Gerber, Eric. "Vietnam, 'Skooks,' Postscripts and the Rest of Us." Houston *Post* (November 18, 1984): 15F. *Brief quotes from Eco on* The Name of the Rose.

Gilbert, Sari. "A Medieval Italian 'Rose' Takes Root." Washington Post (October 9, 1983): F1, F6–F7. *Interview in which Eco discusses the genesis and success of* The Name of the Rose.

Goodman, Walter. "Writers Discuss Myth in Modern Life." New York *Times* (October 13, 1984): 13. *Announcement of Eco speech on "The Semiotics of Symbols."*

Harris, Paul. "Fair Deals for the World's Book Trade." *The Scotsman* (Edinburgh) (October 29, 1983): *Weekend Scotsman* section, 4. *Eco comments on apparent similarities between* The Name of the Rose *and Fuller's* Flying to Nowhere.

Hitchens, Christopher. "American Notes." *Times Literary Supplement* (November 16, 1984): 1310. *Report on PEN "conversation" between Eco and Susan Sontag, as well as discussion of his method and appeal.*

Hutshing, Ed. "Longshot In Book Derby Comes Up Rose." San Diego *Union* (November 6, 1983) *Books* section, 2. *Brief comment on unexpected success of* The Name of the Rose.

Inge, M. Thomas. "He Didn't Even Read the Book." Washington *Post* (July 14, 1984): A17. *A reply to Jonathan Yardley's column attacking the novel. Eco "has proven that it is possible to use the forms of popular culture and fiction to create a piece of literature that is profound in its import and at the same time accessible to ordinary readers."*

Johnson, Hillary. "Royalty Picture Rosy for a Semiotics Prof." *Wall Street Journal* (September 23, 1983): 28. *History of initial rejection and eventual success of Eco's novel.*

Kaylan, Melik. "Umberto Eco . . . Man of the World." *Vogue* 174 (April 1984): 329–30, 393. *Interview in which Eco discusses himself, the Catholic church, philosophy, American versus European thought, deconstruction, and the intellectual capital of the world.*

Linklater, John. "Booker Award Judges Told of 'Similar' Novels." Glasgow *Herald* (October 1, 1983): 1. *Notes similarities of* The Name of the Rose *and John Fuller's* Flying to Nowhere.

McDowell, Edwin. "About Books and Authors." *New York Times Book Review* (July 17, 1983): 26. *Brief mention of quick rise of* The Name of the Rose *on best-seller list.*

——————. "Publishing: New Bloom on the 'Rose.' " New York *Times* (June 15, 1984): C26. *Details success of the paperback edition of* The Name of the Rose.

Mackey, Louis. "The Name of the Book." *SubStance* 47 (1985): 30–39. *Sees* The Name of the Rose *as "Aristotle's lost book on comedy," a "poisoned book whose 'venomous power' turns at last on itself."*

Mitgang, Herbert. "Reading and Writing—A Sly Scholar." *New York Times Book Review* (July 17, 1983): 31. *Interview in which Eco speaks of semiotics and its relation to* The Name of the Rose, *of his boyhood, and of the pertinence of his novel to twentieth-century readers.*

Nathan, Paul S. "Rights & Permissions." *Publisher's Weekly* 224 (August 5, 1983): 35. *Reports winning bid for paperback rights to* The Name of the Rose *(Warner Books, $550,000).*

Okulski, Janice Schuh. "The Name of the Rose: Mystery in Truth." *Eternity* 35 (September 1984): 66–69. *Sees novel as "good, absorbing entertainment."*

Parker, Douglass. "The Curious Case of Pharaoh's Polyp, and Related Matters." *SubStance* 47 (1985): 74–85. *Explores Adso's dream and its two antecedents,* Cyprian's Banquet *and* John's Banquet.

"Prize-Winning Italian Novel Due From HBJ." *Publisher's Weekly* 223 (February 25, 1983): 62. *Announces forthcoming publication of* The Name of the Rose *in June.*

Richter, David H. "Eco's Echoes: Semiotic Theory and Detective Practice in *The Name of the Rose.*" *Studies in Twentieth Century Literature* 10 (Spring 1986):

213–36. *Explores Eco's use of the semiotics of detection, problematic anachronisms, time, and the "Distant Mirror" theme; novel is neither "closed" nor "open" but one in which authors "tell stories about the way stories are built up."*

Robey, David. "Umberto Eco." In Michael Caesar and Peter Haensworth, eds. *Writers & Society in Contemporary Italy*. New York: St. Martin's Press, 1984, 63–87. *Eco "provides a clear and powerful model of the relationship between the intellectual and society, a model that illustrates strikingly the advantages and difficulties of the marriage of theoretical speculation with social practice." Surveys and analyzes several Eco works.*

Romano, Carlin. "Critics Cheer and Eco Hears His Name." Philadelphia *Inquirer* (July 16, 1983): 1-C, 8-C. *Interview in which Eco discusses* The Name of the Rose, *why he wrote it, semiotics, C. S. Peirce, and the role of the intellectual.*

Rosso, Stefano. "A Correspondence With Umberto Eco—Genova—Bologna—Binghamton—Bloomington: August–September 1982–March–April 1983." Trans. by Carolyn Springer. *Boundary 2* 12 (Fall 1983): 1–13. *Topics discussed include "postmodernism," reasonability, James Joyce, essays versus fiction,* The Name of the Rose, *and the semiotics of unlimited semiosis.*

Roy, Klaus G. "A Letter." Cleveland *Plain Dealer* (October 16, 1983): 23-C. *Reply to Alice Metcalf Miller's* Plain Dealer *review of* The Name of the Rose. *Contends novel is very relevant to the present day.*

Rubino, Carl A. "The Invisible Worm: Ancients and Moderns in *The Name of the Rose*." *SubStance* 47 (1985): 54–63. *The message of the novel is that "the burdens of omniscience are too heavy for human beings: the search for the cool rose of the north is an arduous one, and those who brave the quest must pay a high price for their courage."*

Schiavoni, Franco. "Faith, Reason and Desire: Umberto Eco's *The Name of the Rose*." *Meanjin* 43 (December 1984): 573–81. *It is "a semiotic novel, in the Kantean sense that it contains both a representation of the world and a critical discourse on the categories and problems of representation and in the sense that this double discourse occurs in the terms and preoccupations that characterize the modern discipline of semiotics."*

Schulze, Leonard G. "An Ethics of Significance." *SubStance* 47 (1985): 87–101. *The* Name of the Rose *manages "to suggest how the hinge, the always-to-be-articulated word by which we constitute our worlds, is not a logical point, but a narrative process."*

Seidenbaum, Art. "Italian Novel Translates Into Success." Los Angeles *Times* (May 23, 1984): part V, 1,12. *Recounts visit with Eco in Bologna.*

"Umberto Eco to Receive Canadian Unesco Prize." New York *Times* (November 19, 1985): C20. *Eco awarded 1985 McLuhan Teleglobe Canada Award for "achievement in the field of communications."*

Yardley, Jonathan. "Unread Tomes in the Home?" Washington *Post* (July 2, 1984), C1, C6. *Yardley finds it hard to understand why the book is at the top of the best-seller list and can only account for it by "bestselleritis, the dread disease that strikes persons foolish enough to believe that if it's popular, it must be something they'd like."*

Yeager, Robert F. "Fear of Writing, or Adso and the Poisoned Text." *SubStance* 47 (1985): 40–53. *Shows how "fear of writing" functions in two ways in* The Name of the

Rose: *"first, the fear of not writing, . . . and, second, the fear of writing itself . . . of the power of words over life, both as sign and as assurance."*

Zamora, Lois. "Umberto Eco's Revelation: *The Name of the Rose.*" *Humanities in the South* 61 (Spring 1985): 3–5. *Examines Eco's use of the myth of the apocalypse which "underlies the plot structure, the thematic considerations, and the historical context" of the novel.*

Zimmer, Dieter E. "Eco I, Eco II, Eco III. . . ." *Encounter* 66 (April 1986): 68–71. *Interview in which Eco discusses film version of his novel, the similarities and differences between the Middle Ages and the present, the information explosion, the intellectual, writing, the "usable past," and the effects of success.*

II.   Book Reviews of Eco's Works in English Translation

A Theory of Semiotics

Benson, Thomas W. *Philosophy and Rhetoric* 10 (Summer 1977): 214–16. *Eco "proceeds with order, lucidity, and tact."*

Cardwell, Guy A. *Key Reporter* 61 (Summer 1976): 7. *Eco has "a talent for making the difficult accessible."*

Choice, 13 (July/August 1976): 677. *The book's value is "great, not only for its erudition and insight, but most particularly for its grasp of current European scholarship in this field, much of which is not yet available in translation."*

Deeley, John N. "The Doctrine of Signs: Taking Form at Last." *Semiotica* 18 #2 (1976): 171–93. *Review-essay. Eco's notion of "sign-function is not an adequate—let alone necessary—substitute for the classical notion of signum." But Eco's "theory of codes and subsequent theory of sign production . . . contain such wealth of detailed analysis that a reviewer is hard-pressed to convey an adequate sense of the richness and sophistication of this important contribution to, and advance upon, the current state of the semiotic art."*

De Lauretis, Teresa. *Books Abroad* 50 (Summer 1976): 635. *The book "displays an originality of thought which combines scientific rigor with what may be appropriately called creative imagination."*

Fowler, Roger. *Notes and Queries* 26 (April 1979): 163–65. *The book is "an extremely full and reliable account of classical sign theory which, despite its fidelity to its sources . . . embodies a critique of them which anticipates and answers the more sensible criticisms levelled at semiotics."*

Galan, F. W. *Canadian Review of Comparative Literature* 4 (Fall 1977): 354–58. *It is "a fruitless exercise in scholastic taxonomy, grouping various and varied fields of endeavour under arbitrary headings."*

Godzich, Wlad. *Journal of Music Theory* 22 (Spring 1978): 117–33. *"Eco's theory of semiotics provides the unified approach to the problem of signification which semiotics, in the mind of its founders, was supposed to develop and elaborate."*

Graham, Joseph F. "Semiotics and Semantics." *Boundary 2* 6 (Winter 1978): 591–97. *Eco presents "the broad field of semiotics, in the present state of the art, which he proposes not only to survey but also to shape in some way, thereby leaving his mark."*

Hamilton-Faria, Hope. *Modern Language Journal* 60 (September–October 1976): 298. *Basically a descriptive review.*

Hendricks, William O. *Lingua* 43 (November 1977): 293–94. *Despite fact that the book is disappointing, "no one seriously interested in semiotics can afford to avoid {it}."*

Hirsch, David H. "Signs and Wonders." *Sewanee Review* 87 (October–December 1979): 628–38 [629–30]. *Although this is "the* Summa Theologica *of language," its "great flaw" is "the author's inability to define 'sign' or 'signification' in a way that would compel a skeptical reader to accept his definitions."*

Innis, Robert E. "Feature Book Review." *International Philosophical Quarterly* 20 (June 1980): 221–32. *Review-essay. "It is a goldmine of information, hints, clues, heuristic pointers, theses, arguments, and sophisticated questions bearing upon the semiotic project, and it will be indispensable to anyone who wants to get a solid and reliable introduction to what semiotics is all about."*

Juffras, Angelo. *Library Journal* 101 (May 1, 1976): 1123. *Eco "has written a book of impressive erudition (obviously not for the layman), and cites a vast literature."*

Kelkar, Ashok. "Semiotics." *Indian Journal of English Studies* 18 (1978–79): 151–54 [153–54]. *Book is an "abstract but rewarding discussion that takes one from basic and simple notions to complex and advanced ones."*

Lanigan, Richard L. "Contemporary Philosophy of Communication." *Quarterly Journal of Speech* 64 (October 1978): 335–47 [344–46]. *Eco "makes the theoretical connection between communication theory and rhetorical theory. . . . I know of no other book that accomplishes this task with a systemic and systematic set of axioms grounded in empirical evidence that is both linguistic and artifactual."*

Lepick, Julie Ann. "In the Balance—Structuralism and After: Contemporary French Thought and Its Impact on Anglo-American Literary Theory." *Choice* 18 (October 1980): 203–12 [204]. *Brief mention.*

Lepschy, Giulio. *Language* 53 (September 1977): 711–14. *Although it has flaws and weaknesses, "this work is useful and important."*

"New Books." *Drama Review* 21 (March 1977): 120. *This book "could be an important reference and guide for those who are interested in relating semiotics to performance."*

Ray, William. "Reading Theory: The Role of the Semiotician." *Diacritics* 10 (Spring 1980): 50–59 [51–54]. *"Although he ultimately admits the necessity of performance within the theoretical system—that is, the need for interpretation in the midst of theoretical description—he will never fully renounce the objectivist's dream."*

Robey, David. "Signs, Codes and Culture." *Times Literary Supplement* (July 8, 1977): 827. *This is "in many ways a remarkable book, but it will probably turn out to have been the more or less gratuitous expression of an Italian* esprit de système."

Scholes, Robert. *Journal of Aesthetics and Art Criticism*, 35 (Summer 1977): 476–78. *Eco's findings "are neither radical nor startling, but they rest upon a formidable edifice of observation, learning, and reason, opening an immensely fruitful direction for the study of aesthetic texts as acts of communication."*

Sherzer, Dina. *Language in Society* 6 (April 1977): 79–82. *This is a "very erudite and provocative book."*

Silverman, Kaja. "Semiotics Unlimited." *Novel* 10 (Fall 1976): 92–95. *"The book makes its argument accessible at every point—so accessible that the reader cannot fail to grasp the premise that only those things which present themselves representationally fall within the purview of semiotics."*

Sondheim, Alan. *Art Journal* 36 (Winter 1976–77): 180, 186. *This is "easily the most comprehensive survey of the field (as well as the most comprehensive general theory) to date."*

Soufas, C. Christopher. "On the Discrimination of Contemporary Criticisms: An Annotated Introductory Bibliography." *College Literature* 9 (Fall 1982): 231–66 [250]. *This is "one of the most comprehensive studies to date on semiotic theory."*

Strang, Barbara M. H., and Mary Brennan. "English Language." *Year's Work in English Studies* 57 (1976): 11–42 [40]. *Brief descriptive mention.*

"They Select Their Best." *New York Times Book Review* (June 12, 1977): 25, 28. *Indiana University Press picks* A Theory of Semiotics *as one of the five best books it has published in the last two years.*

Watt, W. C. *American Anthropologist* 80 (September 1978): 714–16. *The book succeeds in "extending and firmly consolidating" semiotics' "foundation, making the case for its central position within the study of culture, and whetting one's appetite for future developments."*

The Role of the Reader

Block, Ed, Jr. "The Role of the Reader." *Contemporary Literature* 23 (Winter 1982): 97–99. *This "often humorous and always thought-provoking book provides an informative interaction of reader and text."*

Campbell, Laurence R. "Reviewing Relevant Literature." *School Press Review* 55 (November 1979): 11. *This is "a book for a reader who likes depth study."*

Champagne, Roland A. *World Literature Today* 54 (Spring 1980): 339. *Descriptive mention.*

Choice 16 (December 1979): 1297–98. *"This is an essential book in a rapidly growing and widely applicable field."*

Colomb, Gregory G. "Semiotics Since Eco: Part 2, Semiotic Readers." *Papers on Language & Literature* 16 (Fall 1980): 443–59 [447–54]. *Review-essay.* "If, as it stands, this Reader *is not as substantial as we might like, it is nevertheless very good fare indeed."*

De Lauretis, Teresa. *Clio* 10 (Fall 1980): 93, 94–95. *These essays "complement and enrich" Eco's previously translated work "by providing specificity and a sense of its theoretical development."*

Dolezel, Lubomir. "Eco and His Model Reader." *Poetics Today* 1 (Summer 1980): 181–88. *"Eco makes the difficult concepts of possible-world semantics accessible to many literary scholars and humanists who would find them otherwise impossible to handle."*

F[ell], J[ohn]. *Film Quarterly* 34 (Summer 1981): 59. *Brief mention.*

Forum for Modern Language Studies 17 (July 1981): 288. *This work "takes up again some of the main points made in Eco's previous book,* A Theory of Semiotics.*"*

Hanlon, Lindley. *Journal of Aesthetics and Art Criticism* 38 (Spring 1980): 336. *Eco*

*"strikes a healthy balance between analyses of specific details and structures that can be
located on the page and description of the supposed codes, categories, and culture which we as
readers use to unlock meaning."*

Hawkes, Terence. "Taking It as Read." *Yale Review* 69 (June 1980): 560–576
[564–66]. *Descriptive review.*

Hendricks, William O. "Review Article—Open and Closed Texts." *Semiotica* 35,
nos. 3/4 (1981): 361–79. *Focuses on Eco's notions of open and closed texts; in "the
main," he "continues the structuralist focus on the text itself."*

Hirsch, David H. "Signs and Wonders." *Sewanee Review* 87 (October–December
1979): 628–38 [636]. *"Eco does his old-fashioned explication skillfully; the addition of
statistical and hypothetical readers complicates Eco's rhetorical strategies, but does not in
itself release the meaning of the text."*

I., R. E. *Review of Metaphysics* 35 (September 1981): 126–28. *This is "a welcome
supplement to the materials contained in {Eco's}* A Theory of Semiotics.*"*

Keener, Frederick M. *Library Journal* 104 (May 1, 1979): 1060. *"It is largely delectable
reading—so remarkably learned, puckishly imaginative . . . and amusing is Eco."*

Kintgen, Eugene R. *Stage* 15 (Fall 1981): 479–82. *These essays are "curiously hypothetical"; "caveat lector."*

N[ew], W. [H.] "Last Page." *Canadian Literature* 106 (Fall 1985): 189–91 [191]. *"It
is not a book for the lay reader; it's as dense with theoretical jargon and almost arcane
formula as his novel is rich with incident and character."*

Orr, Leonard. *Philosophy and Literature* 4 (Spring 1980): 138–39. *"This book has a great
deal to offer and should prove to be provocative for anyone interested in narratives."*

Ray, William. "Reading Theory: The Role of the Semiotician." *Diacritics* 10 (Spring
1980): 50–59 [54–59]. *Because Eco refuses to "renounce his semiotician's privilege or
renounce talking about reading in terms of a structure/event interface," this book is "put
into question by its own theory; and therein lies its weakness—and its richness."*

Schwimmir, Eric. *American Anthropologist* 82 (December 1980): 867–68. *The book is
important because it discusses elements "relevant to anthropology."*

White, J. J. *Modern Language Review* 76 (January 1981): 142. *It is "a witty, highly
readable, and sensible illustration of the issues under discussion."*

The Name of the Rose

Adachi, Ken. "Erudite Treatise Disguised as a Murder Story." *Toronto Star* (June 25,
1983) H10. *Review-interview. "The mystery is cunningly constructed; the denouement is
breathtakingly exciting"; but "the heart of the novel resides in Eco's insights into the age."*

Adams, Phoebe-Lou. *Atlantic* 252 (July 1983): 108. *The "real purpose" of the novel is "to
make the reader see the similarities between the fourteenth century and today. The mystery,
while not irrelevant, is frosting on a rather acrid cake."*

Ahern, John. "That Which We Call a Rose." *Commonweal* 110 (November 4, 1983):
597, 600–601. *"One hopes that the popular success of this engrossing, playful, serious,*

multi-layered book will inspire far-sighted publishers to make available in English other parts of Eco's enormous body of work."

Allen, Bruce. " 'Rose' and Other Summer Novels Just as Sweet in the Fall." Chicago *Tribune* (November 13, 1983) Book World sec., 34. *"Eco has combined an engrossing mystery story with a pair of splendid characterizations and a masterly evocation of medieval culture."*

Anderson, Erin. "Medieval Detective." Charleston (West Virginia) *Daily Mail* (September 17, 1983) 4A. *"It is an interesting murder-mystery that, despite its remote time and place, pulls the reader into the story."*

Atchity, Kenneth. "A Medieval Monastic Mystery on the Banks of Allegory." Los Angeles *Times* (June 19, 1983) Book Review sec., 3. *"A book like this seeks to replace the world with itself, and eventually does so, showing the reader that reality, except as vision, is already inaccessible; that only vision matters; that even before he began reading, even before the book was written, the 'world' had already been, long ago, replaced by the word."*

Atwood, Margo. "A Monk Who Solved Murder and Bored With Screeds." York (Pennsylvania) *Record* (October 22, 1983). Eco *"has a sophisticated wit, and loves to play with words, but I wish he had not seen fit to use so many of them."*

Aymond, Stephen. " 'The Name of the Rose'—Spiritless Translation Sabotages First Novel." Shreveport *Times* (June 19, 1983): Sunday Magazine sec., 9-F. *Despite the "spiritless translation,"* Eco *"does a fine job of transporting the reader back into another world in which knowledge was more respected, but man no less fallible than today."*

Barber, Michael. *Books & Bookmen* no. 350 (November 1984): 37. It is *"a gripping high-brow mystery with as many shades of meaning as Finnegans Wake."*

Bernhardt, Susan. "Engrossing Labyrinth of a Novel." Monterey (California) *Sunday Peninsula Herald* (July 31, 1983). *"This is the sort of book that is utterly engrossing while it is being read, and blossoms still further in the memory."*

"Best and Worst Books of the Year." *The Spectator* 251 (December 17, 1983): 52–53. *Harold Acton, Max Hastings, Caroline Moorehead, and Patrick Devlin chose* The Name of the Rose *as a best book of 1983.*

Biasin, Gian-Paolo. *World Literature Today* 55 (Summer 1981): 449–50. *"The labyrinth as an artistic structure" and "play as transgression" are "at the core of the book and explain its powerful appeal."*

Birkerts, Sven. "An Uncommon Mystery." *New Republic* 189 (September 5, 1983): 36–38. *It is a "first class mystery" which is "hard to return to" for a second reading; its characters are "cleverly done cutouts." But it is worth rereading because "the mind is moved from word to word and back, covering in the process more than a few ills."*

Blake, Patricia. "Murders in a Medieval Monastery." *Time* 121 (June 13, 1983): 72. *It is "a monumental exercise in mystification by a fun-loving scholar."*

"Books of the Year." *The Observer* (December 4, 1983): 25. *Philip French and Anthony Burgess chose* The Name of the Rose *among the best books of the year.*

Born, Daniel. "Murder at the Monastery." *Sojourners* 13 (January 1984): 36. *Reading this book is "to wander through a labyrinthine and exotic library created by Eco for our imagination."*

Brennan, Eileen. *North Shore* (November–December 1983). *"Above all is Eco's use of language."*

B[rosnahan], J[ohn]. *Booklist* 79 (May 15, 1983): 1187. *It "resonates from its theological basis into a highly literate and deft entertainment."*

Burgess, Anthony. "Medieval Sherlock." *The Observer* (October 16, 1983): 32. *It "makes no stylistic concessions, assumes a fair erudition on the reader's part, and titilates only intellectually"; it is "a work of genuine literature."*

Burke, Peter. "Cloistered Crimes." *History Today* 34 (May 1984): 56. *Eco has produced "a work of fiction which exemplifies his own theories of literature and has at least as many meanings as medieval theologians found in the Bible—in other words four": the "literal," "allegorical," "moral," and "historical."*

Burns, Rex. "Faith, Mystery Merge in 'Name of the Rose.'" *Rocky Mountain News* (Denver) (August 7, 1983): 31-S. *It is "a fine combination of adventure and fact that entertains and delights."*

Butler, Tom. " 'Rose' Is Enthralling Puzzle, Murder Mystery." Wilmington (Delaware) *News Journal* (July 17, 1983): E2. *"Rarely does a work of serious literature offer so much pure enjoyment. It is humorous, beguiling and frightening. It alternately edifies, enlightens and enrages."*

Bywater, Michael. "A Name Is a Name Is. . . . " *Punch* 285 (November 23, 1983): 77. *"Professor Eco has pulled off a masterpiece, something unique and of . . . magisterial wit and intelligence."*

Carr, Jay. "An Erudite Tale of Murder Behind Monastery Walls." Detroit *News* (August 14, 1983): 2-E. *"The recondite speeches begin by characterizing the various speakers; they end by characterizing an age."*

Carroll, Michael P. *American Anthropologist* 86 (June 1984): 432–34. *"Eco's novel should be especially useful to students who are being brought into contact with semiotics for the first time."*

Caswell-Pearce, Sara. "Novel Set in Abbey Captures 14th Century's Feel." Nashville (Tennessee) *Banner* (August 20, 1983). *"Although I felt at times that I should have an encyclopedia of religion and a dictionary within arm's reach, not knowing everything never hurt my understanding of the book or my ability to follow the intriguing story."*

Caywood, Carolyn. *Voice of Youth Advocate* 7 (April 1984): 29. *"While this is not an easy book, an enthusiastic recommendation will attract readers who enjoy mental games in a world very different from our own."*

Collins, Anne. "Books—Medieval Sleuth on the Murder Trail." *Maclean's* 96 (July 18, 1983): 50. *"Eco has written a compelling whodunit."*

Condini, Nereo E. "Eco's Rose." *Cross Currents* 33 (Winter 1983–84): 461–64. *Eco's "craft and ingenuity, his intellectual clarity and acumen are so sparkling that not only the mystery or the love angle takes life under our eyes, but also science, magic, the doctrinal disputes."*

Cornis-Pop, Marcel. "Through Rose-Colored Glass." *North American Review* 269

(September 1984): 65–67. *"The true theme in* The Name of the Rose *is that of the World as an Intertext, a baffling cultural Labyrinth."* It is an *"imperfect symbol of the greater, vanished library, a kind of 'immense acrostic' that, like his own writing, has salvaged from the 'perfectly level and boundless' desert of death a wealth of 'images' and words."*

Cowart, David. "Multilayered Drama—Eco a Master of Fictive Architectonics." *The State* (Columbia, South Carolina) (July 3, 1983): 7-F. *It has "a simultaneous popular and esoteric appeal."*

Craft, Robert. "A Christmas Roundup." *New York Review of Books* 31 (December 20, 1984): 49–53 [49–50]. *"Eco is perfectly aware that his novel is a string of digressions, and that its popularity can only be attributed to the brilliance of his discourse and his ability, against all obstacles, to sustain suspense."*

Cryer, Dan. "New Italian Novel Literary Discovery." New Haven (Connecticut) *Register* (June 26, 1983): D4; see also *Newsday* (Garden City, New York) (June 19, 1983) Ideas sec., 20. *It is "an exciting detective story, a colorful evocation of medieval life and a lively morality tale on fanaticism, books and the search for truth."* This review also appeared in: Norfolk Virginian-Pilot, (August 7, 1983): C6; Des Moines Register, (July 10, 1983): 4C.

D'Amico, Masolino. "Medieval Mirth." *Times Literary Supplement* (January 9, 1981) 29. *Review of Italian edition. It is "no mere detective story; rather, its framework serves as a vehicle for nothing less than a* summa *of all the author knows about the Middle Ages—and all he wishes us to know."*

Dirda, Michael. "The Letter Killeth and the Spirit Giveth Light." Washington *Post* (June 19, 1983): Book World sec., 5, 14. *"It conveys remarkably the desperation of a dying culture, while at the same time touching on perennial issues of love, religion, scholarship and politics."*

Egan, Thomas M. "Italian Mystery Bares Paradoxes, Tragedy of Medieval Christianity." New York *Tribune* (October 12, 1983): 5B. *"It's good reading and lots to ponder in this tapestry of prose."*

Ellmann, Richard. "Murder in the Monastery?" *New York Review of Books* 30 (July 21, 1983): 11. *It "succeeds in being amusing and ambitious at the same time."*

Ferrucci, Franco. "Murder in the Monastery." *New York Times Book Review* (June 5, 1983): 1, 20. *"The narrative impulse that commands the story is irresistible. . . . Mr. Eco's delight in his narrative does not fail to touch the reader, who may or may not choose to be intrigued with the levels of interpretation crisscrossing in front of him as in a semiotic labyrinth."*

Fitzpatrick, Jan. "Tip Off—On Books." Rochester (New York) *Times Union* (July 18, 1983): 3C. *"Eco demonstrates what many fans of the {mystery story} genre have always suspected, that sometimes a 'low' form of literature can provide the best solution to the labyrinth of the human heart."*

Flieger, Verlyn. "The Name, the Thing, the Mystery." *Georgia Review* 38 (Spring 1984): 178–81. *Review-essay. "Eco's one clear message to the reader" is: "Beware of meaning; it may not be there, and even if it is, it may not be what you think."*

Floyd, Jerry. "Mysterious and Gripping Tale of the 14th-Century Papacy." Washington (D.C.) *Times* (July 5, 1983): 3D, 14D. *It is "both a superb murder mystery and a haunting artistic reflection of contemporary anxieties."*

Fox, Robert. "The Importance of the Past." *Times Educational Supplement* (November 18, 1983). *It is "the most exciting re-creation of fourteenth century Europe in modern fiction."*

——————. "Monastic Murder." *The Listener* 110 (October 6, 1983): 25. *"Few works of fiction written this century can have conjured up Europe of the High Middle Ages so successfully."*

Freedman, Adele. "Elementary, My Dear Monks." Toronto *Globe and Mail* (June 25, 1983): Entertainment sec., 18. *It is "a novel of satisfying playfulness, clarity and imaginative vigor."*

Fuehrer, M. " 'Detection' on a Grand Scale." Minneapolis *Tribune* (September 25, 1983): 17G. *Eco's "style and wit" rescue him from "what could have been a very tedious format."*

Fuller, Edmund. "All Too Contemporary Images from the Middle Ages." *Wall Street Journal* (June 20, 1983): 26. *It is "one of two outstanding novels at the highest literary level of historical fiction."*

Fuller, Richard. "Murder, Mystery, Mayhem." Philadelphia *Inquirer* (June 1, 1984) Weekend sec., 38. *Book is "highly recommended."*

Gingher, Robert. "Book Talk—Biology Secrets, Medieval Mystery." Greensboro (North Carolina) *News* (June 26, 1983): E5. *Novel "reads like Arthur Conan Doyle and Thomas Mann combined forces."*

Goodman, Walter. "Books of The Times—Medieval Mystery." New York *Times* (June 4, 1983): 18. *"No doubt medievalists will find errors in Mr. Eco's vision, and some may be offended by the intrusion of a personification of modern skepticism into the 14th century. But in this novel imagination carries the day."*

Gray, Rick. "Books Are at Center of Rich-Textured Novel." Toledo *Blade* (August 21, 1983). *Novel "repays each and every intellectual stretch that it demands."*

Grosser, Dorothy L. Asbury Park (New Jersey) *Press* (September 18, 1983). *It is "a masterful work, a detective story, a historical novel, classic Gothic literature."*

Harper, Michael. "Nominees, 1983 Fiction Prize." Los Angeles *Times* (November 13, 1983): Book Review sec., 6–7. *" 'Fiction' and 'non-fiction' are closely interwoven in a delightful novel of ideas, and Eco has succeeded brilliantly in creating a work which embodies in its very form the theme which lies at the heart of its many concerns."*

Harris, Roger. "Death in the Abbey." Newark (New Jersey) *Star-Ledger* (June 19, 1983): sec. 4, 23. *"It has both a sense of humor and a sense of excitement, a combination of qualities that is quite rare. But it also has moral and philosophical implications about liberty and tolerance."*

Hartley, Anthony. "Eco's Great Mystery—Secrets of an Old Library." *Encounter* 62 (March 1984): 37–40. *"It is abundantly worthwhile to make the intellectual effort this book requires: to take part in an inquiry where the object of detection is the destiny of man and his capacity to reason."*

Hartman, Zella. "Religious Library Place of Learning and Death." Oklahoma City *Oklahoman* (August 28, 1983). *Descriptive review.*

Hayes, E. Nelson. "Books—Steeped in Mysteries." Boston *Ledger* (June 27–July 4, 1983): 29. *Brief, favorable review.*

Hellwig, Monika K. *Commonweal* 111 (February 24, 1984): 122. *"The characterizations are magnificent and the wisdom paradoxical and profound."*

Hewgley, Joseph. "Mystery Re-creates Turbulent Italy." Nashville *Tennessean* (August 21, 1983): 6-F. *"Though heavy with descriptions of ecclesiastical councils and theological debates, not to mention a frustrating preponderance of untranslated Latin quotations,* The Name of the Rose *is still absorbing reading."*

Hiers, Cheryl. " 'Rose' Weaves Intricate Murder Yarn." Orlando (Florida) *Sentinel* (July 31, 1983): D-3. *"Beautifully written, this tale of 'events wondrous and awful' is imaginative literature that exceeds all the bounds of traditional mysteries."*

Higgins, Fitzgerald. "Medieval Monks and Mayhem." Grand Rapids (Michigan) *Press* (July 3, 1983): 9H. *It is "both an entertaining puzzle and a richly detailed portrait of another world."*

Hill, Reginald. *Books & Bookmen*, no. 337 (October 1983): 30. *It offers "many rich and strange reading pleasures."*

Hobson, Linda. "Mystery Writer Exploits Medieval Scholarship." New Orleans *Times Picayune* (October 30, 1983): sec. 3, 16. *This novel, "a cultivated bloom among sundry weeds . . . rightfully deserves its high ranking."*

Hodiak, Bohdan. "Murder, Monks, Metaphysics." Pittsburgh (Pennsylvania) *Post-Gazette* (September 13, 1983): 25, 28. *"The book is like an expedition. Once you reach the end you begin to forget the mosquitoes, the heat, the unnecessary detours, and remember the adventures, the unique sights and insights, the fascinations."*

Kaufman, James. "Between Soft Covers." *Christian Science Monitor* (July 6, 1984): B8. *Brief review.*

Kearns, George. *Hudson Review* 36 (Autumn 1983): 554. *It is "an extraordinary detective-story* cum *historical novel."*

Kelley, J. Ralph. "Much More than a First-Rate Detective Story." *Catholic Transcript* (November 4, 1983): 4A. *"It may well be that Umberto Eco's first novel . . . will in time take on the stature of a minor classic."*

Kendrick, Walter. "Who Bought Umberto Eco? The Case of the Semiotic Fluke." *Village Voice Literary Supplement* 28 (October 1983): 24. *Descriptive review which speculates on reasons for novel's success.*

Kennedy, Eugene. "Few Thorns in 'The Name of the Rose.' " Chicago *Sun-Times* (August 14, 1983) Show sec., 29. *It is "ideal vacation reading for anyone interested in detective stories, ideas, and the feel of other times and places."*

Kennedy, Joseph P. "Mirror on the World: Eco's Holy Holmes." Houston *Chronicle* (July 3, 1983) Zest sec., 19. *It is a "brilliant demonstration of the power of the word" and "a masterwork by a scholar who knows how to play."*

Kiernan, Suzanne. "The Name of the Name—Eco's Clever Tour From Aquinas to Zadig." *The Age Monthly Review* (Melbourne, Australia) 3 (February 1984): 6–8

"The name of the book is the name of the rose and the name of the rose is the rose is the rose is the post-modern rose squared."

Kirkus Reviews 51 (April 15, 1983): 470. *It is "a rich, fascinating failure—with clever, tapestry-like appeal for a limited, historically minded audience."*

Krauthammer, Charles. *American Spectator* 17 (December 1984): 27. *"If you like your theology, semiotics, and medieval history delivered cunning and sharp, invest a weekend in this one."*

Lantz, Jere. " 'The Name of the Rose' Is Mystery Plus." Rochester (Minnesota) *Post-Bulletin* (September 24, 1983). *"Eco's ultimate gift . . . is not his baroque descriptive style or his voluminous knowledge, but his plea for deep thinking, for refusing to accept the simplistic answers of blind, emotional, unconsidered faith, to arrive at the truth."*

Laski, Margharita. "Their World as in Their Time." *Country Life* 174 (December 15, 1983): 1819–20. *"This is a long . . . and witty book, both learned and clever, and, to anyone who likes both mysteries and medieval cosmology, irresistible."*

Lebowitz, Martin. "Elementary, My Dear William." Los Angeles *Herald-Examiner* (August 14, 1983): sec. F, 5. *"The present reviewer does not share an intense enthusiasm for this novel"; but it is "quite impressive as an expression of the author's encyclopedic knowledge of the Middle Ages."*

Lehman, David. "Medieval Murders." *Newsweek* 102 (July 4, 1983): 72–73. *"He is one textual strategist who knows how to put what he preaches into dazzling practice."*

Leppanen, Linda E. "Novel Brings 14th Century to Life." Worcester (Massachusetts) *Telegram* (July 3, 1983). *"This beautifully written, philosophical as well as intriguing investigation is no mere detective tale, it is a {multifaceted} gem of a novel."*

Lewis, Jim. Houston *Post* (August 14, 1983): 17F. *It is "an absorbing novel; the most compelling feature of it is the author's ability to take the reader back more than 650 years in time and place." This review also appeared in: Trenton (New Jersey) Times (August 7, 1983): magazine, 2; Savannah News (September 25, 1983): 5G.*

Lewis, Roger. "Sign Language." *New Statesman* 106 (November 4, 1983): 27. *Descriptive review.*

Lileks, James. "Anatomy of a Mystery." *Minnesota Daily* (University of Minnesota, September 25, 1983): 25, 27. *"Enter this book hating semiotics and you will leave it hating semiotics. Come in a fan; leave a fan. Enter ignorant, and leave ignorant."*

Linklater, John. "Of Cults and Coincidences." Glasgow *Herald* (October 1, 1983): Weekender sec., 4. *Compares novel to Fuller's Flying to Nowhere: "Eco's brilliantly conceived and executed work is the one which will stand the test of time."*

Lloyd, Pat. "Books—European No. 1 Bestseller Set in Middle Ages." Pensacola (Florida) *News* (July 5, 1983): 1D, 4D. *"The medieval times are fascinating and Eco makes them as readable as today's happenings."*

Lobner, Corinna del Greco. *James Joyce Quarterly* (Summer 1982): 468–71. *"The contents of this brilliant, diachronic, medieval fresco invite readers to create many new structures and new texts."*

McAteer, M. J. "A Mystery from the Dark Ages Sheds Light on Modern Times."

Charlotte (North Carolina) *Observer* (December 25, 1983): 8F. *"It sheds light on a dark age, but its wisdom illuminates our own age, too."*

McClain, Kathleen. " 'Rose' Blooms as Surprise Hit of the Summer." Memphis (Tennessee) *Press-Scimitar* (August 6, 1983). *Although Eco's "approach is at times a bit too complex for reading comfort" and the language "ranges from poignantly beautiful to painfully detailed," he is "a masterful storyteller whose love of language shines through every page."*

McMurtrey, Linda. "Rose's Success a Mystery." Hattiesburg (Mississippi) *American* (October 2, 1983): 2D. *"Eco tells a good story and has a lot to say about such things as intellectual freedom and truth."*

Madrigal, Alix. "Murder and Mystery in a 14th-Century Monastery." San Francisco *Examiner & Chronicle* (July 24, 1983): Review sec., 8. *"It is a brilliantly conceived adventure into another time, an intelligent and complex novel and a lively and well-plotted mystery."*

Maguire, Patrick. "Vitality in Middle Ages." *The Scotsman* (Edinburgh, October 29, 1983): *Weekend Scotsman* sec., 5. *"The novel is brilliantly plotted, its pyrotechnic conclusion an amazing display of virtuosity."*

Marese, Murphy. "Troubles in the Abbey." *Irish Times* (Dublin, October 22, 1983): Weekend sec., 4. Eco *"imparts his vast knowledge with the lightheartedness of a humourist, using it as the context for a gripping mystery story."*

Maurer, Paul. *Best Sellers* 43 (September 1983): 201. *"It's rare and exhilarating to discover a novel so rich in wisdom, elegant in style and unique in format competing so well in the marketplace."*

Meroke. "Book Reviews." *The Cryptogram* 49 (September–October 1983): 3, 18. *Brief descriptive review.*

Miles, Margaret R. *Commonweal* 111 (November 30, 1984): 670–71. *"The mystery is fascinating; and the discussions of philosophy, politics, and theology are interwoven so skillfully with the progression of the plot that the reader is drawn into these discussions in order to understand the plot."*

Miller, Alicia Metcalf. "Eco's 'Rose': Ambitious Failure." Cleveland *Plain Dealer* (August 7, 1983): 16-C. *"Certainly anyone not absolutely mesmerized by the aesthetics of the Middle Ages or who asks more from reading than a ton of facts and occasional bursts of virtuosity, will find* The Name of the Rose *falls resoundingly flat."*

Milligan, Bryce. "Reading—A 14th-century Sherlock Holmes." San Antonio *Express-News* (August 14, 1983): 7-K. *It is "simply a fine act of storytelling."*

Modert, Jo. "By Any Name, It's Delightful and Deadly." St. Louis *Post-Dispatch* (October 30, 1983): 4E. *"It is an intelligent and intellectual masterpiece."*

Morley, Patricia. "Monks' Murders Spice Fine Novel." Ottawa *Citizen* (July 16, 1983): 35. *"Eco combines knowledge with narrative, and wisdom with wit."*

Mystery News (May–June 1983). *Novel is "far-ranging" and "masterful."*

N[ew], W. [H.] "Last Page." *Canadian Literature* 106 (Fall 1985): 189–91 [190–91]. *"It's part mystery, part history, part social parable, and all metafiction: a narrative that is at once conscious of the effect of its own form . . . and able to sweep the reader into the critiques and aspirations of a world remarkably like our own."*

Norris, Timothy J. "Breaking from the Locked Room." *In Print: A Book Review* (September 1983). Eco *"has demonstrated the basic and unshakable need our imaginations have for action and ideas; he has shown the primacy literature still holds over its critics."*

Novelli, Martin. "A Scholar's Rich Novel of Murder in the Monastery." Philadelphia *Inquirer* (July 10, 1983): sec. P, 9. *"Eco has written a novel that celebrates imagination and skepticism, faint but important lights in dark times. He also makes it clear that such qualities are needed just as much now, in our own dark times."*

"Paperback Choice." *The Observer* (November 11, 1984): 24. *It is "audacious, witty, informed and riveting."*

Pate, Nancy. " 'Rose' More than Mere Murder Tale." Wichita *Eagle-Beacon* (June 26, 1983): 5C. *Although, "at times, the book becomes heavy going," Eco "writes with erudition and wit" and "a sure grasp of narrative."*

Pearl, Nancy. Tulsa *World* (August 21, 1983): sec. I, 7. *"Historical fiction at its best, this novel is educational without condescending to the reader."*

Pecile, Jordon. "Discursive Ramble in Thorny Thicket." Hartford *Courant* (August 14, 1983): E10. *"It is a book which many are buying, but which few, I think, will finish."*

Peters, Andrew. *Library Journal* 108 (April 1, 1983): 757. *"The narrative sometimes becomes tiresome in its detail, but the last half redeems most of the excesses."*

Petersen, Priscilla. " 'The Name of the Rose' Reviewed." Nevada (Missouri) *Herald* (November 6, 1983). *"Above all, it is an engrossing mystery, full of visions and biblical symbolism, which builds to a powerful conclusion."*

Peterson, Shirley. "Reviewer's Window." Schenectady (New York) *Gazette* (September 3, 1983). *Descriptive, favorable review.*

Pintarich, Paul. "An Illuminated Manuscript of Murder." Portland *Oregonian* (July 24, 1983): 15NW, 23NW. *"Eco skillfully allows the reader to share in a whodunit while dropping into his plot less light aspects of the Dark Ages."*

Poplawski, Matt. " 'Name of the Rose.' " Charleston (South Carolina) *News & Courier/Evening Post* (July 17, 1983): 6-E. *It is a "masterful work."*

Publishers Weekly 223 (May 13, 1983): 48. *It is "a large, ambitious historical novel of limited but strong appeal for its special audience."*

Quigly, Isabel. "Italian Tapestry." *Financial Times* (October 1, 1983): 12. *It evokes the medieval world "with a force and wit that are breathtaking."*

Rapport, Evelyn M. " 'Name of Rose' Plays Thorny Joke on Reader." Kansas City (Missouri) *Star* (August 21, 1983): 1E, 9E. *"This is an important book. . . . Attention must be paid. However, it is not a notable book. It is cold and violent and bitter, a denunciation of ideas and ideals that died centuries ago in the turmoil of a civilization finding itself. It also is discursive, unfocused and coy. It is pretentious."*

Reedy, Gerard. *America* 149 (August 6, 1983): 75–76. *It is "a masterpiece of sympathy for the past. Its author knows that commitment to discovering any human age in its particularity will lead to universal insight."*

Reilley, R. J. "Library Corner." Parkersburg (West Virginia) *Sentinel* (December 2, 1983). *"In the end, satisfied though one is by the mystery, one does find oneself wishing that Professor Eco had used his considerable talents to weave a historical novel that would have dramatized the waning of the Middle Ages and the collapse of the great scholastic synthesis."*

Roberts, Nancy. "On First Reading—'Rose' by Any Name Would Read as Sweet." Corsicana (Texas) *Sun* (September 9, 1983). *Descriptive, favorable review.*

Ross, Michele. "Medieval Mystery Ignites Thoughts." Atlanta *Journal & Constitution* (July 17, 1983): 10-H. *"The book is amazingly complex, richly textured and unapologetically intelligent."*

Rubin, Merle. "A Rose By Any Other Name." *Christian Science Monitor* (December 2, 1983): B6,B14. It *"owes some share of its success to the fact that it has a great deal to communicate, from the charmingly archaic lore of gems to its treatment of topics just as relevant today as over six centuries ago: censorship, fanaticism, the perils and promises of natural science, and the pitfalls of political intrigue."*

S[chare], J[effrey]. *Harper's* 267 (August 1983): 75–76. It is *"an antidetective-story detective story; as a semiotic murder mystery it is superbly entertaining; it is also an extraordinary work of novelistic art."*

Schirmer, Gregory A. "A Master of Possibilities." *New Leader* 66 (October 17, 1983): 16–17. *"It can be read on so many levels that we are continually forced to remember that our interpretation or understanding of it necessarily ignores many others."*

Schwabsky, Barry. "Semiotics and Murder." *New Criterion* 2 (September 1983): 79–80, 82–83. It *"demands that we question interpretations, and settle for something less than definitial answers."*

Seidenbaum, Art. "Endpapers." Los Angeles *Times* (July 1, 1984): Book Review sec., 11. It is a *"magnificent mystery."*

Shrimpton, Nicholas. "Dr. Eco's House of Blood." London *Sunday Times* (October 2, 1983): 43. *"Intellectual freedom and intellectual play are the values which this novel most energetically asserts. You'll love it."*

Smith, Andy. "Between the Lines." Rochester (New York) *Democrat & Chronicle* (July 17, 1983): 12. *Descriptive mention.*

S[mith], S[herman] W. *West Coast Review of Books* 9 (September–October 1983): 35–36. *"In addition to general reading, it would make an excellent study for college students in the social fields covered by the book."*

Spearman, Walter. "The Literary Lantern." *The Pilot* (Southern Pines, North Carolina, July 6, 1983). *"American readers are hardly likely to find it so intriguing and may well get lost on the sea of words that pour out erudition. Some skipping is both advisable and necessary."*

Staley, Thomas F. "Book Reviews." *Oklahoma Home & Garden* (August 1983): 27. It is *"a rare and compelling work."*

Stephens, Walter E. "Ec[h]o in Tabula." *Diacritics* 13 (Summer 1983): 51–64. *Review-essay. It is "a semiotic duel, a 'showdown' between medieval theocentric semiosis and a vision of Peircean unlimited semiosis." It "acknowledges a theoretical, rather than narrative, debt to Borges."*

Stille, Alexander. "Miracle of the Rose." *Newsweek* 102 (September 26, 1983): 88. *Comments on surprising best-seller status of* The Name of the Rose.

Thompson, Francis J. "Murder in the Monastery." Tampa (Florida) *Tribune & Times* (September 4, 1983): 5-C. *Almost entirely plot summary.*

Toomey, Philippa. "The Case of the Murderous Monks." London *Times* (November 3, 1983). *It is "most entertaining reading."*

Truly, Pat. "By Any Other Name It Would Exude the Fragrance of a Bestseller." Fort Worth *Star-Telegram* (July 17, 1983). *It is "two books—one, an excellent mystery to read before the fire on a rainy evening; the other, an excellent glimpse into a time and issues of which we know little."*

Turner, Edith. *Commonweal* 110 (December 2, 1983): 666–67. *Throughout the novel, "one can perceive the workings of great perennial questions, many of which vex us today."*

Turner, Charles. "Murder in the Abbey." Memphis (Tennessee) *Commercial Appeal* (July 31, 1983): G3. *"An impressive first novel."*

Updike, John. "Baggy Monsters." *New Yorker* 59 (November 14, 1983): 188-97. *"Once this novel is set down, it feels more miniature and toylike than it should considering the large amount of passionate wit and learning poured into its pages."*

van de Wetering, Janwillem. *Parabola* 8 (Fall 1983): 98, 100–101. *"The book is an instant classic, a faultless artifact, a composite of myriad brilliant details bundled into a single ray."*

Vansittart, Peter. "Franciscan Fears." *London Magazine* 23 (October 1983): 100–102. *"Within a mass of theological speculation, scholastic debate, medieval erudition, is a straight, well-developed detective story with suspects, mixed motives, fanaticism, dreadful retribution."*

Vasilask, Gary S. "The Diaphanous Bud." *Chronicles of Culture* 8 (January 1984): 8, 10–12. *"What is remarkable about" this novel "is that it is a book that can sustain the onslaughts of critical inquiry while still existing as a work that can be read and appreciated by the common reader."*

Watson, Chris. "Medieval Mystery Arrives in U.S." Santa Cruz (California) *Sentinel* (August 26, 1983). *"A most ambitious novel," it "succeeds in all avenues."*

Waugh, Harriet. "Dead Monks." *The Spectator* 251 (December 17, 1983): 45. *"It is a fine book with great breadth of vision, moving at a deceptively leisured pace towards an exciting climax."*

——————. "Recent Fiction." *Illustrated London News* 272 (January 1984): 65. *"The author both tells an entertaining, instructive and exciting story and presents an essay on the thought behind post—structuralist thinking . . . made amusingly accessible to the reader."*

Weigel, George. "Murder in the Dark Ages." *The Weekly* (Seattle, Washington, August 17–23, 1983). *"We come away from* The Name of the Rose *enriched by seeing contemporary questions unraveled through a parallel, but distinctive, historical period."*

Wellejus, Ed. "Erudite Story." Erie (Pennsylvania) *Times* (June 23, 1983). *Almost entirely a descriptive review.*

Wilsher, Peter. "The Pleasure of Reading—1984." *New Statesman* 108 (December 21–28, 1984): 43. *Chooses* The Name of the Rose *as the book that gave him the most pleasure in 1984: "a box of delights."*

Windsor, Gerard. "Death in the Thorns of the Rose." *Bulletin* (Australia) 104 (February 21, 1984): 73–74. *"This is a juicy book. It's opulent, it's a brainteaser, it's exciting, it's jokey. It's even educational."*

Wozniak, Maurice D. "Writers Find That Crime Pays." Milwaukee (Wisconsin) *Journal* (September 4, 1983): Entertainment sec., 11. *"It is a credit to Eco's craftsmanship and good humor . . . that the reader will stick with him through detail after obscure detail."*

Yates, John. "Medieval Mystery Has Religious Overtones." San Jose (California) *Mercury* (July 31, 1983): Arts & Books sec., 25. *"If the book at times gets tedious and perhaps too 14th century and scholarly, stick with it because it is all worth it in the end."*

Ziaukas, Tim. " 'Rose' Is a Rare Literary Blossom." Pittsburgh (Pennsylvania) *Press* (August 28, 1983): Magazine sec., 4. *"A brilliant match of method and material,* The Name of the Rose *is that rarest of literary blossoms: a page-turner about ideas."*

The Sign of Three

Baker Street Journal 34 (June 1984): 118. *"Most of the book is new material analysing Sherlockian logic, deduction, and inference."*

Danto, Arthur C. "Guessing Games." *New Republic* 193 (September 16 and 23, 1985): 48. *"The book is re-creative in the highest degree."*

Dillard, R. H. W. *Hollins Critic* 22 (June 1985): 11–12. *"The book is as intellectually exciting as it is instructive."*

Kennedy, J. Gerald. *Philosophy and Literature* 10 (April 1986): 122–23. *The two authors "dabble in the logic of detection with scarcely a glance at the impressive body of theory and criticism on the detective story that has accrued in the last ten years."*

Lauterbach, Edward S. *Modern Fiction Studies* 31 (Summer 1985): 384–85. *"The purpose of this collection of essays is to juxtapose the theory of education put forth by the American philosopher Charles Sanders Peirce with the problem-solving methods of Sherlock Holmes."*

O'Brien, Robert C. *Library Journal* 109 (January 1984): 96. *"A gem for Holmes fans and armchair detectives with a penchant for logical reflection, and Peirce scholars."*

Semiotics and the Philosophy of Language

Bogue, Ronald L. *Philosophy and Literature* 9 (October 1985): 245–46. *It is "a compelling demonstration of the usefulness of semiotics as a framework for linguistic analyses and for understanding the history of the philosophy of language."*

Brink, Jeanie R. *Magill's Literary Annual—1985*, ed. Frank N. Magill. vol. 2 (Englewood Cliffs, NJ: Salem Press, 1985): 807–10. *"Readers interested in literary theory will find much of value in this demanding volume," which "belongs to the tradition of rigorous and humanistic inquiry."*

Choice 21 (June 1984): 1479. *"Lively yet erudite explanation of semiotics for readers who have a familiarity with and fondness for analytic philosophy."*

Lewis, Thomas E. "Semiotics and Interpretation: Before or After the Fact? Umberto Eco's *Semiotics and the Philosophy of Language.*" *Poetics Today* 6, no. 3 (1985): 503–20. *Review-essay.* The book's *"most ambitious aspect" is its "attempt to wrest control of a series of key concepts from those who would wish to pursue semiotics exclusively as a formalist enterprise."*

Posner, Rebecca. "Signs Without End." *Times Literary Supplement* (June 15, 1984): 660. *"On the whole, this collection can be read with pleasure by those unversed in semiotic theory. . . . {It} can be recommended as a most enjoyable read."*

S[cobie], S[tephen]. "Criticism." *Malahat Review* 69 (October 1984): 107–18 [109–10]. *"The final chapter is . . . a fascinating if exhaustive exposition of the reasons why mirror images cannot be regarded as 'signs.'"*

Shapiro, Michael C. *Studies in Second Language Acquisition* 7 (October 1985): 372–74. Though *"informative, thought-provoking, erudite and enlightening,"* the book would be better if *"put forward in a less obscurantist prose style."*

Sturrock, John. "The Name of the Discipline." *New York Times Book Review* (May 13, 1984): 17. Eco has made a *"formidable achievement in writing so dynamically authoritative a guide to a fundamental subject in a language not his own."*

Swiggers, P. *Language* 61 (December 1985): 919–20. *"The essential thing is that Eco stimulates the reader's thinking about fundamental problems of general semiotics."*

Postscript to "The Name of the Rose" (English edition under the title *Reflections on "The Name of the Rose")*

Adams, Phoebe-Lou, *Atlantic* 255 (January 1985): 100. *It "does nothing to regiment the reader's ideas."*

B[rosnahan], J[ohn]. *Booklist* 81 (January 1, 1985): 613. *"Eco's postscript functions on several levels simultaneously, with the amount of both instruction and delight to be derived totally incommensurate with the book's small size."*

Burgess, Anthony. "By Any Other Name." *The Observer* (April 7, 1985): 20. *"Both explains and leaves the inquirer more puzzled than before."*

Byatt, A. S. "Major Reviews." *Books & Bookmen,* No. 354 (April 1985): 8–9. *Descriptive review.*

Craft, Robert. "A Christmas Roundup." *New York Review of Books* 31 (December 20, 1984): 49–53 [49-50]. *Descriptive mention.*

Hainsworth, Peter. "Pleading Guilty." *Times Literary Supplement* (November 29, 1985): 1373. *Laudatory review whose only quibble is with the translation.*

Keefer, Bob. " 'Postscript' Makes Sure No One Misses the Point." Eugene (Oregon)

Register-Guard (November 4, 1984): 5D. *It is a "rambling discussion" which contains "a gem or two."*

Kirkus Reviews 52 (October 15, 1984): 988. *"Very brief, often pedantic musings—and explanations."*

Knight, Stephen. "Eco's Reflections a Mere Echo." Sydney *Morning Herald* (August 10, 1985): 46. *It is "basically a lecture with white space and doubtfully relevant illustrations. At that, a lecture which is not so much a thorough reflection on the novel as a rather faint echo."*

Lee, Jennifer. *Rocky Mountain Review of Language and Literature* 39, no. 2 (1985): 143–45. *It is "a terse, intriguing commentary."*

McCoy, J. S. *Best Sellers* 44 (March 1985): 467. *"This little book is a gem."*

Modert, Jo. "More of the Mysterious Rose." St. Louis *Post-Dispatch* (February 3, 1985): 4B. *"While Eco answers some questions, he raises more, which the reader can only try to solve."*

Peters, Andrew. *Library Journal* 110 (January 1985): 87. *"This postscript is as approximately frank and lucid as the novel was 'mysterious.' "*

Romano, Carlin. "Eco Explains What It All Means." Philadelphia *Inquirer* (November 4, 1984). Books/Leisure sec., 3. *It is a "slim, post-game rumination."*

Scobie, Stephen, *Malahat Review,* No. 72 (September 1985): 145. *"We get a few banal comments on the process of writing a novel, a few more interesting comments on irony and postmodernism, and far too few nuggets of hard information. . . . For addicts only."*

Seidenbaum, Art. "Book Review—A Short Course in the Narrative Form." Los Angeles *Times* (November 30, 1984): V, 30. *It is "a little course in comp lit and art crit, a clever text even in the classroom sense; the ebullient professor from Bologna offers a rich and rollicking lesson in the telling of story."*

Shrimpton, Nicholas. "The Naming of the Rose." London *Sunday Times* (April 7, 1985): 45. *It consists of "anecdotal hindsight."*

Woolley, Benjamin. "And Now the Thorns." *The Listener* 113 (April 11, 1985): 25. *"In a sense, the book is a guide to the mechanics of authorship."*

Travels in Hyperreality: Essays

Adams, Phoebe-Lou. *Atlantic* 257 (June 1986): 83. *Volume provides "pleasure and stimulation."*

B[rosnahan], J[ohn]. *Booklist* 82 (June 15, 1986): 1476. *It "always preserves the scholar's demeanor while descending to more earthbound whimsies, fantasies, and concerns."*

Cohn, Jessica. "Cutting Issues Down to Size." Grand Rapids *Press,* (June 1, 1986): E11. *Eco's comments are "forceful"; he "makes tolerable sense of complex events."*

D'Evelyn, Thomas. "Meditations on Terrorism and Other Signs of the Times." *Christian Science Monitor* (May 14, 1986): 23. *Eco writes out of a conviction that, "as an intellectual, he has a moral obligation to tell others how he sees 'daily life, political events, the language of the mass media.' "*

Frankel, Sara. "Essays On Our Modern World." San Francisco *Chronicle* (June 22, 1986): Review sec., 8. *It is "one of those rare books that combine serious commentary on society and popular culture with first-class storytelling, lightheartedness and a sense of humor."*

Harris, Roger. "From Pap to Philosophy." Newark (New Jersey) *Star-Ledger* (May 25, 1986): sec. 4, 14. *"This is an interesting and stimulating collection."*

Kirkus Reviews 54 (March 15, 1986): 439. *"This is critical writing of a superb order. The range is wide . . . and the writing is provocative and exuberant."*

Klewans, Stuart. "The Disappearing Act." *Nation* 242 (May 10, 1986): 666–67. *"For all his learning and acuity, Eco often performs better as an entertainer than as an analyst."* What's missing from this volume is *"reality itself—that is, ordinary, day-to-day reality."*

Kuczkowski, Richard. *Library Journal* 111 (June 15, 1986): 68–69. *"Though these essays are generally entertaining, they lack the originality and punch of Barthes's* Mythologies *and seem unlikely to find the same popular success as Eco's own* The Name of the Rose.*"*

Markey, Constance. " 'Hyperreality' Is Early Eco and Not a 'Rose' By Just Another Name." Chicago *Tribune* (May 25, 1986): sec. 14, p. 35. *It is "a mixture of solid literary research and shrewd observations on language"; but Eco's observations on culture are "one-sided and condescending."*

Merritt, Robert. "Modern Life & Middle Ages." Richmond (Virginia) *Times-Dispatch* (May 25, 1986): F-5. *This volume "shows a great preference for the Middle Ages, raising compelling questions about our own modernity."*

Publishers Weekly 229 (April 25, 1986): 63. *Eco is "urbane, detached, elegant and sometimes obscure as an essayist."*

Schreiber, Le Anne. "Guilty Secrets." *Vogue* 176 (May 1986): 180–81, 184 [184]. *"In Eco, intelligence and irony are reflexes, and no matter how rapidly fired, they always find their targets: dogmatism and ingenuousness."*

Taylor, Robert. "Umberto Eco Observes a 'Hyper-real' America." Boston *Globe* (May 21, 1986): 77. *Eco is the "European observer of fantastical American culture" and "ranges with grace, erudition and pawky good humor."*

III.   Book Reviews in English of Eco's Works in Italian

Diario Minimo

Cecchetti, Giovanni. *Books Abroad* 38 (Spring 1964): 182. *"Eco watches the sudden enthusiasm for strange notions and propositions characterizing our era, and satirizes them."*

"Structure A to Z." *Times Literary Supplement* (September 27, 1963): 764. *Eco seems to be "parodying himself" and is "absolved from any real art of critical responsibility."*

Opera aperta

Golffing, Francis. *Books Abroad* 37 (Winter 1963): 67. *Descriptive favorable review.*
"Structure A to Z." *Times Literary Supplement* (September 27, 1963): 764. *This "impressively documented study" arouses disquiet by making its point with too much illustration.*

Apoclittici e Integrati

"Pop Goes the Artist." *Times Literary Supplement* (December 17, 1964): 1137–38. *This "remarkably able book" may "introduce the reader to the intellectual effort which Italian critics have devoted to mass culture in the past five years or so."*

Il Caso Bond

"An Englishman's Bond." *Times Literary Supplement* (May 27, 1965): 408. *It is "a useful collection."*

La Definizione Dell'Arte

"Culture as Communication." *Times Literary Supplement* (March 27, 1969): 330. *Brief descriptive mention.*

La Struttura Assente

"Culture as Communication." *Times Literary Supplement* (March 27, 1969): 330. *Eco is at the top of "his word-spinning form" in attempting to "break up the epistemological complacencies and exorcize the demon of Structure."*
Lepschy, G. C. *Linguistics* 62 (October 1970): 109–10. *Praise for Eco's "acumen, originality, and richness of first-hand bibliographical information."*

Il Problema Estetico in Tommaso D'Aquino

"A Scholastic View of Beauty." *Times Literary Supplement* (October 8, 1971): 1211. *Book is "a valuable introduction to the whole field of medieval aesthetics."*

Le Forme del Contento

"The Avoidance of the Real." *Times Literary Supplement* (December 8, 1972): 1510. *Eco's task is "to examine culture not as a privileged area of investigation but as a territory falling* iure naturale *under the rule of semiotics."*

Il Costume Di Casa

"Lessons in Suspicion." *Times Literary Supplement* (October 5, 1973): 1151. *The "most important group of articles is a series of examples of, broadly speaking, applied semiotics."*

Sette Anni Di Desiderio: Cronache 1977–1983

Reid, Gilbert. "Playing the Displaced." *Times Literary Supplement* (October 5, 1984): 1130. *Eco presents elaborate "definitions and distinctions with good-humored verve and old-fashioned precision."*

Carnival!

Burke, Peter. "Codes and Conflicts." *Times Literary Supplement* (June 28, 1985): p. 728. *Brief, descriptive mention of Eco's essay.*

Holquist, Michael. *Latin American Literature and Arts Review* 35 (July–December 1985): 40–41. *Brief mention of Eco's essay, "an eight-page noodle."*

Contributors

_____

Ruth M. Alvarez is completing a dissertation on Katherine Anne Porter at the University of Maryland. She is managing editor of _Resources for American Literary Study_ and has contributed to _American Quarterly._

Helen T. Bennett is Associate Professor of English at Eastern Kentucky University. She is doing research on the application of semiotic and contemporary literary theory to Old English poetry. Her essay, "Deconstructing the Monastery in Eco's _The Name of the Rose,_" will be published in a collection by the University of Minnesota Press.

Jackson R. Bryer is Professor of English at the University of Maryland. He has published extensively on American literature and bibliography and is currently preparing a new edition of his _Sixteen Modern American Authors_ (1974), as well as a selected edition of the letters of Eugene O'Neill.

Michael Cohen is Professor of English at Murray State University in Kentucky. He is author of _Engaging English Art: Entering the Work in Two Centuries of English Painting and Poetry_ (1987) and co-author of _The Poem in Question_ (1983). He is currently writing a book on Shakespeare's _Hamlet._

Joan DelFattore is Associate Professor of English at the University of Delaware. She has written extensively on detective fiction and on such authors as Henry James, Chaim Potok, and Joseph Heller, as well as translating Latin poetry.

Pierre L. Horn is Professor of French at Wright State University. He is author of _Marguerite Yourcenar_ (1985) and biographies of Louis XIV (1986) and Lafayette (1988) and is currently editing a _Handbook of French Popular Culture._ In 1978 he was made a Chevalier dans l'Ordre des Palmes académiques by the French government.

M. Thomas Inge is Robert Emory Blackwell Professor of Humanities at Randolph–Macon College. He is editor of the three-volume _Handbook of_

American Popular Culture (1978–81) and is currently writing a book on Melville in popular culture.

Hans Kellner is Associate Professor of Humanities at Michigan State University. He has published articles on historical and literary theory and is author of the forthcoming book *Language and Historical Representation: Getting the Story Crooked*.

Jocelyn Mann is a doctoral candidate at the University of Houston. Although Ms. Mann mainly writes fiction and poetry, she is currently working on a Bakhtinian analysis of Emily Bronte's novel, *Wuthering Heights*.

Deborah Parker is Assistant Professor of Italian at the University of Virginia. She is presently writing a book on Latin and Italian commentaries to Dante's *Divine Comedy*.

Mark Parker is Assistant Professor of English at Randolph–Macon College. His research interests focus on the English Romantics and on autobiography.

Roger Rollin is William James Lemon Professor of Literature at Clemson University. His most recent publications include a psychoanalytic study of Ben Jonson's poems to Shakespeare and John Donne, and he is preparing a second edition of his study, *Robert Herrick* (1966).

H. Aram Veeser is Assistant Professor of English and Director of Composition at Wichita State University. His research interest are in literary theory, seventeenth-century English literature, and the masques of Ben Jonson, and he is editor of *The New Historicism: Political Commitment and the Postmodern Critic*.

Lois Parkinson Zamora is Associate Professor of Comparative Literature at the University of Houston. She has completed a critical study, *Last Words: Apocalyptic Ends and Endings in Contemporary U.S. and Latin American Fiction*, and a translation of Angelina Muñiz's collection of short stories *Enclosed Garden*.

Index